THE REVELS PLAYS

Former editors
Clifford Leech 1958–71
F. David Hoeniger 1970–85

General editors
David Bevington, E. A. Honigmann, J. R. Mulryne
and Eugene M. Waith

THE SHOEMAKER'S HOLIDAY

MANCHESTER
UNIVERSITY PRESS

THE SHOEMAKER'S HOLIDAY

THOMAS DEKKER

edited by R. L. Smallwood
and Stanley Wells

MANCHESTER
UNIVERSITY PRESS
Manchester and New York

*Distributed exclusively in the USA
by* St. Martin's Press

Introduction, critical apparatus, etc.
© R. L. Smallwood and Stanley Wells 1979

Reprinted 1999

The right of R. L. Smallwood and Stanley Wells to be identified as
the editors of this work has been asserted by them in accordance with
the Copyright, Designs and Patents Act 1988.

First published by Manchester University Press 1979

This edition published by Manchester University Press
Oxford Road, Manchester M13 9NR, UK
and Room 400, 175 Fifth Avenue, New York, NY 10010, USA
http://www.man.ac.uk/mup

Distributed exclusively in the USA by
St. Martin's Press, Inc., 175 Fifth Avenue, New York,
NY 10010, USA

Distributed exclusively in Canada by
UBC Press, University of British Columbia, 6344 Memorial Road,
Vancouver, BC, Canada V6T 1Z2

British Library Cataloguing-in-Publication Data
A catalogue record for this book is available from the British Library

Library of Congress Cataloging-in-Publication Data applied for

ISBN 0 7190 3099 4 *paperback*

06 05 04 03 02 01 00 99   10 9 8 7 6 5 4 3 2 1

Typeset in Hong Kong
by Best-set Typesetter Ltd
Printed in Great Britain
by Bell & Bain Ltd, Glasgow

Contents

THE REVELS PLAYS

General Editors' Preface

Clifford Leech conceived of the Revels Plays as a series in the mid-1950s modelling the project on the New Arden Shakespeare. The aim, as he wrote in 1958, was 'to apply to Shakespeare's predecessors, contemporaries and successors the methods that are now used in Shakespeare editing'. The plays chosen were to include well known works from the early Tudor period to about 1700, as well as others less familiar but of literary and theatrical merit: 'the plays included,' Leech wrote, 'should be such as to deserve and indeed demand performance.' We owe it to Clifford Leech that the idea became reality. He set the high standards of the series, ensuring that editors of individual volumes produced work of lasting merit, equally useful for teachers and students, theatre directors and actors. Clifford Leech remained General Editor until 1971, and was succeeded by F. David Hoeniger, who retired in 1985.

The Revels Plays are now under the direction of four General Editors, David Bevington, E. A. J. Honigmann, J. R. Mulryne and E. M. Waith. Published originally by Methuen, the series is now published by Manchester University Press, embodying essentially the same format, scholarly character, and high editorial standards of the series as first conceived. The General Editors intend to concentrate on plays from the period 1558–1642, and may include a small number of non-dramatic works of interest to students of drama. Some slight changes have been forced by considerations of cost. For example, in editions from 1978, notes to the introduction are placed together at the end, not at the foot of the page. Collation and commentary notes will continue, however, to appear on the relevant pages.

The text of each Revels play, in accordance with established practice in the series, is edited afresh from the original text of best authority (in a few instances, texts), but spelling and punctuation are modernised and speech headings are silently made consistent. Elisions in the original are also silently regularised, except where metre would be affected by the change; since 1968 the '-ed' form is used for non-syllabic terminations in past tenses and past participles ('-'d' earlier), and '-èd' for syllabic ('-ed' earlier). The editor emends, as distinct from modernises, the original only in instances where error is patent, or at least very probable, and correction persuasive. Act divisions are given only if they appear in the original or if the structure of the play clearly points to them. Those act and scene divisions not in the original are provided in small type. Square brackets are also used for any other additions to or changes in the stage directions of the original.

Revels Plays do not provide a variorum collation, but only those variants which require the critical attention of serious textual students. All departures of substance from 'copy-text' are listed, including any relineation and those changes in punctuation which involve to any degree a decision between alternative interpretations; but not such accidentals as turned letters, nor necessary additions to stage directions whose editorial nature is already made clear by the use of brackets. Press corrections in the 'copy-text' are likewise collated. Of later emendations of the text, only those are given which as alternative readings still deserve attention.

One of the hallmarks of the Revels Plays is the thoroughness of their annotations. Besides explaining the meaning of difficult words and passages, the editor provides comments on customs or usage, text or stage-business—indeed, on anything judged pertinent and helpful. Each volume contains an Index to the Commentary, in which particular attention is drawn to meanings for words not listed in *OED*, and (starting in 1996) an indexing of proper names and topics in the Introduction and Commentary.

The Introduction to a Revels play assesses the authority of the 'copy-text' on which it is based, and discusses the editorial methods employed in dealing with it; the editor also considers the play's date and (where relevant) sources, together with its place in the work of the author and in the theatre of its time. Stage history is offered, and in the case of a play by an author not previously represented in the series a brief biography is given.

It is our hope that plays edited in this fashion will promote further scholarly and theatrical investigation of one of the richest periods in theatrical history.

DAVID BEVINGTON
E. A. J. HONIGMANN
J. R. MULRYNE
E. M. WAITH

Preface

Our collaboration has been close, but sections 1 to 4 of the Introduction, and the Appendices, were written by R. L. Smallwood, sections 5 and 6 by Stanley Wells. We worked jointly on the text and commentary, and each has scrutinised the other's work. We are grateful to the late Professor Clifford Leech, who commissioned us; to Professor F. David Hoeniger, who encouraged us in the earlier stages of our work; and especially to Professor E. A. J. Honigmann for his careful criticism of our typescript and for numerous helpful suggestions. We are also grateful to Mr John Banks of the Manchester University Press for his helpfulness and care through the various stages of getting the work into print. Inevitably many other debts are incurred during the preparation of an edition such as this. We should like particularly to thank Professor Arthur Colby Sprague for assistance with the stage history; Dr F. W. Sternfeld for his advice on music; M. Jean Fuzier for help in relation to French translations and performances; and the following librarians: Dr Ingeborg Boltz, of the Shakespeare Bibliothek, Munich; Mrs Alice Bray, formerly of the Shakespeare Institute, University of Birmingham; Mr Hywel Evans, formerly of the University Library, Birmingham; Dr Jeanne Newlin, of the Harvard Theatre Collection; and Mrs Marion Pringle and Miss Eileen Robinson, of the Shakespeare Birthplace Trust. We also gratefully acknowledge research grants from the University of Birmingham and the interest and encouragement of colleagues and friends at the Shakespeare Institute.

Stratford-upon-Avon, August 1978   R.L.S.   S.W.W.

The hope we expressed at the end of Section 5 of our Introduction (p. 52) was soon to be fulfilled. A production at the National Theatre, directed by John Dexter, opened on 19 June 1981. It was reviewed by, among others, Michael Billington, *The Guardian*, 22 June 1981, Irving Wardle, *The Times*, 22 June 1981, Robert Cushman, *The Observer*, 28 June 1981 and Stanley Wells, *TLS*, 26 June 1981.

Stratford-upon-Avon, February 1999   R.L.S.   S.W.W.

Abbreviations

Editions of *The Shoemaker's Holiday* are referred to by the name of the editor only; for publication details, see pp. 58–62 below. Bowers's edition of the *Dramatic Works* is used for all quotations from, and references to, Dekker's other plays and the pageants. Non-dramatic works of Dekker are cited from E. D. Pendry's edition of *Thomas Dekker: Selected Writings* (Stratford-upon-Avon Library, 4, London, 1967) and from *The Plague Pamphlets of Thomas Dekker*, edited by F. P. Wilson (Oxford, 1925). For non-dramatic works not reprinted in these collections, original editions have been used, though for convenience references are also provided to *The Non-Dramatic Writings of Thomas Dekker*, edited by Alexander B. Grosart (Huth Library, 5 vols, London, 1884–6). All quotations from Deloney are from *The Novels of Thomas Deloney*, edited by Merritt E. Lawlis (Bloomington, Indiana, 1961). Unless otherwise stated, linguistic glosses in the Commentary are based on *O.E.D.* and topographical glosses on Sugden. Shakespeare quotations and references are normally from Peter Alexander's one-volume edition of the *Complete Works* (London, 1951). The titles of Shakespeare's plays are abbreviated as in C. T. Onions's *A Shakespeare Glossary* (1911; second edition, Oxford, 1953). Biblical quotations are from the Bishops' Bible, the version likely to have been most familiar to Dekker from its use in church services.

In addition to the above, the following abbreviations are used:

Abbott	E. A. Abbott, *A Shakespearian Grammar*, London, 1869; third edition, 1870.
Chambers, *E.S.*	E. K. Chambers, *The Elizabethan Stage*, 4 vols, Oxford, 1923.
Chapman, ed. Parrott	George Chapman, *The Comedies*, edited by T. M. Parrott, London, 1914.
Dialect Dict.	J. Wright, *The English Dialect Dictionary*, 6 vols, London, 1898–1905.
Henley and Farmer	W. E. Henley and J. S. Farmer, *A Dictionary of Slang and its Analogues*, 7 vols, London, 1890–1904.

Henslowe	*Henslowe's Diary*, edited by R. A. Foakes and R. T. Rickert, Cambridge, 1961.
Herford and Simpson	*Ben Jonson*, edited by C. H. Herford and Percy and Evelyn Simpson, 11 vols, Oxford, 1925–52.
Heywood	Thomas Heywood, *Dramatic Works*, edited by R. H. Shepherd, 6 vols, London, 1874. (References to this edition are to volume and page numbers. Quotations are given from the original editions of Heywood, but for convenience references are also provided to the somewhat unreliable Shepherd edition.)
K.B.P.	Francis Beaumont, *The Knight of the Burning Pestle*, in *The Dramatic Works in the Beaumont and Fletcher Canon*, edited by Fredson Bowers, vol. 1, Cambridge, 1966. (References to this edition are to act and line numbers; scene divisions are not marked.)
Linthicum	M. C. Linthicum, *Costume in the Drama of Shakespeare and his Contemporaries*, Oxford, 1936.
Lyly	John Lyly, *The Complete Works*, edited by R. W. Bond, 3 vols, Oxford, 1902.
McKerrow	R. B. McKerrow, *Printers' and Publishers' Devices in England and Scotland, 1485–1640*, London, 1949.
M.L.N.	*Modern Language Notes.*
M.L.R.	*Modern Language Review.*
M.P.	*Modern Philology.*
N.&Q.	*Notes and Queries.*
Nashe, ed. McKerrow	*The Works of Thomas Nashe*, edited by R. B. McKerrow, revised by F. P. Wilson, 5 vols, Oxford, 1958.
O.D.E.P.	*The Oxford Dictionary of English Proverbs*, third edition, edited by F. P. Wilson, Oxford, 1970.
O.E.D.	*A New English Dictionary on Historical Principles.*
Partridge	Eric Partridge, *Shakespeare's Bawdy*, London, 1947, second edition, 1958.
R.E.S.	*Review of English Studies.*
Ren.Q.	*Renaissance Quarterly.*
S.B.	*Studies in Bibliography.*
S.E.L.	*Studies in English Literature.*

ABBREVIATIONS

Shakespeare's England	*Shakespeare's England*, edited by Sidney Lee and C.T. Onions, 2 vols, Oxford, 1916.
Sh.S.	*Shakespeare Survey.*
S.P.	*Studies in Philology.*
Stow	John Stow, *A Survey of London*, edited by C. L. Kingsford, 2 vols, London, 1908.
Sugden	E. H. Sugden, *A Topographical Dictionary to the Works of Shakespeare and his Fellow Dramatists*, Manchester, 1925.
Tilley	M. P. Tilley, *A Dictionary of the Proverbs in England in the Sixteenth and Seventeenth Centuries*, Ann Arbor, Michigan, 1950.

List of Illustrations

Simon Eyre; A drawing by Roger Leigh, Clarenceux King of Arms, ca. 1446–7 (*Wriothesley MS. Heralds' Roll of Arms, Guildhall Library, London*). Reproduced by permission of the Librarian, the Guildhall Library   *frontispiece*

London, about 1599   *pages 12–13*

The title-page of the first edition of *The Shoemaker's Holiday* (1600)   *page 72*

Introduction

1. DEKKER'S CAREER: THE PLAY IN ITS BIOGRAPHICAL
CONTEXT

Thomas Dekker was probably twenty-seven when, on 15 July
1599, the theatre-manager Philip Henslowe lent £3 to Thomas
Downton to 'bye A Boocke of thomas dickers Called the gentle
Craft'.[1] 'A Pleasant Comedy of the Gentle Craft', better known as
The Shoemaker's Holiday, is one of several plays on which Dekker
worked for Henslowe in the last years of the sixteenth century. Our
first definite record of him is some eighteen months before, when,
on 8 January 1598, he received from Henslowe the sum of 20s for an
unnamed play. One week later Henslowe paid him a further £4 for
a play which he calls 'fayeton'.[2] In September of the same year,
Dekker's name appears alongside those of Shakespeare, Jonson, and
Chapman in Francis Meres's list of those he considers 'our best for
Tragedie'.[3] It seems likely, then, that by the time he came to write
The Shoemaker's Holiday Dekker was an established member of the
group of writers who, in the last years of the sixteenth century and
the first years of the seventeenth, kept Henslowe supplied with a
constant stream of new plays for performance by the Lord
Admiral's men, principally at the Rose Theatre on Bankside.

Of Dekker's life before he joined Henslowe's circle almost
nothing is known. His birth is usually placed in 1572, for he refers to
his 'threescore years' in the dedication to the 1632 edition of *English
Villainies*.[4] Of his origins there is no evidence. His surname may
indicate that he came of a Dutch family, perhaps one of those that
had fled to England to escape religious persecution. Lacy's disguise
as Hans in *The Shoemaker's Holiday* is one of several instances in his
work of acquaintance with things Dutch which seem to increase
the plausibility of this conjecture—but conjecture it remains. Of his
education there is no record, a fact which makes it unlikely that he
attended the university. Apart from a reference in the register of St

Giles, Cripplegate, to the baptism on 27 October 1594 of Dorcas, daughter of 'Thomas Dycker' (who may or may not be the poet), we know no detail of his life until that first mention of him in Henslowe's Diary on 15 January 1598.

But if no detail is certain, one general fact stands out in irrefutable clarity. Dekker was a Londoner, born and brought up in the city which, even more than it does today, dwarfed all others in England.[5] In the Induction to *The Seven Deadly Sins of London* Dekker addresses the city with the declaration 'from thy womb receiued I my being, frō thy brests my nourishment'. Elsewhere he calls London the 'Mother of my life, Nurse of my being'.[6] The intensity of the relationship with London that Dekker here betrays is discernible in nearly all his literary work, revealed now in celebration of the city's past glories and present achievements, now in lamentation of its miseries or castigation of its vices. Mme Jones-Davies, indeed, refers to London as his collaborator rather than his subject (I.27). It seems fitting, therefore, that *The Shoemaker's Holiday*, with its infectious enthusiasm for London customs, its fascination for the trades, the festivals, even the place-names of the capital, should be the earliest of his plays to have survived.

That it was not his first play, however, is clear from a series of references in Henslowe's Diary to several other dramas, all now lost, following the mention of *Phaeton* in January 1598. Even before that, Dekker almost certainly worked, along with Chettle, Munday, Heywood, and Shakespeare on the unpublished play of *Sir Thomas More*.[7] In the years following Henslowe's first mention of him, he seems to have been writing plays with quite astonishing frequency: between 1598 and 1603 more than fifty plays, in a wide variety of genres, all but a handful now lost, have been linked with his name as author, part-author, or reviser.[8] The majority were written for Henslowe, many of them in collaboration with the manager's other regular playmakers Henry Chettle, Michael Drayton, and Robert Wilson. In 1599, the year of *The Shoemaker's Holiday*, we find him working on ten plays: an Introduction to *The Civil Wars of France* (alone) in January; *Troilus and Cressida* (with Chettle) in April and May; *Orestes Furens* (alone) in May; *The Shoemaker's Holiday* (alone) in July; *The Stepmother's Tragedy* (with Chettle) in July and August; *Bear a Brain, or Better Late than Never* (alone) in August; *Page of Plymouth* (with Ben Jonson) in August

and September; *Robert II, or The Scots Tragedy* (with Chettle and
Jonson) in September; *Patient Grissil* (with Chettle and William
Haughton) from October to December; and *Old Fortunatus* (alone)
in November and December.[9] Working under pressure seems to
have been no hardship to Dekker: from this remarkably productive
year came two of his most successful plays, *The Shoemaker's Holiday*
and *Old Fortunatus*, both of them called to Court for the Christmas
revels of 1599–1600, both published (with title-page advertisement
of their Court performances) in 1600, and both somewhat unusual,
in the context of Dekker's overall dramatic work, in being written
independently of collaboration. With *Patient Grissil* (printed in
1603) they are the only plays from this group to have survived.

Dekker's professional diligence during these years with Henslowe, and the successes he achieved, provided him with only a
modest living. As Henslowe's Diary reveals, payments 'in earnest'
were often made during the course of work on a play, with a final
payment for the completed 'book'; but the total payment for any
play was rarely more than £6 or £7, and this was frequently to be
shared among two or more collaborators. On two occasions before
he completed *The Shoemaker's Holiday* Dekker was in gaol for debt:
on 4 February 1598 (it is only the third mention of him in the Diary)
Henslowe had to pay £2 to release him from the Counter in the
Poultry, and again on 30 January 1599 he lent £3 10s to release
Dekker from arrest.[10] This precarious existence on the brink of
poverty and disaster, against which constant hard work is the only
protection, may perhaps be seen as part of the background to *The
Shoemaker's Holiday*. For, as we shall see, Dekker chose to add to the
two optimistic stories which he borrowed for his plot a third, made
from his own invention and, we may imagine, from his own
experience, of a man and his wife saved from poverty and despair
only by hard work and good fortune.

The years which followed *The Shoemaker's Holiday* continued
the pattern of hard work, versatility, and successful achievement,
mixed with failure, that had already established itself by 1599. An
undoubted indication of success, following the Court performances of 1599–1600, was Dekker's participation with the
Chamberlain's Men (Shakespeare's company) in 1601 in the so-
called 'War of the Theatres' with a play against Ben Jonson,
Dekker's former collaborator.[11] *Satiromastix*, again written at

speed, though somewhat distanced for modern audiences by its
topicality and close involvement with the personalities concerned
in the quarrel, reveals nevertheless a deftness of satiric touch,
sharpness mingled with geniality, that is indicative of Dekker's
facility in yet another dramatic genre.

Satiromastix is the first play we know Dekker to have written
outside Henslowe's auspices. In the thirty-one years between its
completion and the burial, recorded in the register of St James's,
Clerkenwell, on 25 August 1632 of 'Thomas Decker, househol-
der'—assumed to be the dramatist—he worked as a free-lance
writer in almost any literary genre from which a living might be
wrung. That the effort sometimes failed is clear from the fact that
seven of these years, from 1612 to 1619, were spent in the King's
Bench prison for debt. Even after his release the threat of poverty
remained constant: in 1626 and 1628 he is in trouble for failure to
attend church, probably through fear of arrest at the hands of
creditors if he appeared in public; and it seems likely that he died in
debt.[12]

The fight against poverty, waged exclusively in dramatic form
in the early period to which *The Shoemaker's Holiday* belongs, was
fought on a broader front in the years that followed. His theatrical
work in the Jacobean and Caroline period is almost entirely collaborative. It is a measure, perhaps, of his professional reputation that
the principal dramatists of the period nearly all worked with him:
Shakespeare and Ben Jonson in the 1590s, Middleton, Webster,
Massinger, and Heywood in the first dozen or so years of the new
century, and then, in the 1620s, there is the new alliance of the
ageing Dekker and the emerging genius of John Ford. Allied to his
work for the theatre is his connection with a number of civic
pageants. The coming of James I saw Dekker's first venture into
this genre when he collaborated with Ben Jonson in *The Magnificent Entertainment Given to King James ... upon the Day of His
Majesty's Triumphant Passage through London*. He was to return to
the creation of pageants for the City of London in 1612, 1627, 1628,
and 1629 when he was responsible for the entertainments offered to
the incoming Lord Mayors.[13]

With the new reign he turned also, probably for the first time, to
pamphlet-writing. In *The Wonderful Year* (1603) he presented a
'picture of London, lying sick of the plague', to which he added

'like a merry epilogue to a dull play, certain tales . . . cut out in sundry fashions'. The formula was one to which he returned in later plague-years.[14] His subsequent non-dramatic work shows enormous variety and versatility. Collections of tales, jest-books, anti-Catholic propaganda, imitations of Nashe, topical pamphlets, exposures of the criminal underworld, war poems, social satires, a collection of prayers, a visionary poem—all are among the genres he explored. The bibliography of his writings (including lost and collaborative works, and some items dubiously assigned to him) comprises more than 140 titles.[15] It is a prodigious output, involving the completion of a work, on average, every three or four months throughout his working life.

To read back into a dramatist's first surviving play characteristics which he reveals over the next thirty years of his writing career is an enterprise of perhaps dubious validity. There are, however, two aspects of *The Shoemaker's Holiday* that may helpfully be illuminated by reference to Dekker's later work. The first and most obvious of these, the vividness of the play's London atmosphere, looks forward to that obsession with the capital which, it has already been remarked, dominates his later writing. The London setting of *The Shoemaker's Holiday* is unusual in Dekker's early work—or it seems to be, so far as one can tell from the titles of lost plays. But the success of it in this comedy might be regarded as Dekker's discovery of his real *forte*. The 'picture of London lying sick of the plague' in *The Wonderful Year*, and the series of pamphlets which followed it, shows Dekker using London as the microcosm which provided him with an ample basis for the exploration of human society. After the first pamphlets, London is used again as the setting for plays—*Westward Ho, Northward Ho, The Roaring Girl*—with the same exploitation of familiar London types, customs, place-names, involving the audience in the dramatic action through the immediacy of familiar response, as he had achieved in *The Shoemaker's Holiday*. A Londoner, offering a portrait of London to his fellow-citizens, the role Dekker assumes so successfully in *The Shoemaker's Holiday*, was to prove the dominant role of his literary career. Even the mayoral pageants of 1612 and 1627–29 were in a sense prepared for by this early play celebrating the life of one of London's former mayors. The same excitement in the city's past and its institutions, constantly shaping and enriching its present, which *The Shoemaker's Holiday* communicates, is still present at the other end of Dekker's career as he begins his last mayoral pageant, *London's Tempe* (1629), with an enthusiastic rehearsal of some of the principal landmarks in the city's development, and in its civic ceremonial.

The second aspect of *The Shoemaker's Holiday* that may helpfully be considered in relation to Dekker's later work is what might be termed the 'economic' one. The overall mood of the play is optimistic—for the most part, indeed, ebullient. To the two stories he found in his source, of a married man getting rich with the help of his wife, and a rich man getting a wife with the help of his money and influence (the stories which he developed into the Eyre and Lacy plots of the play), Dekker has, however, added a third of his own invention. The effect the story of Ralph and Jane has on the play is considered below, but it is worth remarking here how its revelation of the precarious boundary between the cheerful security within the bright circle of Eyre's household, and the poverty and despair outside it, points forward to the exploration of that dark world of penury and suffering, and attendant crime, that we find in some of Dekker's later writing. 'God helpe the Poore, The rich can shift' he declared in the motto on the title-page of *Work for Armourers* (1609), a pamphlet which shows the constant bickering between the Princesses Money and Poverty arriving at open war. Among the recruits in Poverty's army at the start of the campaign are soldiers returning from the Low Countries where 'they had ventured their lives, spent their blood, lost legs and armes . . . not a rag to their backes' and are now left with no alternative but 'to serue *Pouerty*, to liue and dye ẃ her'.[16] Ralph Damport, returning from the wars on his crutches in *The Shoemaker's Holiday*, is more fortunate in his homecoming. But that it should appear to be only good fortune that saves Ralph and his wife from the fate to which the normal operation of society would otherwise condemn them is part of Dekker's intention in *The Shoemaker's Holiday*. He has no solution to offer, of course, for the social conflict depicted in *Work for Armourers*—the wars, indeed, merely peter out, with defections on both sides—any more than the governments of Elizabeth and James I could provide solutions for the problem of poverty in their kingdoms. But one wise counsellor does emerge from the ranks of Covetousness, Parsimony, Deceit, and their fellows, who follow the Princess Money, and the equally disruptive Discontent, Despair, Repining, and the rest, who form the train of the Princess Poverty. This is Industry, whom we find listed among the counsellors of Poverty, though he is always 'seeking . . . to draw *Money* to be stil in league with' his mistress (sig. C3*v*; Grosart, IV.116). This 'deepe scholler, stout in warre, and prouident in peace', who, 'when the Land had beene ready to sterue, hath . . . releeued it, and turned dearth into plenty', and who compels men 'to take paines' rather than 'to liue basely', is Dekker's only answer to the problems of the subjects of the Princess Poverty. It is precisely the answer he had offered ten years before, in *The Shoemaker's Holiday*, when the newly returned Ralph faces his own disablement, and the news of the loss of his wife, with the resolution 'Since I want limbs and lands, / I'll to God, my good friends, and to these my hands' (x.118).

Work for Armourers is one of Dekker's more direct statements on the conflict between poverty and wealth, and has therefore been chosen to illustrate his fuller treatment of a question already touched on, lightly but tellingly, in *The Shoemaker's Holiday*. But dread of poverty, pity for its victims, and fear of the social outrages it provoked, can be discerned throughout much of his work. To the opposite problem, of riches and their proper use, Dekker addressed himself only a few weeks after *The Shoemaker's Holiday*, in *Old Fortunatus*. Here Fortunatus is offered by the Goddess Fortuna a choice of wisdom, strength, health, beauty, long life, and riches. He chooses after only a little hesitation:

> Gold is the strength, the sinnewes of the world,
> The Health, the soule, the beautie most diuine,
> A maske of Gold hides all deformities;
> Gold is heauens phisicke, lifes restoratiue,
> Oh therefore make me rich. (I.i.289)

The play goes on to depict, in light-hearted tone but with serious moral intention, the misuse of Fortune's gifts by Fortunatus and his two sons, Andelocia the squanderer of wealth, and Ampedo the hoarder. Andelocia pronounces his own sentence as he dies:

> Riches and knowledge are two gifts diuine.
> They that abuse them both as I haue done,
> To shame, to beggerie, to hell must runne. (V.ii.173)

The judgement on Ampedo is spoken by the Goddess Virtue:

> those that (like him) doe muffle
> *Vertue* in clouds, and care not how shee shine,
> Ile make their glorie like to his decline:
> He made no vse of me, but like a miser,
> Lockt vp his wealth in rustie barres of sloth . . .
> So perish they that so keepe vertue poore. (V.ii.272)

The golden mean achieved by Eyre in *The Shoemaker's Holiday*, mediating, like Industry (a quality he himself embodies) between the followers of Money and Poverty, using riches to create a fruitful and harmonious balance, stands out more clearly when seen in contrast to some of Dekker's other treatments of the question of wealth and poverty. And in his addition to the characters he took over from his main source of two of the followers of poverty, Ralph and Jane, who show the harmony and balance represented by Eyre momentarily threatened, Dekker has emphasised the importance of that harmony, and, perhaps, its precariousness. In the dedication to *Dekker His Dream*, the strange, disturbing poem he published soon after his release from prison in 1619, Dekker wrote: 'There is a *Hell* named in our Creede, and a *Heauen*, and the *Hell* comes before: If we looke not into the first, we shall neuer liue in the last' (sig. A2v; Grosart, III.8). To see *The Shoemaker's Holiday* in the context of the hardships of Dekker's own life, of the suffering and social disharmony which he confronts in some of his other writing and which is allowed momentarily to cloud the cheerful world of Eyre's London, may serve to define, more sharply, and perhaps more poignantly, the briefly vivid optimism of its vision.

2. DATE: THE PLAY IN ITS HISTORICAL AND LITERARY CONTEXT

Henslowe's record of the payment on 15 July 1599 of £3 to 'bye A Boocke of thomas dickers Called the gentle Craft' establishes the date of completion (and, incidentally, the authorship)[17] of *The Shoemaker's Holiday* beyond reasonable doubt. Both Chambers and Greg regard the 15 July entry as the record of a final payment, and Arthur F. Kinney's attempt to reverse their judgement is unacceptable.[18] Kinney's intention is to link the play with Christmas festivities, and he finds completion of it in September, when 'such troupes as the Admiral's Men were beginning to choose plays for the Queen's Christmas festivities', more in keeping with this suggestion. Whether a play started in the middle of the year is more likely to be influenced by thoughts of Christmas than one finished then may be debatable. More important, the evidence of the Diary points the other way. Kinney rightly says that £3 represents only about half of Henslowe's usual payment to Dekker for a play. But he then argues from this that the 15 July entry must record the first payment, with others following during the months up to September. The Diary entries, however, seem to be extremely full from July to the end of the year; the hiatus before late May, as Chambers (III.292) argued, is much more likely to conceal payments. The wording of the 15 July entry also seems to suggest a final payment. Henslowe almost invariably accompanies entries for advances on work in progress by the words 'in earnest'; the 'to bye' of *The Shoemaker's Holiday* entry, though unusual, seems much more akin to the phrase 'in payment of' or 'in full payment of' with which Henslowe habitually records the last transaction with the author of a play. Thus for *Old Fortunatus*, the other surviving 1599 play of which Dekker was sole author, the Diary records payments 'in earnest' on 9 and 24 November (£2 and £3 respectively), with Dekker receiving a further sum of £1 on the thirtieth 'in full payment of his booke'.[19]

If the Diary entries for *Old Fortunatus* for three weeks or so before completion can be regarded as a possible parallel, we may tentatively surmise that Dekker wrote *The Shoemaker's Holiday* in the few weeks on either side of midsummer 1599. The intense activity of that year, with its clear evidence that he was working with extraordinary speed and vigour, seems to argue for rapid composition—though it has to be remembered that the probable publication date of his principal source (see Appendix A, p. 203) would have permitted a longer period of work on the play. The title-page of the first quarto records a performance of *The Shoemaker's Holiday* at Court on 1 January 1600. One assumes, though direct evidence is lacking, that it had proved successful on the public stage before being offered at Court. The likelihood is that it was first performed at the Rose in the late summer or autumn of 1599.

There is a nice appropriateness in the fact that a comedy which ends in a cheerful assertion of English unity, a unity embracing monarch, nobility, merchants, and apprentices, should have been written in the final year of a century which had seen such enormous progress towards the achievement of this ideal. By 1599 the long Elizabethan struggle for political and religious stability was plainly over; the great trial for which all the earlier part of the reign had, in a sense, been a preparation had passed with the triumphant repulse of the Armada in 1588. During the 1590s other armadas had threatened—there were even rumours of renewed Spanish preparations in 1599 itself—but they had not materialised. Philip II of Spain, for so long the arch-enemy, had died in 1598. In all but outward declaration, the succession question too, so troublous to the earlier years of the reign, was settled. A mood of self-confidence in national unity accompanied the sense of danger past and victory achieved, and lent its flavour to the literature of the decade, in particular to the great series of plays on English history—a genre to which (so Henslowe's records inform us, though the plays are lost) Dekker was himself a prolific contributor. With the turn of the century the mood was shattered in the tragic futility of Essex's rebellion, his misconceived and abortive uprising, and prompt execution, harshly closing a chapter to which the Queen's own death provided the epilogue. But in the summer of 1599 Essex was still, in the eyes of many observers, the symbol of England's national strength. Probably only a few weeks before Dekker completed *The Shoemaker's Holiday*, Shakespeare, bringing to a close his great cyclic dramatisation of English history, was anticipating Essex's triumphant return from Ireland, .'bringing rebellion broached on his sword'.[20] Essex's sudden and ignominious return to England at the end of September, with his Irish campaign, and his career, in ruins, was soon to make a bitter end of such hopes. In this last summer of the century, however, the sense of national confidence which informs the presentation of political events in *Henry V* harmonises interestingly with the optimism of Dekker's portrayal of social affairs in *The Shoemaker's Holiday*. The massive Poor Law legislation of two years before should remind us of the malaise underlying the cheerful surface, a malaise which is allowed its brief appearance even in *The Shoemaker's Holiday* and which, as we have seen, Dekker was to explore more widely in his later work.

　　The concern with poverty, which Dekker reveals in his story of Ralph and Jane, and with the proper use of wealth in society, which pervades the play, make their appearance in other publications of the last years of the sixteenth century. Among them are several works, all published in the year before Dekker's play, by the poet Richard Barnfield, with titles of rather aggressively self-evident purpose: *The Encomium of Lady Pecunia, or, The Praise of Money*; *The Complaint of Poetry for the Death of Liberality*; *The Combat between Conscience and Covetousness*. In the same year too, there appeared, pseudonymously no doubt, in the curious collection *Tyro's Roaring Meg, Planted against the Walls of Melancholy*, a racy prose attack on niggardliness, and an assertion of the social importance of liberality, under the title *The Mean in Spending*. More sedately, in the previous year, a pious Yorkshireman, Henry Arthington, had come into print with a pamphlet called *Provision for the Poor, Now in Penury, out of the Storehouse of God's Plenty* in which he offered an analysis of the causes of poverty and a remedy for it in a return to what he regarded as the neglected virtue of charity. It is the failure of charitable giving that all these, and other, writers constantly find responsible for the problem of poverty, and, as with Arthington, the remedy proposed is usually the revival of the alleged godliness and generosity of the past. But in the successive Poor Law enactments through the reign of Elizabeth one sees the development of the process by which the state was gradually forced to recognise the fact that the old system had irretrievably failed to deal with a new situation, and to take over control of the organisation of poor relief which had previously been dispensed by private institutions and individuals.[21] Dekker's Simon Eyre, of course, is a most confident assertion of the old tradition of individual munificence.

But though a longer perspective makes clear the decline of that tradition, and though a little delving reveals that the apparent harmony and optimism of the social surface at the end of the century was precarious and fragile, for the moment it still seemed possible in 1599 to enjoy the fruits of the Elizabethan achievement. Four years later, in *The Wonderful Year* (1603), Dekker describes the sense of national harmony that Elizabeth had established by contrasting it with the shock of her death:

> For having brought up even under her wing a nation that was almost begotten and born under her, that never shouted any other *ave* than for her name, never saw the face of any prince but herself, never understood

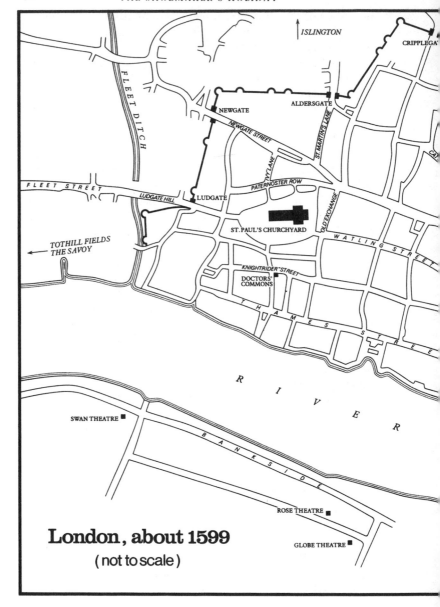

ISLINGTON

CRIPPLEGATE

FLEET DITCH

NEWGATE

ALDERSGATE

NEWGATE STREET

ST. MARTIN'S LANE

IVY LANE

FLEET STREET

LUDGATE HILL

PATERNOSTER ROW

LUDGATE

OLD EXCHANGE

TOTHILL FIELDS
THE SAVOY

ST. PAUL'S CHURCHYARD

WATLING STREET

KNIGHTRIDER STREET

DOCTORS'
COMMONS

THAMES STREET

R   I   V   E   R

SWAN THEATRE ■

B A N K S I D E

ROSE THEATRE ■

London, about 1599
(not to scale)

GLOBE THEATRE ■

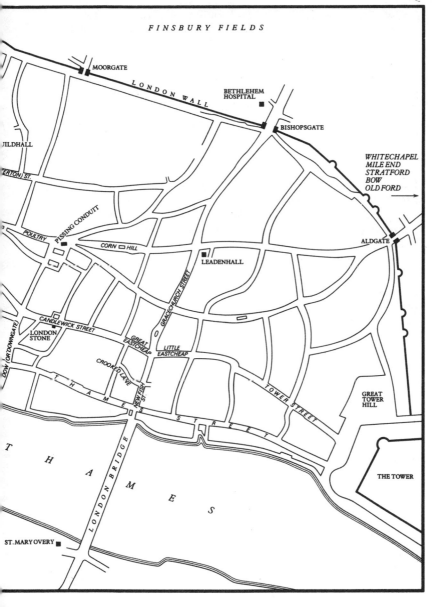

FINSBURY FIELDS

MOORGATE

LONDON WALL

BETHLEHEM
HOSPITAL

BISHOPSGATE

UILDHALL

ERTON ST.

WHITECHAPEL
MILE END
STRATFORD
BOW
OLD FORD
→

PISSING CONDUIT

POULTRY

CORN ☐ HILL

LEADENHALL

ALDGATE

GRACECHURCH STREET

CANDLEWICK STREET

LOW (OR DOWNGATE)

LONDON
STONE

GREAT
EASTCHEAP

LITTLE
EASTCHEAP

CROOKED LANE

T H A M E S

NEW FISH ST.

STREET

TOWER STREET

GREAT
TOWER
HILL

LONDON BRIDGE

T

H

A

M

E

S

THE TOWER

ST. MARY OVERY ■

what that strange outlandish word 'change' signified—how was it possible but that her sickness should throw abroad an universal fear, and her death an astonishment? (Pendry, p. 33)

The growing confidence of the sense of national identity which the history plays of the 1590s had exploited, and which provides a general context for *The Shoemaker's Holiday*, is linked and over-shadowed in Dekker's play by an apparently more recent pheno-menon—the exploitation of the local patriotism of Londoners. That obsession with London that came to dominate Dekker's own work had made its theatrical presence felt only recently, in William Haughton's *Englishmen for My Money* of 1598. Haughton, like Dekker, was a member of Henslowe's regular team of playwrights; a few months after the completion of *The Shoemaker's Holiday* they collaborated in the writing of *Patient Grissil*.[22] It seems safe to assume that Dekker would have known his colleague's work.

Englishmen for My Money appears to be the first of the London citizen comedies.[23] If it is, it shows the genre emerging fully fledged. It is full of London place names, so that we know where many of the characters live and could plot the action on a map, and punctuated by familiar London sounds, such as the bells of the Royal Exchange, or Bow Bell. The audience are being offered the pleasures of familiarity, a play set in the streets through which they had just walked to the theatre, punctuated by the sounds that measured out their daily lives. And with this flattery of local self-consciousness goes an overall flavour of national patriotism as the sisters, whose affairs form the central interest of the play, make fools of their foreign wooers and succeed in marrying the Eng-lishmen of their choice (and of the play's title).

The formula established by Haughton quickly became a fashion. Within a year came *The Shoemaker's Holiday*, and during the next two decades an enormous number of plays with London settings were written. 'Our scene is London, 'cause we would make known, / No country's mirth is better than our own' Ben Jonson announced in 1610 in the Prologue to *The Alchemist*—and by that date there was a large body of plays to support the assertion. The great development of London plays in the early years of the seventeenth century is in some ways a logical progression from the history plays which had dominated the preceding decade: for where the histories had satisfied the curiosity of their audiences for knowledge of their country's past, and flattery of its achievements, the London plays frequently offered instruction in the history of the city and flattery (with increasing elements of satire) of citizen values and local patriotism. In the lesson on the origins of the Leadenhall market and of the Shrove Tuesday holiday in *The Shoemaker's Holiday* Dekker makes excellent dramatic use of these semi-didactic elements.[24]

The growing self-awareness of Londoners that lies behind *The Shoemaker's Holiday*, and the citizen comedy in general, and at which Dekker directed much of his later writing, is evidenced also in the publication in 1598 of that most famous of all works of London topography, John Stow's *Survey of London*. Stow's reputation had been established in the composition of historical chronicles, and his turning from national history to London history interestingly parallels the movement we have observed in the drama. That his book should have appeared in the same year as Haughton's first London play is another nice coincidence. The *Survey* was certainly used as a source by later writers of London plays, and Dekker seems to have turned to it for some items of information in *The Shoemaker's Holiday* (see notes on *Dramatis Personae*). It concerns us here not only because of its obvious significance as a milestone in the development of Elizabethan Londoners' interest in their own city, but also because of Paul C. Davies's suggestion that it may have had a direct influence on Dekker as rather more than a casual source of information. In his edition of *The Shoemaker's Holiday* Davies proposes (p. 8) that Dekker's play may be in some sense a development of the 'Discourse' that Stow appended to the *Survey*, 'by way of an Apologie (or defence) against the opinion of some men, which thinke that the greatnes of that Cittie [London] standeth not with the profit and securitie of this Realme'. The picture of London life that Stow presents in answer to this charge shows some interesting similarities to that offered by Dekker in *The Shoemaker's Holiday*. He describes the citizens, 'by profession busie Bees, and trauellers for their liuing in the hiue of the common wealth', their various classes 'friendly enterlaced', and from the fact that Londoners 'be generally bent to trauell' he 'draws hope' that 'they shall escape the vices which idle people do fall into'. Since the 'greatest part of them be neyther to rich nor too poore', he concludes that 'the Prince needeth not feare sedition by them'. Merchants and retailers do not 'profit themselues only, for the prince and realme both are enriched by their riches'.[25] And so he goes on, painting a picture of the social harmony of industrious citizens, achieving, through the fair accumulation and proper distribution and use of wealth, the general good of the nation and its capital. Whether this 'Discourse' influenced the similar sentiments of Dekker's play it is impossible to say; it is clear, however, and perhaps more important, that both draw on the same mood of optimistic pride in London that is one of the most important formative influences on *The Shoemaker's Holiday*.

Before turning to the direct narrative sources of the play, a number of other possible literary influences may be noted. Most of these are dramatic, but the pamphlets and tales of Thomas Nashe from the earlier years of the decade, with their vivid, robust, effervescent prose and their good-humoured name-calling, must certainly be counted among the most important formative influences on Dekker's own prose style, both in his later pamphlets and in the role of Simon Eyre in *The Shoemaker's Holiday*. As for dramatic influences, Dekker was an active worker in the small world of the London theatre, and is likely to have been aware of what other dramatists were doing. The war background to *The Shoemaker's Holiday*, with characters leaving to fight in France, may owe something to Shakespeare's *Henry V*, completed, probably, a few months, or weeks, earlier; it seems likely that we should have Henry V in mind when the King appears at the end of the play (see below, p. 24); and the sense of comradeship and cheerful harmony that Dekker establishes around Eyre in the final scenes is slightly reminiscent of the mood that Shakespeare suggests in the Agincourt episodes of his play. The verbal ostentation of Eyre occasionally recalls Ancient Pistol, who had achieved enough success in *2 Henry IV* to be mentioned on the title-page of the first quarto, as well as to reappear in *Henry V*. But Pistol's self-important verbosity derives from a sham and borrowed rhetoric, concealing hollowness, while Eyre's verbal fecundity seems to be a just representation of the inner man. The Bastard Faulconbridge in Shakespeare's *King John* affords a closer parallel. The 'madcap' qualities he displays in the early scenes (the very term is applied to him at I.i.84, as it is more than once to Eyre), the verbal gusto of his role, words and epithets tumbling from him, ensure that he takes the play almost by storm, in much the same way that Eyre does in *The Shoemaker's Holiday*. And like Eyre, too, Faulconbridge comes to control his play, to shape its course, and to provide its conclusion. On a smaller scale, the Host of the Garter in *The Merry Wives of Windsor* shares the same delight in words, the intoxicating piling of epithet upon epithet, that is Eyre's most remarkable characteristic. That Dekker should have remembered, in his comedy of London life, Shakespeare's citizen play of two years earlier,[26] with its vivid evocation of the town in which it is set, seems very likely. He may well have remembered also Ben Jonson's ostentatiously verbose shoemaker Juniper from *The Case is Altered*, first performed about 1597–98. Cobblers and shoemakers seem, in fact, to have been popular on the stage both before and after *The Shoemaker's Holiday*.[27] Two of the plays in which they appear are of more particular interest for containing episodes that may have influenced Dekker: at the end of *George à Greene, The Pinner of Wakefield* (*c.* 1590) there is a scene reminiscent of *The Shoemaker's Holiday*, as the King arrives to meet the shoemakers of Bradford and confers on their profession the name of 'the Gentle Craft' because they have drunk with him and thus achieved gentility; and in *The Famous Victories of Henry V* (*c.* 1586) there is an impressment scene involving John Cobbler and his weeping wife, pleading to be released from service in France, which resembles the opening scene of *The Shoemaker's Holiday*.[28] The influence of Paris in *Romeo and Juliet* (*c.* 1595) on Dekker's conception of Hammon, another rival wooer, has also been plausibly argued.[29] Possible verbal echoes from this and other plays are discussed in the Commentary.

3. THE USE OF SOURCE MATERIAL

When one turns from possible dramatic influences to the immediate narrative sources of *The Shoemaker's Holiday*, vagueness is replaced by clarity. Of the three plots that Dekker interweaves in his play, two are drawn directly from Thomas Deloney's *The Gentle Craft* and the third, though largely of Dekker's own invention, shows some traces of its influence. Deloney's title-page reference to the motto 'A shoemaker's son is a prince born', which Dekker transforms into Eyre's catch-phrase, his dedication to 'all the good yeomen of the Gentle Craft', followed by Dekker in his epistle 'To all good fellows, professors of the gentle craft, of what degree soever', his first tale of St Hugh and of the use to which the shoemakers put his bones, alluded to at several points in the play, his frequent presentation of shoemakers' songs which Dekker follows with his 'three-man's songs',[30] and his overall cheerful celebration of the shoemaking trade, which Dekker fully endorses, indicate the pervasive influence of Deloney's book on *The Shoemaker's Holiday*. Dekker's more concrete debt was to the second and third of the three stories that make up Part I of *The Gentle Craft*, the story of Crispine and Crispianus, and the story of Simon Eyre. A summary of the former, and a text of the latter, are provided as Appendix A to this edition.

Dekker's use of this material in constructing *The Shoemaker's Holiday* is brilliant in its economy and integration. He uses the strong, simple story-line of Eyre's rise to power as his solid centre. But just as Deloney feels it necessary to vary the apparent inevitability of Eyre's rise by adding the amusing, irrelevant adventures of his household servants (see Appendix A, pp. 204–5), so Dekker uses the Eyre story only as the central anchor to which he attaches the two stories of the contrasted pairs of lovers, Lacy and Rose, and Ralph and Jane. The interdependence of these parts is made possible by an amalgamation of the roles of Eyre and his wife with those of the shoemaker and his wife in the Crispine–Crispianus tale, and by the invention of a rival wooer in both love-plots, whose interference keeps the tension alive, thus postponing, and making more welcome, the happy ending. The treatment of the source-material in the three plots of *The Shoemaker's Holiday* is worth examining in some detail.

The Crispine–Crispianus story provides Dekker with the Rose–Lacy plot. Crispine becomes Lacy, and though the other brother virtually disappears, a vestige remains, perhaps, in Askew, Lacy's companion, who goes off to fight in France. Dekker's identification of Crispine's master with the Simon Eyre of Deloney's next story necessitates the movement from Kent to London. The hostile father Maximinus is thus transformed from Emperor to Lord Mayor. In Stow's *Survey of London* (II.173) Dekker would have found 'Robert Oteley, Grocer' listed as Lord Mayor in the same year (1434) as Eyre became sheriff. The compression of the time-scheme allows Dekker to suggest that Oatley is mayor throughout the whole period of Eyre's rise (and, apparently, his immediate predecessor in office (see xxi.76)). Oatley thus doubles the roles of the hostile father in Deloney's story of Crispine and of the Lord Mayor who feasts Eyre in Chapter 11 of *The Gentle Craft*. The danger of incongruity here is averted by giving Oatley a fierce pride in citizen caste: he can thus oppose a courtier's suit for his daughter and at the same time celebrate the success of a fellow citizen. In Deloney's story Maximinus is anxious that his daughter Ursula should marry 'some worthy Romane' (p. 120), and Ursula herself is at first horrified that a princess should feel affection for a shoemaker. Dekker retains this disruptive sense of class-consciousness, but reverses it, so that Oatley objects to Lacy as someone whose social station he cannot equal. The addition of an uncle for Lacy, the Earl of Lincoln, who also opposes the marriage through class-prejudice, emphasises this aspect of the story, so that the happy ending, producing from this class-jealousy a universal harmony, is the more striking. The love element of the plot is brought in at once, and strengthened, by having Lacy go into disguise as a shoemaker, not from fear, as Crispine does, but in order to remain close to Rose. The necessity for the long apprenticeship that Crispine and Crispianus serve is removed by giving us the story of Lacy's having learned the trade of shoemaking during a visit to Wittenberg (i.29). (This may derive from the first story in *The Gentle Craft*, in which St Hugh, rejected by Winifred, goes abroad and becomes a shoemaker.) The idea of Lacy's Dutch disguise under the name Hans is obviously suggested by the presence of Haunce in Deloney's story of Eyre's servants; interestingly Dekker prefers to amuse his audience, as he amuses Firk (iv.51), with Dutch 'gibble-gabble' rather than with its French equivalent as provided by John the Frenchman in Deloney.[31] The love of Rose and Lacy is apparently of long standing when the play opens. Dekker thus has no need to follow Deloney in showing its development, and uses Lacy principally in his disguise role. He does, however, repeat Deloney's amusing device of having the lovers plan their marriage during a shoefitting (sc. xv; Deloney, ch. 6). And it is in the matter of a secret wedding, not a secret childbirth, that Lacy seeks his shoemaker-master's help, thus providing the play with a more traditionally romantic conclusion. The fact that the lovers are kept apart for most of the action leads to the invention of Sybil as a dramatically useful message-carrier. But Dekker's inventiveness also gives the role that comic sauciness which, on a small but vivid level, produces theatrical life. Another addition to this plot, Lincoln's toadying informer Dodger, is also a role with theatrical potential (see below, pp. 51–2). The last of the additions to this plot, the rival wooer Hammon, representative, with his insignificant companion Warner, of the class which Oatley approves, provides Rose with a rare moment of dramatic vigour as she reveals the strength of her love for Lacy in defying her father's choice. Hammon is important, too, as the principal link between this plot and the story of Ralph and Jane.

The second of Dekker's love-stories is the only area of the play not dependent for plot material on Deloney. Only a few hints in the story of Ralph and Jane come from *The Gentle Craft*. The sudden removal from the shoemaker's home of Crispianus, pressed to the wars in France, is precisely the fate of Ralph at the beginning of *The Shoemaker's Holiday*—though the return of Crispianus in glory contrasts sharply with Ralph's limping back as a cripple. Some elements in the story of John, Haunce, Nicholas, and Florence (see Appendix A, pp. 204–5) may also be discerned in the Ralph–Jane plot: Jane, like Florence, is a maid in the Eyre household; the planned wedding which ends the two stories is preceded in both by a meeting of shoemakers at an inn (xvi.159–60; Deloney, ch. 14); and the wedding itself is prevented by the unexpected reappearance at the church-door of a spouse thought dead (John's wife in Deloney, Jane's husband in Dekker). But in all but casual details of this sort the story of Ralph and Jane is quite unlike anything in Deloney. No doubt Dekker drew this material from real life as much as from literature. The soldier maimed in the service of his country is referred to with unfailing regularity as the epitome of the deserving poor by writers on poverty during the period, and the figure was already enough of a stage stereotype by 1599 for Pistol's fraudulent adoption of the role (*Henry V*, V.i.84–5) to be readily recognisable to an audience.[32] Wherever he drew his inspiration from, however, Dekker's importation of this material into his play has a profound effect on the mood, and the overall shape and atmosphere, of *The Shoemaker's Holiday*.

Of the three plots of *The Shoemaker's Holiday* the one closest to Deloney is obviously that which deals with the rise of Simon Eyre from shoemaker to Lord Mayor. Even here, however, Dekker's changes are revealing. The integration of Deloney's two stories means that the disguised Lacy takes the place of the Frenchman John in helping to buy the ship's cargo and in thus setting Eyre on the road to riches. More significant, however, in this first phase of the story, are Dekker's changes to the means by which Eyre procures the cargo. In Deloney, John's role is simply that of interpreter—the Greek captain understands French and not English. In the play the ship and its captain are Dutch, but Hans/Lacy acts as more than go-between: it is his loan of twenty portagues 'as an earnest-penny' which makes possible Eyre's entering into the transaction (vii.23–4). The plan, verging on sharp practice, by which Deloney's Eyre dresses up as an alderman in order to acquire the cargo (Appendix A, pp. 209–10), a plan which is entirely the invention of Eyre's wife, is reduced by Dekker to a relic (vii.107 ff.) which might have been better omitted, since it is probably incomprehensible without the source. The substitution of vagueness, and a generous loan, for female cunning and ambition, seems a significant alteration: in a play which is to be concerned with the proper use of wealth, Dekker may have preferred to avoid any suggestion of impropriety in its original acquisition. Lacy's loan also permits Eyre's gratitude later (xvii.13 ff.), when, with his journeyman turned noble, he is in a position to give him help in return. Such tightening of the plot is typical of Dekker's method throughout.

The order of the second and third stages of Deloney's story—the Lord Mayor's feast for Eyre and Eyre's promotion to sheriff—is reversed by Dekker. The invitation to become sheriff is not something Eyre is goaded into accepting by his wife and the London councillors, as in Deloney, but an apparently spontaneous offer, cheerfully accepted and joyfully announced, which the celebratory feast appropriately follows. The enthusiastic acceptance of civic office by Dekker's Eyre seems also to provide a romanticised view of the normal situation in Elizabethan London: there is evidence that during the 1590s elected sheriffs bought themselves out of the duty of serving their term in office.[33] Interestingly, Dekker finds the acceptance of civic responsibility, though made possible by wealth, rather than the acquisition of wealth itself, the appropriate cause for rejoicing. And at Dekker's feast, Eyre and his household are the only guests; master and men together celebrate his rise. In

Deloney, Eyre, with his wife, finds himself, somewhat self-consciously, at a full-scale civic banquet. Dekker's small alteration here
looks forward to his complete transformation of the last stage of
Deloney's story.

Deloney's rather disappointing final chapter begins with the
statement that 'Within a few yeeres after', Eyre, 'changing his
copie . . . became one of the Worshipfull Company of Drapers'—
the company to which Stow (II.174) also assigns him. Predictably,
Dekker entirely ignores any suggestion of such apostasy as he builds
up the climax of his play from Deloney's hurried conclusion. Most
of the events of the final scenes are in the source—the report of
Eyre's becoming Lord Mayor, his Shrove Tuesday feast, his building of Leadenhall and establishment of the leather-market there.
But in the play these disparate elements are brought together: the
feast for the apprentices is planned to take place at the Leadenhall
itself (or so xviii.190–200, 216 imply), and at the feast we find Eyre
still among his own workmen; it is a celebration of his own
triumph as well as a feast for the apprentices. This simultaneity of
celebration is crowned by the coming of the King (whose presence
in the play is entirely Dekker's invention) to bestow a name on the
new building and to grant its market privileges. The concluding
harmony and festival, which involves the participants in all three
plots and includes monarch, nobility, citizens, and apprentices,
shows Dekker moving a long way indeed beyond his sources.

The plot-changes in this third area of the play are accompanied
by significant additions and alterations to the characters. The creation of the vivid human beings who make up Eyre's household
gives the play much of its life. Purely of Dekker's invention are
Hodge, stolid, dependable, though not without a sense of humour
at his mistress's expense, and Firk, whose bawdy mischievousness is
clearly intended by Dekker to make a direct appeal to the audience:
he shares most of his jokes and tricks with us, at the expense of the
other characters around him. The Madgy Eyre of the play, self-
important, excitable, a little shrewish but fundamentally good-
hearted, is a remarkable development from Deloney's portrait of
Eyre's acquisitive and slightly domineering wife. The most splen-
did transformation of all, however, is the creation of Eyre from the
money-counting nonentity, sanctimoniously quoting scripture as
he gives thanks for his wealth, that Dekker found in his source. As

we have already noted, the verbal ostentation of Eyre may owe something to the stage successes of the period immediately preceding *The Shoemaker's Holiday*. But whatever hints Dekker may have derived from other plays, the role of Eyre remains peculiarly his own, intensely theatrical, though retaining human credibility, voluble without being ranting, dominant without becoming overpowering. The creation of this role to provide at once the structural backbone of the play and its essential mood is the most striking example of Dekker's brilliant development of his source material in *The Shoemaker's Holiday*.

The combination of two stories from Deloney and one of his own invention leaves Dekker with problems of time-scheme and of setting. The period of several years which, it is clear from Deloney, intervenes between Eyre's purchase of the ship's cargo and his becoming Lord Mayor is scarcely compatible with the rapid sequence from wooing, to marriage, to childbirth in the Crispine story. And the setting of the Crispine story in rural Kent during the Roman occupation seems a long way from the mid-fifteenth-century London in which Eyre lived. Dekker solves the problem of the time-scheme—or, rather, allows it to remain unsolved—simply by the process of plot-combination itself. The movement of the scenes among the three plots gives the impression that time has passed in one plot while one's attention has been diverted from it by another. There is no particular incompatibility in the time-schemes of the two love-stories, and the movement from Eyre's acquisition of wealth to his appointment as sheriff is plausible enough. The speed of Eyre's rise from sheriff to Lord Mayor is less susceptible of close scrutiny.[34] At Scene xxi.76, the King, welcoming Eyre into his newly acquired rank, refers to Oatley as 'our last Mayor'. Dekker has deliberately glossed over the eleven years (and eleven mayors) that separated Oatley's holding of the office in 1434 (when Eyre was sheriff), and Eyre's mayoralty in 1445. One of his devices in making the rapidity of Eyre's rise seem more acceptable is the report of the illness and death of seven of the aldermen (xiii.39–40; xv.15). The existence of an historical precedent for this fifty years after Eyre's time[35] is less successful in making us accept it than the fact that we hear of it casually, as events in the other two plots—Ralph's first intimation that Jane is still alive, Lacy's first on-stage meeting with Rose—are coming to a head. By the time it has become a reality (and, indeed, a necessity, if Lacy's affairs are to be brought to a happy conclusion), the idea is familiar and we take it in our stride. Dekker's treatment of the compatibility of setting among his plots involves more positive decisions than his treatment of the time-scheme. The amalgamation of Simon Eyre and Crispine's shoe-maker-master of Faversham makes inevitable the movement of the whole play to London. Dekker is then faced with the choice of an historical period. Deloney had been vague about this: 'somtime there was' is how he begins his story of Eyre. Dekker is a little more precise. He seems to have turned to Stow for his knowledge that Oatley was Lord Mayor at the time that Eyre was sheriff. But general plausibility rather than the precise historical accuracy suggested by Chandler[36] was probably the limit of his intention, as is clear from his treatment of the King. Dekker leaves him nameless, and the real significance of the role (one of Dekker's additions to the Eyre story as he found it in Deloney) is to approve and confirm the happiness that Eyre has established. This general dramatic signifi-cance overrides the historical fact that the King under whom Eyre served as Mayor was Henry VI—a name that Shakespeare's history plays must have caused to be linked in the popular theatrical imagination with failure. Dekker's vagueness allows the image of Henry V, probably just presented on stage in Shakespeare's play when *The Shoemaker's Holiday* was written, to influence our recep-tion of the King here, without specifically identifying him with the victor of Agincourt. Obviously, the ability to mix affably with his subjects, the successful wars with France, and the vigour with which they are taken up again at the end of the play, even the joking allusion to the tennis balls (xxi.25), all suggest Henry V rather than Henry VI. But the fact that Agincourt itself is not mentioned is in keeping with Dekker's care not to make the identification too precise. For a timeless quality is necessary at the end of the play as Dekker seeks, with the help of a monarch's blessing, to establish the immediacy and relevance of Eyre's achievements for the audience of 1599; a king too firmly placed in the past might have obstructed his wish simultaneously to suggest the past and the present.[37]

The vagueness that permits an easy movement between past and present in time is supported by the care of Dekker's setting in place. Having brought all his characters, from Deloney and elsewhere, into a London setting, he keeps them firmly there. We hear of the doings of some of them in France, and in Ralph's case see the results of absence from London, but no scene of the play takes place outside the capital or its immediate surroundings. Perhaps following William Haughton's example in *Englishmen for My Money*, Dekker fills his play with London place-names—streets, buildings, taverns, nearby villages. Some thirty-five separate places are mentioned in the play's twenty-one scenes, many of them several times. Most of them apply equally to the London of Eyre's time and the London of Dekker's; none is confined to fifteenth-century London; a few are exclusively Elizabethan.[38] There are less than half-a-dozen London place-names in Deloney's story, and Dekker's generous provision of topographical detail (typical, as we have seen, of the London citizen comedies) is plainly designed to establish a sense of familiarity in his audience. The interchangeability of past and present is set against the everyday reality of the familiar landmarks of London.

Dekker's care to give a sense of immediacy to the life of a long-dead Lord Mayor of London makes plausible the suggestion that a topical source for the Oatley/Lacy plot may coexist alongside Deloney's story. In the spring of 1599, a few weeks before Dekker finished *The Shoemaker's Holiday*, Sir John Spencer, who had been Lord Mayor of London in 1594, had been temporarily committed to the Fleet for mistreating his only daughter Elizabeth, whose contract of marriage to the Second Lord Compton, a young courtier close to the Queen, he bitterly opposed. Spencer continued to do all in his power to hinder the match after his release.[39] He had been an unpopular Lord Mayor—there are records of violent clashes with the London apprentices—and a firm opponent of the theatres, and the affair was the subject of gossip. It is not unlikely, as Novarr suggests, that the opening scene of *The Shoemaker's Holiday*, with a Lord Mayor doing his best to prevent his daughter's marriage to a courtier, would have struck a familiar chord with its first audiences, and that there would have been little doubt about the direction of their sympathies.

To suggest a rigid identification between the Spencer case and *The Shoemaker's Holiday* would be to confine the play too narrowly; Dekker perhaps glances at a notorious contemporary example, but the general situation was a familiar one. This is typical of his entire approach to his sources: in his choice of material, both general and specific, and in his arrangement of it in dramatic form, Dekker has achieved a coherent and flexible combination of popular legend, civic and national history, contemporary city scandal, and the latest dramatic fashions. The nature and success of this combination remain to be considered.

4. THE PLAY

The entry of Simon Eyre, with his family and servants, in the first scene of *The Shoemaker's Holiday*, brings together characters from all three of the play's plots. Dekker has already launched the story of Rose and Lacy in the opening conversation of Lincoln and the Lord Mayor; now, in the confrontation of Eyre and Lacy over the fate of Ralph, we are introduced to the other elements that Dekker is to weave into the dramatic pattern. After this initial conjunction of the plot-strands of the play, the stories separate until the end, when the characters are again brought together in the final, inclusive celebration. Eyre and his followers, in the first scene a small group, powerless, in the great world of politics and military discipline, to prevent one of their number being taken from them, have come, by the end, to dominate the play's world and to include King and nobles, commons and spectators, within their sphere. The grief and separation of the opening are transformed to the joy and marriage of the close. Dekker's control of his plot material, and the care he takes in the interaction and interrelationship of its parts, form the basis of this developing, expansive movement. Any consideration of the concerns and the achievement of *The Shoemaker's Holiday* must therefore begin with an examination of the play's structure.[40]

Dekker's debt to Deloney, and his alterations to the main outlines of his sources, have already been considered. It is through the blending of these ingredients into a unified whole that he gives his play its vitality and power. The two love-plots, of Rose and Lacy and of Ralph and Jane, one involving the higher classes, one involving the lower, both influenced by the war, both threatened by the same rival wooer, both involving shoemakers (real or pretended), both brought to a conclusion by the comic ingenuity, shared with the audience, of Firk, develop in easy conjunction, their contrasting moods sounding antiphonally through the play, the threads of both joining in the overall plot of Eyre's steady rise to wealth and power, the inexorable expansion of his world. The turning-point of each of the love-plots occurs within the context of the Eyre plot: the return of Ralph, wounded, from the wars in the excited scene in which Madgy Eyre awaits news of her husband's becoming sheriff; and Rose's recognition of Lacy, in disguise as Hans, in the dancing at Old Ford that celebrates Eyre's becoming sheriff. The climax of the Ralph plot in the shoemakers' interruption of Jane's wedding to Hammon impinges on, and its comedy and satisfaction are immediately followed by, the climax of the Rose plot as Oatley and Lincoln enter to break up the wrong wedding, only to learn that Rose and Lacy have already been married elsewhere. And from this climax the move is smooth and easy into the denouement, where the third plot, of Eyre, is brought to its fulfilment as the King comes to give his blessing to all Eyre's projects. Here, as folk-hero and monarch meet in a patriotic and celebratory climax, the two love-stories are subsumed into the general atmosphere of feasting and celebration.

The neatness and symmetry of this structure emerge more clearly if one looks at each plot in turn. The story of Rose and Lacy has the same simple motif as the Deloney tale from which Dekker derived it: its account of true love temporarily thwarted exists rather on the level of romance or fairy-tale. It is introduced at a late point of its development, and is very lightly treated. The lovers see little of each other during the course of the play, and after their marriage-plans have been revealed to us in Scene xv, Dekker can even afford to omit their marriage scene itself (he has another, more startling, wedding to dramatise). The main focus of the love-story is on the feelings of class-consciousness that it provokes. It was Dekker's own alteration to place Rose, the commoner, and Lacy, the nobleman, in different social classes, and the exploration of the conflict between the lovers' parents (Rose's father, Lacy's uncle) occupies the dramatist's attention much more than the love theme itself, which is taken for granted. This stiffening of the story makes it a part, also, of the general consideration of social questions that pervades the play, and shifts its climax away from the marriage of the lovers to the reconciliation of their parents in the final celebration of harmony and love. Lacy's disguise too moves him away from the simple love-tale in which the role begins: as Hans he has an important part to play in another of the plots, and is also swept up into the world of mirth and industry that surrounds Eyre's household. The little story of Rose and Lacy thus takes its part in the general shape of the play, supporting its structure and sharing its concerns.

The second of Dekker's love-plots, created, as we have seen, almost entirely from his own invention, is economically told. The story of Ralph and Jane occupies only five scenes—and some of these contain matter relevant to the other plots. It is, for much of its length, a sad, sometimes a painful, story. Husband and wife are separated in the first scene of the play and are not reunited until the last scene of their plot. And the cause of their separation, in contrast to the traditional barrier of parental opposition that separates Rose and Lacy, is in the social organisation that they are powerless to fight. Ralph cannot escape his obligation to military service in France in the way that Lacy escapes his, for he is not of high enough social rank to do so. Ralph goes out of the play, in the first scene, with Lacy's promise 'Thou shalt not want, as I am a gentleman' (i.185); his wife is reassured, by Lacy again, that 'God, no doubt, will send / Thy husband safe again' (i.186); and he leaves Jane to the care of his master: 'As you have always been a friend to me, / So in mine absence think upon my wife' (i.208). And he returns in the middle of the action, lamed by his service to his country, to find that his wife has been allowed to leave the security of Eyre's household to fend for herself in the harsh friendlessness of London. Dekker's deliberate incorporation of these episodes into his play necessarily has a powerful effect in sharpening its tone. Ralph's lameness, for example, becomes the butt for some uncomfortable jokes from Firk: 'Thou do for her? Then 'twill be a lame doing, and that she loves not' (xiii.26); 'Thou lie with a woman—to build nothing but Cripplegates!' (xiv.72). But Dekker, in introducing this note of harsh reality, has also carefully controlled it. We should react, for example, with more than the tolerant sympathy for Jane that the news of Ralph's death provokes in Scene xii if we had not already been shown that the news is false. Similarly, certain scenes, essential to the development of the story, are reported but not shown, and in each case one can see that Dekker's decision not to dramatise an event is made with careful attention to the overall mood: the quarrel between Jane and the Eyres, reported at x.91–6, might have upset our regard for the Eyres; Jane's acceptance of Hammon, which must occur between the wooing scene and the wedding, might have affected our attitude to her; the episode of Ralph's fitting Jane's shoe, reported at xviii.8–14, would have distracted attention from the climax of the wedding scene and the lovers' reconciliation.

The story of Ralph and Jane, then, introduces real grief, without cheapening it, into the basically happy fabric of *The Shoemaker's Holiday*. Its sharpness of social realism—London must have been full, in the late 1590s, of soldiers maimed by service in France, the Netherlands, or Ireland, and of their widows trying to scratch a living, and Dekker, as we have seen, elsewhere shows his awareness of such suffering—offsets the conventional romanticism of the first love-story, while linking with, and deepening, the social overtones of the Rose/Lacy plot. Yet Dekker's rigid control of mood keeps its effect in balance: through the separation of Ralph and Jane he shows us unhappiness, but in their reunion, and reabsorption into the Eyre world, he reinforces the movement towards celebration which controls the third, and most basic, of his plots.

The play's story of Simon Eyre is again, considered on its own, extraordinarily simple. His movement up the social scale is steady, rapid, and apparently inevitable. Dekker has, as we have seen, omitted or blurred certain stages in the story that are clear in Deloney—the precise means of Eyre's acquiring the cargo, for example, or the slow rise from sheriff, to alderman, to Mayor, made so rapid in the play with the help of those conveniently dying aldermen. The story itself, indeed, is complete six scenes from the end of the play, when we learn that Eyre is already Lord Mayor (xv.16). It is not, however, the step-by-step plotting of Eyre's story that Dekker is concerned with, but the expansion of the mood which it brings with it. Most of Eyre's scenes take place in his shop. As the play progresses, the shop's atmosphere of conviviality, industry, and good cheer comes to encompass a wider and wider area, until, in the final scenes, it includes the characters of the other two plots, the whole play, indeed, and everyone in it, in the general celebration of craft, city, nation, ratified by the King himself and demanding the assent of the audience. The simple structural function of the Eyre plot as the centre from which the other branches of the story emanate (both lovers, for example, work for Eyre), is

overshadowed as the action progresses by its linguistic and thematic
dominance, providing the life-spring of the play.

The widening circle of Eyre's influence is something to be
considered later. It develops naturally from the control and subtlety
with which Dekker interweaves these three plot-strands, using
them to strengthen and enhance the effect of each other. The
significance of their interaction in making the time-scheme acceptable, in giving Lacy (through his association with the shoemakers)
the vitality he would otherwise lack, and in deepening the effect of
one love plot and absorbing the harshness of the other—these
things have already been noted. The inclusion of elements of
different plots in the same scene frequently allows Dekker to
exploit the contrast of their moods: one thinks of the mixture of
Ralph's wonder and joy and Firk's cheerful obscenity in the scene
where the order for Jane's wedding-shoes is brought; the noisy
music and dancing of the shoemakers as the background for the
romantic encounter of Rose and Lacy at Old Ford, with Ralph,
lame, doing his best to be part of the morris; or the scene of
Hammon's wooing of Jane, with her tenderness and loyalty and
his affectedly patterned rhyming as he seeks to overcome her
best instincts while the audience waits tensely for the outcome,
knowing that Ralph is alive. It is one of the play's most remarkable qualities, this overall mixture and delicate control of moods;
traditional romantic love and simple homely affection, the convivial industry of the shop and the pageants and feasts of the
end, the partings and reunions, the obscenities, the songs, the
dances, all those things which give the play its often-praised vitality
can be seen to stem from Dekker's success in the control of
his plot material and the skill with which he has interwoven its
strands.

The effect of the interaction of the plots and of their contrasting
moods is nowhere better revealed than in the scene of Ralph's
return from the wars (sc. x). The scene is beautifully paced, beginning with Madgy's bustling self-importance, the new-found pom-
posity of her addressing 'good Roger' instead of the accustomed
'Hodge', and her anxiety about the capacity of her figure to support
the new finery that she intends to heap upon it. And into this
turbulent, happy atmosphere comes, not the looked-for Firk with
news of the election of the sheriff, but the totally unexpected Ralph,

unseen since the play's first scene and almost forgotten, maimed by the wars which he was sent off to in such high spirits and with such promises of safety: '*Enter Ralph, being lame.*' Poor Madgy does her best to greet him as he should be greeted, but her mind is elsewhere, and Dekker captures the mood precisely, Madgy obviously just falling short of really caring about anything but the news from the Guildhall. The awkwardness and tension of the moment are there, neatly, in that bawdy joke that fails to be funny: 'The left leg is not well. 'Twas a fair gift of God the infirmity took not hold a little higher, considering thou camest from France—but let that pass' (l. 72)—her catch-phrase, for once, supremely appropriate. The mood of the play hangs in the balance until Ralph begins to sense that he is back in the Eyre world of good will:

> I thank you, dame. Since I want limbs and lands,
> I'll to God, my good friends, and to these my hands. (l. 118)

It is a sentiment which expresses one of the most fundamental concerns of the play, and we shall return to it later. And it is immediately followed by the arrival of Firk and Hans, tumbling in with the news of Eyre's election to the office of sheriff, so that, just as suddenly as the mood of sadness and tension settled, it is lifted, and we are once again swept up into the world of excitement and 'madness', now beginning its great movement outwards from the immediate confines of Eyre's shop. The scene closes with Eyre himself, expansive with words, voluble, cheerful, bringing in merriment and celebration with his gold chain of office.

This sense of excitement, of 'madness', that accompanies Eyre, growing and expanding as the action progresses, is the ruling force of the play's development. *The Shoemaker's Holiday* is a progress towards celebration, a process leading towards the enthronement of Eyre as monarch of the festival.[41] At the beginning of the play, as we have seen, Eyre and his followers are a small, tightly-knit circle, conspicuously powerless against the military and political processes that they try to divert. Eyre's final domination represents a victory over forces which must be driven out before the establishment of 'holiday' is possible. Simply stated, the play depicts the victory of individuality over class, of honesty over affectation, of good fellowship and love over divisiveness and war.

The forces that oppose Eyre at the beginning of the play are clear enough. Fundamental to them all is the war that lies behind the action, breaking up the unity and love of Eyre's household, separating husband and wife.[42] Ralph returns to the play from his experience of war maimed, pitiful; only his re-entry to the Eyre household restores his cheerfulness and determination. War, too, threatens to separate Rose and Lacy; only through entering a new conflict, that between love and honour (a conflict from which, at the end of the play, Eyre again provides the rescue), can Lacy escape its power. The presence of war beyond the confines of the play, outside the world of Eyre's London yet impinging upon it, is important in defining that world and sharpening its focus.

Linked with war in denial of the freedom and individuality represented by Eyre, is poverty. Poverty prevents Ralph from paying for a substitute for himself in France, as Lacy pays Askew. Poverty divides the shoemakers from the nobles and citizens, as they send their representative to battle: the sixpences and shillings given to Ralph contrast sharply with the pounds and 'portagues' given to Lacy. And, later in the play, poverty makes Jane, absent from the security of Eyre's household, vulnerable to Hammon's wealth. Poverty is a divisive agent in *The Shoemaker's Holiday*: it is conspicuous that Eyre must become rich before he can begin the process by which his values come to dominate the play.

War and poverty are the great destructive agents that exist around the play's world. But there are conflicts closer to the centre of its action, and the opening dialogue immediately reveals one of them. The bitter class-war of Lincoln and Oatley destroys love by imposing separation on Rose and Lacy. The social division and hostility with which the play begins, and which provide the necessary complications for its plot, trace their origins ultimately from contemporary social conditions and attitudes. The savage conflict between rich and poor, fashionable and homely, that is taken for granted in such a work as Greene's *Quip for an Upstart Courtier* (1592), reflects the clarity with which class-divisions were discernible in Elizabethan society. 'A poor physician's daughter my wife! Disdain / Rather corrupt me ever!' is the horrified response of the noble Bertram when confronted with the love of Helena in *All's Well that Ends Well* (II.iii.113–14), perhaps two or three years after Dekker's play. And in *The Merry Wives of Windsor*, Shakespeare offers us a picture of class-consciousness from the opposite point of view in the resentment felt by the citizen Pages against the courtier Fenton's coming to woo their daughter. It is notable, however, that in both these plays, as in *The Shoemaker's Holiday*, love finally triumphs over class feeling, and such literary treatments of the defeat of class-consciousness perhaps owe something to everyday reality as well as to romantic wish-fulfilment. The Spencer case referred to above is only one of many examples in the period of marriages between peers and commoners, and though motives for these were no doubt frequently more financial than emotional, there is little in the class situation in Dekker's play that is wholly beyond the realms of credibility in its contemporary context.[43] The main exception to this is Lacy's turning to the trade of shoemaking on his visit to Germany (i.29–30), and using it to further the pursuit of his love. It is quite unthinkable in Elizabethan terms that an earl's nephew and heir should become a shoemaker.[44] Dekker's use of this idea, derived ultimately, as we have seen, from the disguised Prince Crispine in Deloney's story, takes further that intermixing of classes, that sense of social harmony and buoyancy, which he is throughout intent on creating and emphasising. 'Though you be lords, you are not to bar by your authority men from women, are you?' demands Hodge of Lincoln and Oatley at the failure of their attempt to prevent an inter-class marriage (xviii.122). At the end of the play Dekker brings on the King himself to provide the final, authoritative answer to this question: 'Where there is much love, all discord ends' (xxi.121). Without class-consciousness and class-division as a readily recognisable aspect of social organisation Dekker could not have written the play, for its plot and intrigue are wholly dependent on these things; but in his optimistic portrayal of the impulses and forces that work for social harmony, he is clearly anxious to suggest the aridity and unnaturalness of these divisive elements.[45]

We see this immediately in that opening dialogue introducing the idea of class-division. The conflict between Lincoln and Oatley even destroys the possibility of honest communication and mutual understanding: their conversation is founded on distrust, on sniping innuendo. Words are used dishonestly, to mean more, or less, than they say. Oatley's 'Too mean is my poor girl for his high birth' (l. 11) is sarcastic, his suggestion that a courtier will consume wealth in purchasing 'silks and gay apparel' (l. 13), though ostensibly self-effacing, is intended as a jibe at the whole courtier class. And Lincoln's reply, with its implication that his nephew's noble tastes would dispose of Oatley's mere citizen fortune in twelve months (l. 35), is similarly double-edged. By the end of the conversation the undercurrent of hostility is breaking the courteous surface in the form of asides (ll. 38, 44), as it does in the next scene between the two men (xvi.22). 'How far the churl's tongue wanders from his heart!', Lincoln there remarks. The class warfare of Lincoln and Oatley imprisons them in isolation; the ordinary contact of honest discourse is denied them, for words can no longer be trusted. Even expressions of love are subject to the corrupting force of hypocritical self-interest. As Oatley leaves the stage in the first scene he promises a gift of £20 to Lacy 'to approve our loves / We bear unto my lord your uncle here' (l. 67). Lincoln's withering comment on this, exposing its emptiness, his advice to his nephew to match Oatley's real emotion of hatred with his own (ll. 78–80), and his harsh description of Rose as a 'gay, wanton, painted citizen' (l. 77), reveal the sterility to which language can be reduced when it is used to break rather than forge links between human beings.

More subtle, but equally opposed to the advancement of what Eyre represents, is the misuse of language revealed in Hammon. His role is rather curious. Dekker has added it to those he derived from Deloney, and as the rival wooer in both love-plots Hammon is obviously of great structural importance. But he appears on the surface to be a harmless, if rather feeble, young man, and the harshness with which he is driven out of the play in Scene xviii has sometimes been thought unnecessary. As the principal barrier to the successful conclusion of both love-plots he has, of course, to be removed. But the contempt and ferocity with which this is done might be thought to border on the excessive. Considered within the developing pattern of the play as a whole, however, and in particular of its language, the sharp expulsion of Hammon is appropriate.

As Donald S. McClure[46] has shown, Hammon is consistently presented in terms of linguistic artifice; verbal ornament hides real purpose, so that the rapid switch in his ardent love-making from Rose to Jane becomes acceptable and unsurprising. His wooing of Jane in Scene xii, for example, displays elaborate verbal trickery: even the soliloquy that precedes it is full of word-play, and much of it is in the couplets which, McClure demonstrates, are associated by this point with the trite and the shallow. The wooing itself is conducted largely in couplets, Jane following Hammon's lead, so that the dialogue is drained of real emotion. Only when Jane speaks of her husband (ll. 70 ff.) does the comparative normality (and sincerity) of blank verse return, affecting both of them as the dialogue turns to the news of Ralph's death. But, the moment passed, Hammon returns to his wooing couplets, their glib artificiality seeming more offensive in contrast with Jane's grief.

Hammon is the one major character in the play who never meets Eyre. The pusillanimous artifice of his language is carefully isolated from the vigour of Eyre's prose. In his final appearance (sc. xviii), however, he confronts Eyre's fellow shoemakers. In spite of Hammon's finery, the contest is pathetically unequal, for by this stage of the play the world they represent is irresistibly ascendant. Amid their prose Hammon's couplet to Jane and Ralph stands out absurdly:

> Pardon me, dear love, for being misled.
> 'Twas rumoured here in London thou wert dead. (l. 47)

His attempt to buy Jane for £20 in ready cash reminds us of that other conflict of which he has been a part. For Hammon is of the wealthy citizen class into which Oatley wished to marry his daughter:

> This Hammon is a proper gentleman,
> A citizen by birth, fairly allied. (vi.60)

His threat to the Rose/Lacy plot is primarily the disruptive threat of class. And his threat to the restoration of the union of Ralph and Jane is also based on his social position. The wealth and security represented by Hammon contrast sharply with the poverty of Jane in her shop, selling her wares 'Cheap . . . Good cheap'. His wooing begins with a suggestion that she should name the price at which she will sell her hand (xii.27). As a marriage proposal it comes close to being an invitation to prostitution, and Jane's resistance to it is the resistance which the whole play endorses, of individual integrity to disruptive social pressures. The same temptation of wealth is placed before Ralph in Hammon's final scene, but here in a form so absurdly crude that Ralph can dismiss it contemptuously. The terms in which he does so, however, remind us of Hammon's original proposal to Jane: 'Sirrah Hammon, Hammon, dost thou think a shoemaker is so base to be a bawd to his own wife for commodity?' (xviii.92). A few lines earlier Jane has made her choice between social ease and loyalty to herself:

> Thou art my husband, and these humble weeds
> Makes thee more beautiful than all his wealth. (l. 64)

The scene depicts the triumph of integrity, and of love, in Jane, Ralph, and the shoemakers, over the wealth and insincerity represented in Hammon and his followers. Hammon's uniformly-liveried servants are an image of the stifling of individuality which the play, through Eyre, has fought against. Hammon is driven out, still addressing us in couplets, still playing on words, the distancing effect of his verbal artifice still suggesting hollowness and denying any emotional response. And the vow couched in these final couplets, that 'during my life . . . no woman else shall be my wife' (l. 101), is, appropriately, a self-dedication to sterility. From this the scene moves, contrastingly, to the news of a marriage just accomplished, and then out, beyond, into the universal feast of love and mirth and fellowship at the end of the play.

The role of Hammon, then, combines within itself the antitheses of many of those principles which the play, through Eyre, asserts. Insincerity, denial of individuality, the divisiveness of class, all meet in Hammon. Conspicuously, in a play filled with scenes of men working, he is always idle, standing, observing Jane in her shop, affecting the pursuits of the nobility at his first entrance in the hunt. His expulsion from the play is the necessary prelude to the final celebration.

Hammon, as we have observed, never meets Eyre. But in the banquet scene at Old Ford (sc. xi) Eyre unknowingly offers a character of him: 'Those silken fellows are but painted images, outsides, outsides, Rose. Their inner linings are torn' (l. 43). Ironically, he thinks he is arguing with Oatley in favour of Hammon and against Lacy. In fact, Lacy is with him in the scene, about to take part in a morris dance with his fellow shoemakers, the wholesomeness of his 'inner linings' vividly demonstrated in his capacity for honest industry and good fellowship—the very qualities that will come to dominate the play's world as Eyre rises above the social divisiveness of which he is here still a victim. It is Hammon who represents the 'painted image', the ornate exterior. On the clash of his world with Eyre's the play is built; through the victory of Eyre's world it reaches its conclusion in celebration.

War, poverty, class, insincerity, affectation, and the denial of freedom for self-expression that they all involve, are met and vanquished by the Eyre world in *The Shoemaker's Holiday*. Eyre's weapon in the battle is language. His entrance in the first scene is an immediate indication of the ground on which the battle is to be fought. Prose is his medium, and it comes with a refreshing vigour after more than a hundred lines of verse, much of it used as a cloak for insincerity and deceit. It is prose of the most straightforward kind, spoken without fear of its audience ('I'll speak to them an they were popes'), providing unequivocal information about himself, his followers, and their intentions:

> I am Simon Eyre, the mad shoemaker of Tower Street. This wench with the mealy mouth that will never tire is my wife, I can tell you. Here's Hodge, my man and my foreman. Here's Firk, my fine firking journeyman; and this is blubbered Jane. All we come to be suitors for this honest Ralph. Keep him at home and, as I am a true shoemaker and a gentleman of the Gentle Craft, buy spurs yourself and I'll find ye boots these seven years. (l. 129)

The expansive conclusion is questioned by his wife, only for the honesty of its intention to be reasserted: 'peace, I know what I do.' Eyre knows what he does throughout the play, and never fails to make it clear in words. His self-revealing directness of utterance is a vivid assertion of personal identity, sharply differentiated in its idiosyncratic vigour from the language of any other character. It intrudes at first unexpectedly into the verbal flatness of the opening scene, but as the play moves forward we begin to be swept up into its prolific and expansive good humour. It is a language which turns meanness into plenty: at Oatley's feast, for example, the 'bad cheer' the Lord Mayor self-effacingly, and depressingly, offers is miraculously transformed by the operation of Eyre's language: 'Good cheer, my Lord Mayor, fine cheer; a fine house, fine walls, all fine and neat' (xi.4). Oatley's reply is truer than he is aware:

> It does me good, and all my brethren,
> That such a madcap fellow as thyself
> Is entered into our society.

That quality of 'madness' which Eyre often ascribes to himself suggests an extravagance of gaiety, a wholeness of personality; it implies that Eyre is a law unto himself. And the refreshing, beneficial qualities represented by 'madness', by absolute honesty of self-expression, by 'being oneself', are endorsed at the end of the play by the King, as they were by Oatley earlier:

> 'tis our pleasure
> That he put on his wonted merriment. (xix.14)

> be even as merry
> As if thou wert among thy shoemakers.
> It does me good to see thee in this humour. (xxi.13)

From Eyre's shop come the qualities that are to control the play and establish the final festival. Our first view of this establishment is of Eyre's calling his household to take their places in it at the beginning of Scene iv. Behind his excitable torrent of words is the simple call to work. Upon work, a respect for and pride in work, Eyre's success is built. 'The Gentle Craft is living for a man' remarks Lacy (iii.24) as he takes on his disguise as Hans the shoemaker. The line immediately precedes the first work-scene in Eyre's shop, and is later expanded by Eyre into the bold assertion that 'the Gentle Trade is a living for a man through Europe, through the world' (xi.49). Honest industry is seen in the play to be the necessary prelude to happiness. Lacy, through his disguise as Hans, shows his ability to enter this world of work, to disregard the barriers of class in his search for 'living' as a 'man'. With work goes mirth, that expansive joviality which emanates from Eyre even as he sets his workers to the business of the day. 'Mirth lengtheneth long life', says the dedicatory epistle, wishing it to 'all good fellows, professors of the Gentle Craft, of what degree soever'. The inclusiveness of that is important: the good fellowship provided by mirth, in conjunction with work, is shown by the play to be all-embracing. Eyre's world accommodates both the rich nobility of Lacy and the crippled poverty of Ralph, working together in the shop, dancing together at Old Ford. It is a vital, bawdy, immediately attractive world, full of catch-phrases which give an audience (as catch-phrases always do) the pleasure of familiar recognition. Madgy's constant 'but let that pass' operates as an open invitation to join Firk in the detection of double-entendre; Eyre's own catch-phrase provides, in a sense, the pervasive metaphor of the play. 'Prince am I none, yet am I princely born' is a denial of class as the whole play comes to be a denial of class, and an assertion of sovereignty as the whole play comes to be an assertion of Eyre's festival sovereignty.

Eyre's shop, then, is a community of work, good fellowship, and mirth. Eyre exists through and in community, a community expressed through language—in contrast to Oatley, Lincoln, and Hammon, whose language is the negation of community. Through entry to this community, and work and good fellowship in it (a good fellowship vividly expressed in his generosity to Eyre in the matter of the Dutch cargo), Lacy achieves the help he needs to gain his love. Through his restoration to this community, Ralph begins to recover from the misery to which his departure from it has subjected him: 'Since I want limbs and lands, / I'll to God, my good friends, and to these my hands' (x.118). There it is in a nutshell, the formula of work and good fellowship—and it is through the help of his fellows that Jane is found again. For the conviviality of the shop is one of the manifestations of love in the play. 'Use thyself friendly, for we are good fellows' (iv.109) says Hodge in welcoming Lacy into the company of Eyre's workmen; and his following remark—'if not, thou shalt be fought with, wert thou bigger than a giant'—asserts that honest antipathy to whatever threatens this expansive good fellowship which will later be responsible for the victory over Hammon. Through the fraternal love of Eyre's workshop, marital love is restored and romantic love rewarded. And to the feast of conviviality, of fraternal love, at the end of the play, all are welcomed.

The lavish abundance of the feast, however, depends on the means to provide it. Eyre's success in language is matched by his success in business; the progression through good fellowship to happiness is linked with the movement through work to prosperity. The crippled Ralph sees this as he puts his trust in the 'hands' with which he can still exercise his craft, just as Eyre is prompted by it in the determination with which he rouses his household and sets them to work. Within the world of the play the success of the formula provides its own justification. To see Eyre as 'Shylock masquerading as Falstaff '[47] is to bring to the play concepts wholly alien to its mood. Neither the self-centring, sterile acquisitiveness of Shylock, nor the amoral social anarchism of Falstaff has any place in

The Shoemaker's Holiday, in which one of Dekker's concerns is to explore the proper use of wealth in society. The means by which Eyre becomes rich are, as we have seen, made deliberately vaguer than they are in Deloney. Commercial sharp practice is replaced by Lacy's generosity (by good fellowship again), and a general sense that 'fortune favours the brave'. Dekker is more interested in the use to which wealth is put than in the means by which it is acquired. Even in the first scene, various misuses of wealth are touched on: its waste on 'gay apparel' by the courtier; Oatley's possessiveness and fear that his daughter's marriage will deprive him of it; its use, by Lincoln and Oatley, in the attempt to buy Lacy's absence, thus destroying love. Money is here a source of division. Later, in Hammon's attempt to buy love and in Madgy's comic desire to buy social position through fashion, we see other aspects of the corrupting power of wealth. The properly balanced attitude to wealth is Eyre's. For him it is a source of gaiety and of harmony: 'Let your fellow prentices want no cheer', he tells Firk in Scene xx, and adds, 'Hang these penny-pinching fathers, that cram wealth in innocent lamb-skins' (l. 10). His is the proper combination of the mirthful and the mercantile spirit, the combination suggested in the second three-man's song:

> Ill is the weather that bringeth no gain,
> Nor helps good hearts in need.

'Gain' put to social good, 'madness' justified by industry, wealth shared in mirth and good fellowship—the play is a celebration of these things, showing them working together to overcome the obstacles of discord, isolation, disharmony, that are personified in Oatley, Lincoln, and Hammon. The successive defeats of these three in Scene xviii by the shoemakers and apprentices lead forward to the triumph of love and the establishment of holiday. In Eyre's rise the barriers of social class are breached: Madgy, fetched 'from selling tripes in Eastcheap' (vii.69), becomes Lady Mayoress; Hodge, the foreman, becomes the master; Firk, the journeyman, becomes the foreman. The final feast is a harmonious mixture of all social classes in celebration of the victory of love—romantic love and fraternal love—over divisiveness. 'Where there is much love, all discord ends' (xxi.121), says the King, as he brings even Oatley and Lincoln into Eyre's festival. Through Eyre's combination of work and good fellowship, and through the language that expresses it, discord has been replaced by holiday.

The feast which ends *The Shoemaker's Holiday* is the last of a series.[48] The first scene begins with Lincoln telling Oatley 'My Lord Mayor, you have sundry times / Feasted myself and many courtiers more'—feasts, apparently, with a socially-limited invitation list, and based on the ill-concealed hostility between Oatley and the courtier class. At Old Ford in Scene xi we have another feast, with Oatley still as host. The good cheer of the occasion, however, is all supplied by the guests, who bring the music, and the dancing, and the ability to deny Oatley's suggestion of the poverty of his own welcome by the exuberance of their good fellowship. Conspicuously, Oatley finds that 'urgent business' (l. 69) calls him away from the merry-making. The final feast has Eyre as host, and it is a general revel, with an unlimited invitation list and a lavish abundance of good cheer. The linguistic vitality of Eyre, which has been ably seconded by Firk, now seems to animate even the comestibles:

> There's cheer for the heavens—venison pasties walk up and down piping hot like sergeants; beef and brewis comes marching in dry fats; fritters and pancakes comes trolling in in wheelbarrows, hens and oranges hopping in porters' baskets, collops and eggs in scuttles, and tarts and custards comes quavering in in malt shovels. (xviii.207)

Eyre's feast is open to all; a 'crew of good fellows' will 'dine at my Lord Mayor's cost', and apprentices will 'be bound to pray for him and the honour of the Gentlemen Shoemakers' (xviii.201, 204). The holiday he establishes is a holiday for all, its essence is inclusiveness. '*All* the prentices in London' (xviii.217) have been invited; there is no suggestion that the feast, and the holiday, are for Eyre's own trade alone. Though the absence of the apostrophe, permitted by Elizabethan orthography, in the play's original title might be thought to leave the matter vague, it seems clear that this is 'the Shoemaker's holiday', not 'the shoemakers' holiday'—a celebration of the festival that is Eyre's gift to the whole city, linked with the Shrove Tuesday festivities that were still a great apprentice holiday in Dekker's London (see commentary to xvii.48–55).[49] Dekker takes from Deloney this placing of Eyre's feast on Shrove Tuesday, but his projection of it from the past to the present is wholly his own; 'every Shrove Tuesday is our year of jubilee; and when the pancake bell rings, we are as free as my Lord Mayor. We may shut up our shops and make holiday. . . . And this shall continue *for ever*' (xviii.221). The lines launch the play on its final expansive movement, and lead into the little scene of the King, preparing to follow the apprentices to Eyre's festival.

The presence of the King in the final scene is, as we have seen, Dekker's deliberate invention. He comes to endorse and confirm Eyre's achievements in those three areas of love, mirth, and industry through which he has dominated the play. The royal confirmation of the marriage of Rose and Lacy involves also the final overthrow of class division. The image of the monarch as the bringer of harmony was used again by Dekker a few years later in the pageant he wrote to welcome James I to London. The 'peacefull presence of their King' there brings factious elements again to order, so that 'our globe is drawn in a right line again'.[50] The King's role in the final scene of *The Shoemaker's Holiday* is the same. To Lincoln's last and most extreme statement of class hatred—'Her blood is too too base' (l. 104)—he replies:

> Lincoln, no more.
> Dost thou not know that love respects no blood,
> Cares not for difference of birth or state?

In the restoration of harmony in love, epitomised in the reconciliation of Lincoln and Oatley and asserted in the King's declaration that 'Where there is much love, all discord ends' (l. 121), the first phase of Eyre's achievement is confirmed. In the King's agreement to join Eyre's banquet (l. 190), and the earlier demand (ll. 13–15) that his 'madness' should continue unchanged, Eyre's role as the 'brave lord of incomprehensible good fellowship' (xviii.219) receives royal assent. And thirdly, in the naming of the Leadenhall, and in the granting of the leather-markets, Eyre's achievements in commerce, and in the life of the city, are approved.

The naming of the Leadenhall, however, has a wider significance. The linking of past and present in Hodge's joyful prediction that the Shrove Tuesday holiday will 'continue for ever' (xviii.227) is now given substance by the addition of the concrete details of Eyre's legacy to the city. The Leadenhall market was a fact of everyday life to the first audiences of *The Shoemaker's Holiday*. The revelation of the origins of that familiarity invites their participation in the stage excitement of Eyre and his fellows at the granting of the name and the privileges of the building whose anonymity has been carefully preserved up to the ceremonial moment (see xvii.44; xviii.199, 216; xxi.130–1). In recounting what might seem to a modern audience the mundane details of the markets, Dekker is showing that Eyre's achievement still exists in the present, to be shared by the spectators, as well as the characters, of his play. And if these things, like the London place names with which the play abounds, have a continuing and familiar validity, so too can the audience be a part of the festival of love and mirth which Eyre has established and which the King has come to confirm and perpetuate.

The arrival of the King, then, brings comprehensiveness and inclusiveness to Eyre's festival. The focus of loyalty on one guild, or one city—revealed, for example, in the strictly local patriotism of the farewell to Ralph in the opening scene (i.221–7)—is broadened into a more general nationalism through loyalty to the King. And yet, in a sense, the arrival of the King also signals the end of the festival. The sovereignty of the play has hitherto belonged to Eyre, the 'incomprehensible lord of good fellowship'. Now the supremacy passes to a king whose thoughts, even in the midst of the festival, are wandering beyond its confines. Between his naming of Eyre's Leadenhall and his granting of its market privileges, he turns (ll. 139 ff.) to the war, and to his determination to make France 'repent'. As the play ends, and even as he agrees to share Eyre's banquet, he announces the end of the festival:

> Come, lords, a while let's revel it at home.
> When all our sports and banquetings are done,
> Wars must right wrongs which Frenchmen have begun.

The war that began the play ends it, the holiday only a temporary respite in the surrounding discord. Outside the world that Eyre has established lies the world of reality which Dekker allowed Ralph and Jane to enter, a world in which, as Jane sternly remarks, one 'cannot live by keeping holiday' (xii.31). Despite the fact that they have been rescued from it, that world of reality is still there, recognised in the second three-man's song, probably sung as part of the final festival. 'Cold's the wind, and wet's the rain' is an acknowledgement of its uncompromising severity. But against its harshness the song sets the refuge of good fellowship, the helping of 'good hearts', the conviviality of trolling the jolly bowl. 'Let's be merry whiles we are young. Old age, sack, and sugar will steal upon us ere we be aware' (xi.23) was Eyre's own formulation in the scene of the convivial revelling at Old Ford, and the holiday atmosphere of *The Shoemaker's Holiday* depends upon its being recognisable as an escape from reality, an assertion of the holiday spirit by dramatist, players, and audience.[51] Outside Eyre's world lie poverty, and war, and discord, and old age, just as they lie outside the theatre where their defeat has been celebrated. But this recognition of the limits of the holiday does not devalue it. On the contrary, it sharpens its focus, defines its poignancy, and asserts its importance.

5. THE PLAY ON THE STAGE

The original staging

The printed text of *The Shoemaker's Holiday*, since it appears to derive from an authorial manuscript that had not undergone play-house annotation or revision, tells us rather how Dekker imagined the play's staging than how it was staged. It is easy to suppose, for example, that if the script had been marked up by the theatre's book-keeper it would have included a direction for trumpets to be sounded for the King's first entrance, at the beginning of Scene xix, as well as the direction '*A long flourish or two*' (which might well have been made more precise) at the beginning of the final scene. And we should certainly have expected to be told when the songs were sung, perhaps with some revision of the surrounding dia-logue.

While we cannot speak with certainty of the details of the play's original staging, it is clear that Dekker had in mind the basic structure of the public theatres of his time, and that he made no exceptional demands of it. The play requires as its setting no more than a platform with, at the back, a wall containing entrances, one at least of which can also serve as a discovery space. Entries of a processional nature may have been intended to be made from the yard of the theatre rather than from openings in the tiring-house wall (see i.246.2, n.). This wall seems to be thought of as having three, if not more, apertures. For instance, the stage direction at xii.o.2 uses the phrase 'another door' (not 'the other door' as we might have expected if only two doors were envisaged).

Perhaps the most interesting features of the staging concern the scenes set in, or outside, shops. Scene iv is set in the street outside Eyre's shop (which is also the house where he lives with his wife, servants, and workmen). The setting of Scene vii is not initially defined, but before long it is clearly in the workshop. Scene x, with its many comings and goings, could more easily be imagined outside than inside the shop, though the conventions of the Elizabethan stage would permit a shifting, non-realistic setting. Scene xii opens with Jane '*in a Semsters shop working*'. Richard Hosley sees this as an example of 'a discovery . . . without curtains in a tiring-house whose doors open out upon the stage'.[52] He supposes the doors to be seven or eight feet wide. After being revealed, Jane might well come forward and play the bulk of the scene on the main stage. This is especially likely since the following scene opens with a similar discovery: '*Hodge at his shop boord, Rafe, Firk, Hans, and a boy at work*'. This probably means that all the characters were to be revealed together, especially since the scene opens with concerted singing. The location is either inside or just outside the shop (or even both, given the fluid conventions of scene-localisation). After Eyre becomes Lord Mayor, the workshop aspect of his establishment is forgotten.

So the only certain evidence we have as to how Dekker intended either of the two shops—the sempster's and the shoemaker's—to be represented is by the presence of a shop-board. This could mean either a counter hinged to a window or a movable work table. Elizabethan shop windows were 'without mullions' and 'had wooden shutters hinged at the top and bottom which formed a counter when they were open during the day and an excellent protection against thieves when closed at night'.[53] Eyre refers to such windows at iv.9 and xvii.54. The direction '*Hodge at his shop boord*' could refer to either a counter or a work table. If to a table, it would have to be moved in or discovered before the scene began. Shop scenes are not uncommon in plays of the period, but it is not clear precisely how they were presented. The opening stage direction of Jonson, Marston, and Chapman's *Eastward Ho* (1605; quoted from Herford and Simpson) includes '*At the middle dore, Enter Golding discouering a Gold-smiths shoppe, and walking short turns before it'*, and a direction at the opening of Act Two, '*Touchstone, Quicke-siluer, Goulding and Mildred, sitting on eyther side of the stall'*, also suggests a staging similar to that required at the beginning of Scene xiii of our play. Clifford Leech sees this as 'an indication of a middle entry with some sort of a booth displayed'.[54] Middleton's *A Chaste Maid in Cheapside* (1611–13) opens with '*a Shop being discouered'* (first edition, 1630). R. B. Parker, in his Revels edition (Intro., pp. lxiii–lxvi) suggests a number of ways in which the shop setting might have been represented at the Swan, and he too appears to envisage the shop as a booth or stall. Certainly some plays seem to require an independent structure: Heywood's *2 If You Know not Me, You Know Nobody* (1605) has '*Enter in the shop 2. of Hobsons folkes, and opening the shoppe*' (first edition, 1606). Such a structure may have been what Dekker required for *The Shoemaker's Holiday*, but a discovery at a work table would have been enough to indicate a shop setting. One possibility that seems not to have been suggested is that one or more of the stage doors was fitted with practicable shutters. This would give added point to Eyre's 'Open my shop windows!' (iv.9), though it is not a necessity.

    The Shoemaker's Holiday reveals Dekker's professionalism in its calls upon the resources of the professional acting company, the Admiral's men, for which it was written, and which was the main rival to Shakespeare's company, the Chamberlain's (later the King's) men, throughout its career. Much is known about it because of the survival of the account books and other papers of its chief financier, Philip Henslowe. Its leading actor from about 1590 to 1597, and 1600 to 1605, was Edward Alleyn. From about 1594 to 1600 it had almost exclusive use of the Rose theatre, on Bankside. In 1600 it moved to the Fortune, a popular theatre outside the City bounds north of the river. The size of the cast of *The Shoemaker's Holiday* would neither have strained nor under-employed the resources of the Admiral's men at this period (cf. Chambers *E.S.*, II.156). A number of musical instruments are required—a drum, horns, tabor and pipe, trumpets (for the 'flourish or two', xxi.0.1)—but, as Manifold shows, this is no more than normal; and the wardrobe and property departments would no doubt have been able to provide what Kinney calls Eyre's 'successively grander' garments, and enough working clothes and tools of the trade to characterise his workmen.[55]

All we know of the play's early performances derives from the title-page statement that it was presented at Court on New Year's Day, 1600. This presumably followed successful performances at the Rose. The copy of Q1 now at Harvard has manuscript notes allocating the roles to actors of the Admiral's men and attributing the play to Dekker and Robert Wilson. An article about these notes appeared over the signature 'Dramaticus' in 1849. Greg cast doubt upon their authenticity; in 1923 they still troubled Chambers. Since then, Fredson Bowers has convincingly demonstrated that the notes were forged by J. P. Collier, and that he also wrote the article.[56] The five reprints of the play up to 1657 may reflect the continuing success of the play on the stage, but we have no evidence of any performance between 1600 and the closing of the theatres.

Later stage history

In the twentieth century *The Shoemaker's Holiday* has become perhaps the most frequently performed non-Shakespearian play of its period. It has been especially popular with amateur groups in schools and universities, and many of its performances have left little trace. We are concerned here only with some of the more important. The earliest we have found was given in April 1898 at Cambridge, Massachusetts, by an all-male cast of the Delta Upsilon Fraternity of Harvard University. The production was also shown at the Bijou Opera House, Boston. A reviewer found that many of the players 'succeeded in fulfilling their difficult task very praiseworthily'.[57] A performance during an 'Elizabethan May-day Fête' on 1 May 1906 at Bryn Mawr University, Pennsylvania is recorded by O. L. Hatcher, who found that 'the personality of Simon Eyre is not sufficiently interesting to compensate for the lack of dramatic vitality in the plot'.[58] The O.U.D.S. production of C. K. Allen's version (see below, p. 59) was given at the New Theatre, Oxford from 29 January to 4 February 1913. The actor of Firk (decorously renamed Frisk) made a particularly strong impression; a reviewer called the role 'the fattest low-comedy part in any Elizabethan play'.[59] Allen directed and played Simon Eyre.

In 1919 Miss C. M. Edmondston, who prepared the Bankside edition (see below, p. 59), directed a performance at the Birkbeck Theatre, Chancery Lane, which she claimed as 'the first recorded performance of the play in London for over three hundred years'.[60]

The all-female cast was drawn from members of the Graystoke Players, who for twelve years had been devoting themselves 'to the study and production of Old English plays seldom or never staged'.[61] The influence of William Poel (who never produced the play) may be detected in this production 'given on a draped stage, with such necessary accessories only as plenty of leather and various appliances in use by members of "the gentle craft" '. 'The genial and jovial character' of Simon Eyre 'was brought out admirably by Mrs L. M. Bateman', and Miss Daisy Judge was 'quietly, yet most effectively humorous throughout' in the far-from feminine role of Firk. The play 'was received with justifiable enthusiasm'.[62] The amateur actors of the Hampstead Garden Suburb Play and Pageant Union, who gave the play in April 1920, were congratulated on having 'suffered no sophistication from their necessary acquaintance with the manners and methods of the London stage'.[63]

The play's first professional production in modern times seems to have been A. E. Filmer's at the Birmingham Repertory Theatre, which played for two weeks from 25 November 1922. The designs were by Paul Shelving, and the *Birmingham Post* (1 December) printed a letter from a J. M. Lloyd Thomas saying that the play was 'staged in the Elizabethan manner, with a curtain background, an inner stage, and a balcony above, so that there is no waste of time in changing scenes, and the atmosphere of the old times is preserved without pedantic antiquarianism. The music, which belongs to the period, has exquisite charm, and the morris dancing is a revel of delight.' According to the critic of the *Birmingham Post* (27 November), Cedric Hardwicke 'played Simon Eyre with vigour and zest, and made him a living man of hearty and vulgar good nature', and the *Era* (30 November) felt that his performance 'set the seal on his reputation as one of our rising actors'. The *Birmingham Gazette* reported that Isabel Thornton 'was inimitable as Mistress Eyre, and swam into high society most magnificently in a wonderful farthingale'. The production was uniformly praised, though the Birmingham *Evening Despatch* (27 November) found 'now and again a tendency to burlesque'.

The play reached the professional London stage in a highly successful production at the Old Vic in March 1926. Lilian Baylis wrote that the Worshipful Company of Cordwainers 'helped us in every possible way, from showing the "prentices" how to handle the shoes, to allowing us to display their coat of arms'.[64] She found that performing 'this joyous comedy gave us all fresh vitality'. Baliol Holloway, who had played Falstaff in *The Merry Wives of Windsor* three years previously, was Simon Eyre. 'H.H.' (Horace Horsnell) wrote that he was 'Part Falstaff, part Pantaloon in appearance',[65] and James Agate, describing the character as 'a hurly-burly of a man compounded in equal parts of Falstaff and Pistol', found that Holloway 'gave us all there is in the part'.[66] This was a dominant performance; 'to hear him address Miss Evans as "Lady Madgy!" alone is worth the money!', wrote H.H. Ralph was played with proper seriousness. Neil Porter 'put extraordinary passion into the scene in which he rediscovered his wife', and 'throughout the whole play . . . contrived to wear that shining look with which St. Dunstan's and other hospitals have made us familiar, and to suggest, in his voice, trials bravely endured'.[67] The King was played as Henry V. Agate reserved his highest praise for Edith Evans, who 'found Margery a sketch of a part, and turned her into a complete woman'. 'Miss Evans has this characteristic of all good acting—that she takes hold of her dramatist's conception, absorbs it, and then gives it out again re-created in terms of her own personality and delighted imagination, so that you get the twofold joy of one fine talent superimposed upon another. "How shall I look in a hood?" asks the new-enriched dame, to be answered, "Like a cat in the pillory".[68] Whereupon Margery has the astonishing, irrelevant, "Indeed, all flesh is grass". Hear Miss Evans say this . . . and you reflect, first, that Dekker was a good playwright, and, second, that the best wit in the world gains when it is delivered by a witty actress.'

A performance in Boston, Massachusetts, in December 1932 by an all-female cast of Emerson College is worth noting for the presence of a 'haughty, though silent, Queen Elizabeth accepting from her throne, set among us spectators, the pleasures of Master Dekker's revels'.[69] One of the best English amateur societies, the Norwich Players, chose the play for its silver jubilee celebrations in June 1936. It was given in the open air, and had 'real pace, so much pace in fact, that it seemed hardly necessary to have cut so drastically'.[70]

The most important American revival was directed by the twenty-two-year-old Orson Welles at the Mercury Theatre, New

York in January 1938.[71] The text was adapted and severely shortened; played with no interval, it lasted no more than an hour and a half. It was acted at a 'breathless pace', wrote Brooks Atkinson,[72] with, as scenery, 'a sunny suggestion of a London Street'. There were 'three curtained recesses for shops and streets and guild halls'.[73] Almost all the reviews were enthusiastic. Among the actors, highest praise went to Hiram Sherman as Firk, who gave 'the finest, because the funniest, interpretation of an Elizabethan low comedy character' that John Mason Brown had ever seen.[74] The dominance of the role may have owed something to cuts in other areas of the play. For all the enthusiasm of the reviewers, it is clear that success was often achieved at the play's expense. John Mason Brown, who refers to the 'sadly cut role of Margery', acknowledges that Welles had 'taken liberties with the text' but feels that he 'justified them by restating what remains of it in generally hilarious terms'. As Hammon, Vincent Price began 'quite seriously in a romantic vein' but finally gave 'a sharply edged, often enormously funny performance'. Ivor Brown, as visiting critic on the *New York Times* (23 January), was more censorious: 'I protest against the habit of laughing with Dekker and at him simultaneously. The players have no business to be winking at the audience in order to get laughs on the side and love-scenes should not be burlesqued in the manner of Beatrice Lillie. . . . This is not the real "Shoemaker's Holiday." It is a Busker's Night Out!'

The play appeared again in London at the Playhouse in November 1938, directed by Nancy Price in a production which had mixed notices. The *Evening News* (5 November) referred to its 'senseless bawling heartiness' and *The Times* (5 November) found that 'excellent performances' in some roles were 'balanced by the failure of some others to make more than recitations of their parts'. The actor playing Firk (Hedley Briggs) had a great success: 'This is a clown in the great tradition, cousin to Touchstone and Autolycus, collateral ancestor to Sam Weller, but like all that distinguished and thoroughly national line, a unique individual' (*The Times*). A wartime production by a company led by Walter Hudd was given at the Lyric, Hammersmith, in May 1944, after a provincial tour, with some success. Nevill Coghill directed a successful O.U.D.S. production at the Playhouse, Oxford, in March 1948.[75] Representatives of ten City dramatic societies gave the play at Guildhall,

London, in July 1951 as part of the Festival of Britain. A Bristol Old
Vic production by Denis Carey which opened on 16 March 1954
brought the play as close as possible to the period of its composition, with the King played, unusually, as Henry VIII.

Probably the production to have been enjoyed by the greatest
number of people was that directed by Raymond Raikes for the
Third Programme of the B.B.C., first heard on 30 November 1958
and re-broadcast on 1 January and 28 June 1959, 27 August 1961, 11
March 1968, and 20 September 1970. Eyre was splendidly played
by Donald Wolfit.

On 5 March 1959 Georges Wilson's production of a French
version by Michael Vinaver was given by the Théâtre National
Populaire at the Palais de Chaillot, Paris. A single performance
directed by Paul Daneman at the Old Vic in 1962 'pummelled and
squeezed the genial, sentimental old piece for every possible leer of
bawdiness and trick of banter'.[76] Cicely Bumtrinket made an
appearance and was also to be seen in David William's production
at the Mermaid, London which opened on 24 July 1964. According
to *The Times* (25 July), 'Denise Coffey transforms the wordless
maid's part . . . into an abject spectre of resentment in the midst of
gaiety, whose calamitous skid with a platter of bright red stew
raises the King's entry to a comic climax'. The direction was both
inventive and interpretative. The upper-class lovers were presented
as 'posturing ninnies' and the King as 'pansified and narcissistic'.[77]
Much business was added; *The Times* found most of it 'consistent,
necessary, and funny', but Richard Roud in the *Guardian* (25 July)
wrote: 'Elegant elaborations of the text like audible urination,
various emptying of garbage, and be-spattering with bird dung are
not what I would call funny.' Dodger became 'irresistible in the
black-cloaked figure of Robert Gillespie, flitting into dark corners
with superfluous stealth and delivering his announcement of disaster with a broad grin' (*The Times*).

This was an over-elaborate, over-interpreted version, revealing,
like Orson Welles's, a distrust of the play's ability to stand up for
itself. In the Introduction to his edition of the play J. B. Steane
praises the director's handling of Ralph's return from the wars ('it
would take a very imaginative reading of the printed page to make
one realise just how supple and lifelike this scene can be'), but feels
that the production as a whole was 'not . . . at all satisfactory', and

that 'words were given little time to register or even to be fully audible' (p. 20). It was revived, re-directed by Robert Gillespie, in March 1965.

A musical version presented at the Orpheum Theater, New York, in March 1967, for which the cast includes 'Flossie Frigbottom, Madge Mumblecrust, and Cicely Bumtrinket' was unfavourably reviewed in the *New York Times* (4 March). A Marxist German version by Tankred Dorst was performed in 1967 at Essen. A production at the Phoenix Theatre, Leicester, in September 1968 used locality boards, and had male actors as Margery Eyre (described to us by A. C. Sprague as 'excellent') and Sybil. A production by the National Youth Theatre at the Shaw Theatre, London, in August 1971 was badly received: again the cast was 'directed into such overacting and such a wealth of obscene gestures, camp minnying [sic], falsetto voices, nudges, winks, and the constant speaking of words in audible inverted commas that Dekker's play is buried, almost without trace'.[78] On 2 September 1971 the *Daily Telegraph* printed a letter from the head of the Department of Boot and Shoe Manufacture at Northampton College of Technology, stating that in a production by the Northampton Repertory Players, 'five years ago' Eyre's apprentices had been played by six students who 'were actually making shoes on the stage'. In July 1972 a production from the Crucible Theatre, Sheffield was given at the temporary Bankside Globe Playhouse with little success. Douglas Campbell directed and played Eyre as 'a roaring nonentity' (Irving Wardle, *The Times*, 4 July). A modest production by the Worcester Repertory Company at the Swan Theatre, Worcester in November 1973 came closer to the heart of the play; Cicely appeared again, and the comic potential of the role of Dodger was once more demonstrated.

The best professional productions seem to have been those in Birmingham in 1922 and at the Old Vic in 1926. In more recent years directors have betrayed unease and distrust either of the play or of their audiences' possible reactions. Apparently embarrassed by the play's emotional directness, they have laboured too hard to sophisticate it with comic and interpretative business. Reviews make it clear that the most rewarding roles are those of Simon Eyre, his wife, and Firk. Some of the smaller parts, including Ralph (especially on his return from the wars), the King, Hammon, and even Dodger can make a good effect. The play offers ample scope for idiosyncratic character acting, but detail must not overwhelm the design; the commonest complaints have been of over-fussiness, excessive heartiness, and caricature. But the play's continuing record of performance shows that it has a greater appeal to non-specialist audiences than most other plays by Shakespeare's contemporaries.[79] It would be pleasant if future historians could record performances by the National Theatre or the Royal Shakespeare Company.

6. THE TEXT

Early editions

The first quarto edition of *The Shoemaker's Holiday*[80] was not entered in the Stationers' Register. It was printed with a title-page dated 1600, and has forty leaves, collating A–K4. The title-page (A2) reads:

> THE / SHOMAKERS / Holiday. / OR / *The Gentle Craft.* / With the humorous life of Simon / Eyre, shoomaker, and Lord Maior / of London. / As it was acted before the Queenes most excellent Ma-/iestie on New-yeares day at night last, by the right / honourable the Earle of Notingham, Lord high Ad-/mirall of England, his seruants. / [Device: McKerrow 142.] / Printed by Valentine Sims dwelling at the foote of Adling / hill, neere Bainards Castle, at the signe of the White / Swanne, and are there to be sold. / 1600.

On A3 is the unsigned epistle, printed in roman beneath a pair of ornaments and with an initial K, and headed 'To all good Fellowes, Professors of / *the Gentle Craft; of what degree* / soeuer.' The basic fount for the remainder of the volume is black letter. The songs are on A3v and A4, each with an ornament at the head and foot of the page. On A4v is '*The Prologue . . .*', also set between a pair of ornaments. The text starts on B1 under the head-title 'A pleasant Comedie of / *the Gentle Craft.*' within a compartment. It opens with an initial M. The text of the play is in black letter with roman for speech prefixes and italic for stage directions. There is no division into acts and scenes. Of the preliminaries, only A3 is signed; thenceforward the first three leaves of each sheet are signed. The running title is '*A pleasant Comedie of / the Gentle Craft.*' After the

last line of the play is 'FINIS.' with, at the foot of the page, the pair
of ornaments also used on A3.

In the printing of the quarto there are signs of care in presenting
the play and in preparing it for the reader. Presumably Dekker was
asked to supply the unsigned Epistle which, as Bowers says, 'there
seems every reason to assign to Dekker' (p. 9). Certainly its tone
seems designed as an extension to that of the play. Though the
'argument' it gives is perfunctory, it makes something of a point of
including the songs, and provides a forename for Sir Hugh Lacy
which occurs nowhere in the text of the play as we have it.[81] Also
of interest is the reference on the title-page to performance at
Court. Dekker was on the crest of a wave. *Old Fortunatus*, also
performed at Court during the twelve days of the Christmas season
of 1599/1600, was entered on the Stationers' Register on 20 February 1600[82] and was printed in 1600. The phrase 'this present
Christmasse' in the Epistle to *The Shoemaker's Holiday* may indicate
that the Epistle was composed during the Christmas season. It
seems reasonable to conjecture that publication of both plays followed soon after Court performance, which was both an honour
and a source of publicity, though Dekker's authorship of *The
Shoemaker's Holiday* is not acknowledged, and his name occurs only
at the very end of *Old Fortunatus*. The apparently authorised
publication of plays while they were still likely to do well on the
public stage is a little surprising, though less so from a dramatist
who was not formally attached to a particular company.[83]

The printer and publisher of the first quarto, Valentine Sims, was
active as a stationer from 1594 to 1612.[84] By 1600 he was an
established printer of plays, though his work also extended to other
popular literature and to religion, law, history, and other topics.
For Henslowe's company he printed, besides *The Shoemaker's Holiday*, Chapman's *An Humorous Day's Mirth* in 1599 and *1 Sir John
Oldcastle*, by Munday and others, in 1600. His dramatic output in
1600 also includes the first quarto of *2 Henry IV*, the first quarto of
Much Ado About Nothing, and the second quarto of *The First Part of
the Contention Betwixt . . . York and Lancaster*. His only other printing of a work by Dekker was in 1604, when he issued the first
quarto of *1 The Honest Whore*, with a second edition the following
year. He continued to print plays, his later work including the first
quarto of Marlowe's *Dr Faustus* in 1604.

On 19 April 1610 Sims transferred his rights in *The Shoemaker's Holiday* to John Wright, who published the second quarto in that year, the third in 1618, the fourth in 1624, and the fifth in 1631. His brother Edward entered the transfer of the copy to himself on 27 June 1646; on 4 April 1655 it passed to William Gilbertson, who published the sixth and last quarto edition in 1657. Full bibliographical information, along with lists of surviving copies of these early editions, is given by Greg.[85]

Internal evidence suggests that the copy handed to Sims for printing was authorial, not theatrical. There are permissive stage directions of a kind that suggests the author rather than the prompter, e.g. '... *Sibill ... and other seruants*' (xi.0), and '*fiue or sixe shoomakers, all with cudgels, or such weapons*' (xviii.0). There are irregularities in speech prefixes, such as variations between 'Roger' and 'Hodge'. Lacy's speeches are sometimes ascribed to himself while he is disguised as Hans, sometimes to Hans when he has dropped his disguise. The imperfect state of Eyre's speech at xxi.178 ff. suggests a manuscript that had not been finally polished. The fact that there are no obvious cues for the songs in the text of the play itself (see note to the songs, p. 78) suggests that they were afterthoughts, added to the play after it had been completed without them, and perhaps after the manuscript had been handed over to the company. The evidence supports and strengthens Bowers's conclusion 'that the author's papers may have been used, possibly the "foul papers" '. As he says, 'a transcript of these cannot be ruled out of the question' (p. 9), but there is nothing positively to suggest one.

Bowers (pp. 10–11) discusses the relationships between the early quartos, and provides full collations. The second, third, and fourth quartos all show signs of editorial revision, but Bowers successfully demonstrates that this is almost certainly without authority, as also that the Q2 variants cannot reasonably be credited to unknown press variants in Q1. The fifth and sixth quartos are straight reprints.

It follows that the sole authority for the text of the play is Q1, though an editor is likely to feel that some of the revisions in the later quartos represent genuine though unauthoritative reversions to what Dekker wrote, and so should be adopted.

In the first issue of his edition, Bowers reported the results of a compositorial analysis of Q1 with the aim of determining 'the exact degree of corruption . . . requiring emendation'. He notes 'at least eleven' instances where words are apparently omitted, or verse lines shortened (e.g. by printing 'lets' instead of the metrically more satisfactory 'let vs', i.195). One (x.63) was 'corrected' in Q1; three (i.41 and 195, vi.25) in Q2; three (ii.28, x.1 and 119) in Q3; and one (i.179) in Q4. Modern editors have filled out some of the remaining lines (v.7; xi.36; xv.41), whether necessarily or not. (To the lines noted by Bowers should be added i.1, i.204 ('corrected' in Q2), viii.36 (as Davies points out), viii.53 (emended by Fritsche), x.66, x.173, xxi.92 (a broken line of verse), and xxi.121. Other possible additions are verse lines such as i.181, xii.48, and xiv.61, which include words of uncertain syllabic value.)

What Bowers legitimately hoped to discover by his compositorial analysis was whether more than one compositor set the copy and, if so, whether one appeared to be more liable to errors of omission than the other. A clear result might have helped to determine whether some of the abbreviations stemmed from the copy or from the printing-house, and would have influenced the editor in his decision whether, for example, to fill out short verse lines which make sense as they are. Unfortunately Bowers's investigations are, as he admits, inconclusive: 'The investigation, therefore, brings one back to where one started with little more information than that the possible errors are at least not divided between two regularly alternating workmen, though they are not strictly confined to one' (p. 14).

Bowers's distribution of the text between two compositors is modified by W. Craig Ferguson.[86] Ferguson assigns rather more of the text to an alternate compositor than Bowers, who, in an additional note to his volume IV (incorporated into the notes on the play in reprints of his volume I) appears to accept Ferguson's conclusions. But Ferguson's modifications of Bowers's conclusions do not suggest any significant differences in compositorial practice such as could be applied by an editor in emending the text. The present text is based on a fresh collation of the five known copies of Q1: British Library, formerly British Museum (B.M.), copies 1 (161.b.1) and 2 (C.34.c.28; lacking sigs. K3 and 4); Folger Shakespeare Library (Folg.; photostat); Harvard University Library (H.D.; John Payne Collier's copy, containing his forgeries of actors' names; microfilm); and Henry E. Huntington Library (H.E.H.; microfilm).

The state of the variant sheets is as follows; corrected readings are given to the left of the square bracket:

Sheet C, inner forme (uncorrected, B.M.[1]; corrected, B.M.[2], H.E.H., Folg., H.D.)

Sig. C1*v*

[ii.53] ſouldiers,] ſouldiers

Sig. C2

[iii.12] ſhooemaker?] ſhooemaker:

[iii.13] be:] be

[iii.18] ſight.] ſight,

[iii.22] ſprites,] ſprites

Sig. C4

[iv.113] hoe,] how

[iv.128] readie?] readie,

[v.1] Cosen,] Cosen

[v.1] brake,] brake

[v.1] far,] farre

Sheet E, inner forme (uncorrected, B.M.[1]; corrected, Folg., B.M.[2], H.E.H.; partially corrected, H.D., which has the corrected reading on sig. E2 but the uncorrected one on sig. E4)

Sig. E2

[ix.45] gloue at] gloue at gloue at

Sig. E4

[x.62] huſband: why how now,] huſband, why how,

Sheet G, inner forme (corrected, B.M.[1], B.M.[2], H.E.H., H.D.; uncorrected, Folg.)

Sig. G2

[xiii.35] would] wonld

Sig. G4

[xv.19] conſummate] conſumate

Note: The catchword on G1*v* is 'but' in Folg.; the 't' has dropped out in each of the other copies, presumably as a result of the press corrections.

Of these variants, only those at iv.113, ix.45, and x.62 affect the sense. Although, as Bowers rightly points out, the corrections were not necessarily made with reference to copy, we have preferred the 'corrected' reading in each case.

Our collations differ from Bowers's in three respects. We record an additional variant on the inner forme of Sheet C (iii.22), the dropping of a letter from the catchword on G1v, and the existence of the partially corrected inner forme of Sheet E in the Harvard copy (said by Bowers to be fully corrected). It may also be noted that minor errors have crept into Bowers's edition, affecting some of the textual information.

Later editions

The Shoemaker's Holiday has often been reprinted, though interest in it was slow to develop by comparison with many other plays of its period. Charles Lamb included no extracts from it in his *Specimens of English Dramatic Poets* (1808)[87] and the first reprint after 1657 was edited by H. Fritsche and published at Thorn, Germany, in 1862. He used an imperfect copy of the 1618 quarto and modernised the text, making some of the necessary basic emendations and relineations. He has some notes, in German. R. H. Shepherd claimed to have collated Q2, Q3, and Q5 for the generally unsatisfactory reprint in Dekker's *Dramatic Works* published by J. Pearson (4 vols, 1873). He hit upon a few corrections, but made many errors of his own.

The first thorough study of the text came from Germany in the edition of 1886 by Karl Warnke and Ludwig Proescholdt, which includes an introduction and notes in English and an old-spelling text based on a careful collation of all the early editions except that of 1624, which was not known to the editors. Within the limits of the scholarship of the age, this is an excellent edition. In the following year, Swinburne's essay on Dekker was published in *The Nineteenth Century* and there also appeared the Mermaid volume devoted to Dekker, in which many English readers have made their first acquaintance with the play. The editor, Ernest Rhys, comments appreciatively on it in his introduction, describing it as 'one to be remembered with the score or so of the best comedies of pure joy of life which were produced by the Elizabethans'. He says that his reprint is based upon the text of Warnke and Proescholdt, 'the excellence of text, notes and introduction leaving little beyond the modernising and some elucidation here and there to be done'.

A purified version, removing all traces of obscenity, appeared in *Famous Elizabethan Plays, Expurgated and Adapted for Modern Readers* by H. M. Fitzgibbon in 1890. There were editions by G. E. and W. H. Hadow in 1907, by Charles W. Eliot (with indebtedness to both Warnke and Proescholdt and Rhys) in 1910 (Harvard Classics, New York), and by W. A. Neilson in 1911. In 1913 appeared C. K. Allen's version 'as arranged for the O.U.D.S.', who performed it that year. It too is expurgated.

Fresh work on the text was undertaken by A. F. Lange for his careful, old-spelling edition in volume III (New York, 1914) of C. M. Gayley's *Representative English Comedies*. He consulted Warnke and Proescholdt, but made new collations, while still not knowing of Q4. There is a modernised edition based on Rhys's by C. B. Wheeler in *Six Plays by Contemporaries of Shakespeare* (World's Classics, 1915), and J. S. P. Tatlock and R. G. Martin included it in their *Representative English Plays* (New York, 1916).

The first French translation, as *Le Mardi Gras du Cordonnier*, was made by Georges Duval and appeared in *Les Contemporains de Shakespeare* (Paris, 1920). C. M. Edmondston, who had directed the play in 1919 (see p. 47), published an unambitious acting edition in 1924 (The Bankside Playbooks). 1926 saw the important Old Vic production, and there are many reprints during the next ten years. W. J. Halliday prepared a sensibly annotated school edition for Macmillan's English Classics in 1927; his text is based on Warnke and Proescholdt, with some expurgations. There are other school editions, by W. T. Williams (Methuen's English Classics) in the same year, and by Guy N. Pocock for the King's Treasuries of Literature (undated, but apparently also of 1927). Expurgation continued. Even according to Wheeler's World's Classics text, presumably intended mainly for adult readers, Cicely Bumtrinket 'f—ts in her sleep'. Halliday makes her snore; Pocock deprives her of her surname and her 'privy fault', and expunges references to 'bum', so that 'Loaden thy bum' becomes 'Loaden thyself'. Similarly, Firk's 'my codpiece point is ready to fly in pieces' (xviii.181) is silently removed by some editors (e.g. Eliot, Pocock) and romanticised by Halliday into an allusion to his heart.

G. B. Harrison is unsqueamish in the prettily printed, lightly annotated text which he 'prepared for reading' for The Fortune Play Books (still 1927), in which he expands the stage directions in the fashion, doubtless influenced by Barrie and Shaw, that J. Dover Wilson was following at the time in the early volumes of the New [Cambridge] Shakespeare. 1928 saw a school edition by G. A. Sheldon (Wells of English), a text edited by H. F. Rubinstein in *Great English Plays*, another edited by H. C. Scheikert in *Early English Plays* (New York), and J. R. Sutherland's helpfully annotated edition published by the Clarendon Press.

After eight editions in two years, there was a brief pause. Between 1930 and 1932 the play was included in four collections all published in New York: G. R. Coffman's *Five Significant English Plays* (1930), E. J. Howard's *Ten Elizabethan Plays* (1931), the second, revised edition (1931) of F. E. Schelling's *Typical Elizabethan Plays*, and E. C. Dunn's *Eight Famous Elizabethan Plays* (1932), which reprints, without acknowledgement, the text and notes of Wheeler's World's Classics edition. Also in 1932 it was published in Nelson's Playbooks series, edited by John Hampden, and in a version adapted by Arnold Salter for the Kidlington Historical Play Society (Oxford). In the following year it appeared in two much-used anthologies: *English Drama 1580–1642* (Boston), edited by C. F. Tucker Brooke and N. B. Paradise, where it has a brief introduction, limited annotation, and a statement in the General Preface that 'The texts rest upon a careful new collation of the original editions'; and Hazelton Spencer's *Elizabethan Plays* (Boston), for which the Harvard and Folger copies of Q1 were consulted, and which has limited but careful annotation. C. R. Baskervill's edition in *Elizabethan and Stuart Plays* (New York, 1934), edited by Baskervill along with V. B. Heltzel and A. H. Nethercot, is confessedly based on Lange's. In the same year, the play appeared in a second World's Classics volume, *Five Elizabethan Comedies*, edited by A. K. McIlwraith. In 1935 it was included in *The English Drama*, edited by F. W. Parks and R. C. Beatty (New York), and was adapted for children by R. Vallance as *Shoemakers' Progress* in *Little Plays from the English Drama*. In 1936 it appeared in *The Literature of England* (Chicago), edited by G. B. Woods, H. A. Watts, and G. K. Anderson.

These twenty-one versions in ten years, some of them often reprinted, satisfied demand for a while. A Swedish version, *Alla Skomakers dag . . . För svenskteater av Sven Hallström* was published in Lund in 1947, and a second French translation, by Pierre Messiaen as *La Fête du cordonnier*, appeared in Paris in 1948. The next edition of the original play seems to be that in Volume 1 (1953) of Fredson Bowers's *The Dramatic Works of Thomas Dekker* (4 vols, Cambridge, 1953–61), which represents a landmark in the history of its textual treatment. Bowers's old-spelling edition includes a full collation of all the early editions. Its standard of accuracy is high, but the text would occasionally have been better if Bowers had had to explain the meaning of what he prints. He fails to consider well-supported emendations at viii.23 and x.160, and offers annotation only in reference to selected textual points.

Two bilingual editions, in English and French, followed: A. Koszul's, in prose and verse (as *Fête chez le cordonnier*, Paris, 1955), and J. Loiseau's, in prose (as *Le Jour de fête du cordonnier*, Paris, 1957; based on Bowers's text). Michael Vinaver's French translation (as *La Fête du cordonnier*) for the Théâtre National Populaire was published in the T.N.P. Répertoire series in Paris in 1959. The British Library possesses a Russian translation of 1959, and a Hungarian one, by M. J. Szenczi, of 1961. *The Shoemaker's Holiday* was reprinted in several anthologies around this time: *Four Great Elizabethan Plays*, with an introduction by John Gassner (New York, 1960); *Six Elizabethan Plays*, edited by R. C. Bald (Boston, 1963); *Four Famous Tudor and Stuart Plays*, edited by Louis B. Wright and Virginia La Mar (New York, 1963); *Earlier Seventeenth-century Drama*, edited by Robert G. Lawrence (Everyman's Library, 1963); and *Elizabethan and Jacobean Comedy*, edited by Robert Ornstein and Hazelton Spencer (Boston, 1964). J. B. Steane's edition (Cambridge, 1965) is clearly intended for senior schoolchildren;[88] by this date, the need to expurgate is no longer felt. The influence of Rhys's Mermaid edition is still strong in the reprint of the play in John Gassner's *Elizabethan Drama* (Bantam World Drama, New York, 1967). There is an old-spelling text with oddly-partial annotation by Paul C. Davies (Fountainwell Drama Texts, Edinburgh, 1968), and another, with Introduction and notes in Italian, by Vittoria Sanna (Bari, 1968). M. L. Wine includes the play in his *Drama of the English Renaissance* (New York, 1969). A facsimile of the B.M.[1] copy of the 1600 quarto was issued by the Scolar Press (Menston, 1971). D. J. Palmer's New Mermaid edition (London, 1975) offers a modernised version, occasionally unreliable in details, of Bowers's text, along with light annotation and a sympathetic introduction. A ballad opera based on the play and performed by the Minnesota Theatre Company in 1967 was published in New York by Boosey and Hawkes (undated). The words of the songs in the play have been included in many anthologies.

This list of over fifty editions, adaptations, and translations is probably not exhaustive. It might suggest that a new edition is unnecessary. But, in the absence of the promised commentary to Bowers's edition, the only editions with anything approaching to a full commentary for English-speaking readers are Sutherland's, dating from 1928, and Steane's, which has many limitations and is very much a school edition. So we have not felt the preparation of an edition according to the principles of the Revels Plays to be a work of supererogation.

The present text

The present text follows the conventions of the Revels series in modernising spelling and punctuation.[89] Since the speeches in which Lacy, disguised as Hans, seems to speak Dutch are a mixture of Dutch and English, we have not been able to apply to them a simple process of modernisation. We have preserved the original spelling with greater fidelity than we should have observed if they had been either pure Dutch or pure English. But we have made it more consistent (for instance, printing 'you' throughout, though Q1 also uses both 'yow' and 'yo') on the grounds that compositorial (and, indeed, insignificant authorial) inconsistencies may occur in these passages as elsewhere. We have done something to increase intelligibility for the reader when this involves only trivial alterations, for instance spelling out 'you' when Q1 prints 'v' (for 'u'), a typographical device that would be meaningless in performance, and printing 'fol' for 'wol' (meaning 'full', vii.2). Pseudo-Dutch passages are italicised in the text and translated in the Commentary. Obviously the actor has to find a way of conveying their meaning while sounding foreign.

The collations indicate all substantive departures from the copy-text, Q1, including those of verse-lineation but excluding additions to stage directions indicated by square brackets in the text. Most of these departures have been anticipated either in the later quartos or in modern, edited versions. In accordance with the principles of the Revels series, an attempt is made to credit each alteration to the edition (in the case of the quartos) or the editor who first suggested or adopted it. With a much reprinted play such as this, the task is particularly difficult. We have, of course, collated all the editions mentioned in the preceding section that have any claim to originality. But even the editors of popular reprints occasionally introduce new readings. It is interesting, for instance, that the French translator, Koszul, who is not primarily concerned with textual matters, claims—accurately, so far as we know—to be the first to divide the Prologue into its two stanzas. We have felt no need, and less inclination, to attempt a complete collation of every edition and reprint of the play. Nevertheless, we are confident that our collations are more informative in their attributions than those of Bowers, the most recent editor to have made a similar attempt, as may be suggested by the fact that he lists only nineteen editions up to his own, as opposed to our list of thirty-seven up to that point. We also collate plausible emendations that we have nevertheless not adopted, again attributing them to the first edition or editor to propose them.

Act-and-scene divisions

The six early quartos of *The Shoemaker's Holiday* make no division into acts and scenes. The stage is cleared twenty times during the action, so the play can be divided into twenty-one scenes. Its first modern editor, Fritsche, divided it into twenty scenes, without act divisions. Like some later editors, he made no break at the end of our Scene xiii, presumably regarding the action as continuous. Baskervill divides into nineteen scenes, making no break at the end of our Scenes v and xv, where too the action may be regarded as continuous. Wine does the same.

Most editors have indicated division into five acts. The tradition, originating with Warnke and Proescholdt, is to break after Scenes i, vi, xi, and xvi. This creates acts of very uneven length. Bowers moves the first break to the end of Scene iv, creating a first act of an appropriate proportion. He moves the end of Act II to the end of Scene viii, instead of Scene vi, for similar reasons. He gives a more specific reason for ending Act III with Scene xii instead of Scene xi, saying that both Scenes xii and xiii 'clearly must have employed the inner stage'. So 'it seemed to me better to insert a hypothetical act interval between them to allow time for changing the few necessary properties'. But he admits 'that the difficulty in successive scenes without a break could have been overcome if at some point in the first scene Jane had come out to Hammon and the curtains had closed behind her', and this is in accord with most modern thought about the acting of discovery scenes. In any case, we have no evidence that there was likely to be a longer break in performance after an act than after a scene within an act.

We know that the division into acts of Elizabethan and Jacobean plays was often imposed in the printing-house, or by later editors. The ease with which Bowers can propose a radical rearrangement of the traditional division of *The Shoemaker's Holiday* suggests that this is a superficial division, corresponding to no structural principle in the mind of the author as he disposed his material.

That the concept of the scene existed in Dekker's mind is indisputable. Indeed, except for certain more complex scenes, such as the first and the last, it is easy to summarise very briefly the narrative function of each scene. For instance, Scene ii establishes Rose's love for Lacy and sends Sybil off for news of him; Scene iii shows us that Lacy has disguised himself as a Dutch shoemaker in order to be near Rose; and Scene iv shows him establishing himself among Eyre and his men. But we have discerned nothing in the play's design to suggest that in composing it Dekker had in mind a five-act structure such as was recommended by some dramatic theorists and practitioners of his time. Consequently we have omitted act-divisions from the text, though the customary editorial divisions into acts and scenes are given below. What we call the 'traditional' division originates with Warnke and Proescholdt, and is followed among the more important editions by Rhys, Lange, Brooke and Paradise, and Spencer. Wheeler varies from this by running together IV.ii and iii, so that IV.iv becomes IV.iii, and IV.v becomes IV.iv. Harrison varies by running together IV.ii and iii as IV.ii and IV.iv and v as IV.iii. Bowers is followed by Lawrence, Steane, Davies, Sanna, and Palmer (except that Palmer ends Act III with Scene xi).

This edition	'Traditional' division	Bowers's division
Sc. i	I.i	I.i
Sc. ii	II.i	I.ii
Sc. iii	II.ii	I.iii
Sc. iv	II.iii	I.iv
Sc. v	II.iv	II.i
Sc. vi	II.v	II.ii
Sc. vii	III.i	II.iii
Sc. viii	III.ii	II.iv
Sc. ix	III.iii	III.i
Sc. x	III.iv	III.ii
Sc. xi	III.v	III.iii
Sc. xii	IV.i	III.iv
Sc. xiii	IV.ii	IV.i
Sc. xiv	IV.iii	IV.ii
Sc. xv	IV.iv	IV.iii
Sc. xvi	IV.v	IV.iv
Sc. xvii	V.i	V.i
Sc. xviii	V.ii	V.ii
Sc. xix	V.iii	V.iii
Sc. xx	V.iv	V.iv
Sc. xxi	V.v	V.v

NOTES

[1] Henslowe, p. 122.

[2] Henslowe, p. 86. The lost play of 'fayeton', or *Phaeton*, has frequently been regarded as the first version of the Ford/Dekker collaboration *The Sun's Darling* (c. 1624). M. T. Jones-Davies, in her indispensable study *Un Peintre de la vie londonienne: Thomas Dekker*, 2 vols (Paris, 1958), II.405, argues persuasively against any connection between the two plays.

[3] Francis Meres, *Palladis Tamia*, edited by Don Cameron Allen (Urbana, Illinois, 1933), p. 78.

[4] *English Villainies Discovered by Lantern and Candlelight* (1632), ed. Pendry, p. 179. The inference that Dekker was born in 1572 is accepted by Mme Jones-Davies (I.28), on whose work this account of Dekker's life depends. There is vaguer corroborative evidence from 'S.R.', author of *Martin Markall, Beadle of Bridewell* (1610), who, in discussing one of Dekker's publications, refers to 'wordes vsed fortie yeeres agoe before he was borne' (sig. E1*v*). On the possibility of a 1626 edition of *English Villainies*, with the same dedication, thus bringing Dekker's date of birth six years earlier, see Pendry, pp. 325–6.

[5] London's population in 1593–94 was over 150,000; Norwich, the second English city, had less than 20,000 (figures cited in Jones-Davies, I.17).

[6] *The Seven Deadly Sins of London* (1606), sig. A3v (Grosart, II.13); *A Rod for Runaways* (1625), ed. Wilson, p. 146.

[7] On Dekker's contribution to *Sir Thomas More* see Jones-Davies, II.339–41.

[8] Jones-Davies, II.344–65.

[9] Henslowe, pp. 103–29.

[10] Henslowe, pp. 86, 104.

[11] On Dekker's part in the 'War of the Theatres' see Jones-Davies, I.39–50.

[12] His widow renounced the administration of his estate, a way of avoiding the inheritance of debts (see Jones-Davies, I.71).

[13] On Dekker's London pageants, see David M. Bergeron, *English Civic Pageantry, 1558–1642* (London, 1971), pp. 71–89, 163–78.

[14] See *Plague Pamphlets*, ed. Wilson.

[15] See the bibliographical appendix in Jones-Davies, II.339–416.

[16] *Work for Armourers* (1609), sig. C4 (Grosart, IV.117). Dekker's social concerns, and in particular his views on poverty, are discussed, with some over-emphasis of his radicalism, by Kate L. Gregg, *Thomas Dekker: A Study of Economic and Social Backgrounds*, University of Washington Publications, Language and Literature, vol. 2, no. 2 (Seattle, 1924).

[17] The belief that Robert Wilson was part-author with Dekker has been disproved (see below, p. 47). Dekker's sole authorship of the play can be confidently accepted.

[18] Chambers, *E.S.*, III.292; Greg, in his review of volume I of the Bowers edition of Dekker, *R.E.S.*, New Series 5 (1954), 414–19 (p. 415); Kinney, 'Thomas Dekker's Twelfth Night', *University of Toronto Quarterly*, 41 (1971), 63–73 (p. 72, note 4).

[19] Henslowe, pp. 126–7. Dekker received a further payment of £1 on 31 [sic] November for alterations, and on 12 December £2 more for 'the eande of fortewnatus for the corte' (pp. 127–8).

[20] *Henry V*, Chorus to Act V, l. 32. On the date of the play, see the new Arden edition by J. H. Walter (London, 1954), p. xi. Walter believes the play was written 'nearer March than September' 1599.

[21] On the problems of poverty in the period, and the development of the Poor Laws, see J. B. Black, *The Reign of Elizabeth*, second edition (Oxford, 1959), pp. 265–7. In his *Drama and Society in the Age of Jonson* (London, 1937), L. C. Knights is concerned with these and related economic and social questions as a background to the drama.

[22] Henslowe, pp. 64–5.

[23] Haughton's claim to priority is discussed in Albert Croll Baugh's edition of *Englishmen for My Money* (Philadelphia, 1917), pp. 40–1, and by Alexander Leggatt in his *Citizen Comedy in the Age of Shakespeare* (Toronto, 1973), p. 7. Leggatt's book provides a useful general survey of the dramatic genre to which *The Shoemaker's Holiday* belongs.

[24] See below, pp. 41–3. The chronicle play *Jack Straw* (c. 1591), which concludes with a lesson on why London's Lord Mayors are always knighted, and why the City's arms include a bloody dagger, is an interesting early example of this phenomenon.

[25] Stow, II.207, 208, 211. (References are to the Kingsford edition cited on p. xiv.)

[26] A date of 1597 for *The Merry Wives of Windsor* is argued by William Green in his *Shakespeare's 'Merry Wives of Windsor'* (Princeton, 1962), and in his Signet edition (New York, 1965), and is supported by H. J. Oliver in his new Arden edition (London, 1971). If the contention of G. R. Hibbard is accepted, that only the last act

of the play is so early, with the remainder dating from around 1600, then any influence between Eyre and the Host of the Garter would be in the opposite direction (see Hibbard's New Penguin edition (Harmondsworth, 1973)).

[27] According to Mme Jones-Davies (II.98–9) the following plays before *The Shoemaker's Holiday* feature shoemakers (except where indicated all are anonymous; dates are from Alfred Harbage, *Annals of English Drama*, revised by S. Schoenbaum (London, 1964)): *The Famous Victories of Henry V* (1586); *George à Greene, the Pinner of Wakefield* (1590); Robert Wilson's *The Cobbler's Prophecy* (1590); *Locrine* (1591); *A Knack to Know a Knave* (1592); *The Cobbler of Queenhithe* (1597); Jonson's *The Case is Altered* (1597). After Dekker's play come Samuel Rowley's *When You See Me You Know Me* (1604), William Rowley's *A Shoemaker a Gentleman* (1608), and Massinger's *Love's Cure* (1625). Shakespeare's only shoemaker (or cobbler) appears among the turbulent citizens in the first scene of *Julius Caesar* (usually thought to date from the same year as *The Shoemaker's Holiday*).

[28] The case for a connection between the two scenes is argued by W. L. Halstead, 'New Source Influence on *The Shoemaker's Holiday*', M.L.N., 56 (1949), 127–9.

[29] See R. A. Law, '*The Shoemakers' Holiday* and *Romeo and Juliet*', S.P., 21 (1924), 356–61.

[30] Among the qualities of a good shoemaker listed at the end of the first of Deloney's tales in *The Gentle Craft* is the ability to 'beare his part in a three mans Song' (p. 115; references are to the Lawlis edition cited on p. xii).

[31] Comic pseudo-Dutch occurs in several plays of the period, including Haughton's *Englishmen for My Money* (which, it has already been suggested, probably influenced Dekker in other ways) and, among later plays on which Dekker collaborated, *Westward Ho, Northward Ho,* and *The Roaring Girl.* Foreign garbling of the English language is also present in *Henry V* (whence it may have influenced Dekker in his play of the same year) and *The Merry Wives of Windsor.*

[32] All the writers from the late 1590s referred to above (p. 11) treat the subject of wounded veterans: see Arthington, sig. B4; Tyro, sig. F4; Barnfield, *Complaint of Poetry*, sig. C1. See also C. G. Cruickshank, *Elizabeth's Army*, second edition (Oxford, 1966), pp. 183–8 and, for the figure on the stage, Paul A. Jorgensen, *Shakespeare's Military World* (Berkeley and Los Angeles, 1956), pp. 208–14 and Thomas L. Berger and William C. Bradford, Jr, *An Index of Characters in English Printed Drama to the Restoration* (Englewood, Colorado, 1975), s.v. 'Soldiers'.

[33] See Frank Freeman Foster, *The Politics of Stability: A Portrait of the Rulers in Elizabethan London*, Royal Historical Society, Studies in History (London, 1977). Foster's thorough study of the government of Elizabethan London offers useful background to the play (and confirmation that Dekker tends to present a generally romanticised picture of Eyre's career in civic politics).

[34] Foster (pp. 61–3) makes it clear that sheriffs were normally elected from among the aldermen and lord mayors always so, in strict order of seniority. Apart from his assumption of the disguise of alderman (vii.107 ff.), this preliminary stage in Eyre's civic rise is one that Dekker omits, though at xiii.39–43 the assumption seems to be made that Eyre has aldermanic rank and will succeed to the mayoralty through the decease of those senior to him.

[35] In his article 'The Sources of the Characters in *The Shoemaker's Holiday*', M.P., 27 (1929), 175–82, W. K. Chandler cites the death (from sweating sickness) of two Lord Mayors and six aldermen in 1485 as a precedent that 'reduces the absurdity of Dekker's use of such means' (p. 177).

[36] Chandler ('Sources of the Characters', p. 182) laboriously tries to show that

The Shoemaker's Holiday 'is historical in so far as the source of the characters is concerned'. As he suggests, Dekker might well have found some of the play's surnames in Stow, where they occur close to that of Oatley. But for other surnames (most of them common in Elizabethan England) Chandler proposes sources unavailable in print in Dekker's time. It is possible that Dekker may have consciously chosen names with an historical flavour remembered from the history plays on which he had recently been working for Henslowe, but the degree of deliberation implied by Chandler seems unlikely. (See also the notes to the *Dramatis Personae*.)

[37] See below, pp. 42–4. The frequency of allusions to contemporary plays (see ii.46; xx.54, 59, 60; xxi.23) and contemporary customs (tobacco-pipes (x.58–61), drinking at the Swan (vii.10, 99), etc.) makes it clear that Dekker has no wish to cultivate the historical. Chandler's concern with his thesis leads him firmly to identify Dekker's King with the historical Henry VI. This is properly challenged by Michael Manheim in 'The King in Dekker's *The Shoemakers' Holiday*', *N. & Q.*, New Series 4 (1957), 432, but he, in turn, seeks too firm an identification with Henry V.

[38] Notes on individual places are provided in the Commentary, which draws attention to those which are exclusively Elizabethan; a general study of this aspect of the play is in W. K. Chandler's essay 'The Topography of Dekker's *The Shoemaker's Holiday*', *S.P.*, 26 (1929), 499–504.

[39] The possibility of a connection between the Spencer case and Dekker's play is discussed in David Novarr's article 'Dekker's Gentle Craft and the Lord Mayor of London', *M.P.*, 57 (1960), 233–9. For further information on the affair, see Lawrence Stone, 'The Peer and the Alderman's Daughter', *History Today*, 11 (1961), 48–55. G. R. Hibbard argues for the influence of the Spencer scandal on Shakespeare's *The Merry Wives of Windsor* (see his New Penguin edition, pp. 38–42).

[40] The fullest treatment of the structure of *The Shoemaker's Holiday* is in James H. Conover's *Thomas Dekker: An Analysis of Dramatic Structure* (The Hague, 1969), pp. 19–50. More concerned with thematic intention as revealed through structure is Michael Manheim's article 'The Construction of *The Shoemakers' Holiday*', *S.E.L.*, 10 (1970), 315–23. The following account is indebted to the work of both scholars.

[41] This aspect of the play has been described by Joel H. Kaplan in his article 'Virtue's Holiday: Thomas Dekker and Simon Eyre', *Renaissance Drama*, New Series 2 (1969), 103–22. The following remarks owe a good deal to Professor Kaplan's excellent essay.

[42] On the importance of war in the play, see Frederick M. Burelbach's essay, 'War and Peace in *The Shoemakers' Holiday*', *Tennessee Studies in Literature*, 13 (1968), 99–107.

[43] In *The Crisis of the Aristocracy, 1558–1641* (Oxford, 1965), Lawrence Stone has demonstrated (p. 627) that between the years 1570 and 1599 two-thirds of the marriages of titular peers and their heirs were to commoners. Curiously this is the highest proportion in the whole period with which his study is concerned, and adds support to Patricia Thomson's discernment (in her essay 'The Old Way and the New Way in Dekker and Massinger', *M.L.R.*, 51 (1956), 168–78) of a hardening of the social climate between the optimism of *The Shoemaker's Holiday* of 1599 and the harshly satirical tone of Massinger's *A New Way to Pay Old Debts* written in the early 1620s. Dr Thomson's essay offers an illuminating comparison of the two plays, though its discussion of the class struggle in *The Shoemaker's Holiday* is largely confined to the Rose/Lacy plot, with little to say on the important contribution of this theme to other areas of the play.

[44] A general negative statement of this kind is, of course, difficult to document. We are grateful to Professor Joel Hurstfield who (in a personal communication) has kindly offered his immense knowledge of Elizabethan social conditions in corroboration of this.

[45] For a contrary view of the play, see Peter Mortensen's essay 'The Economics of Joy in *The Shoemakers' Holiday*', *S.E.L.*, 16 (1976), 241–52. Mr Mortensen's determinedly grim reading attempts to make the background of war, poverty, and separation (used by Dekker to throw into relief the happiness achieved by the main characters) into the play's dominant motif.

[46] Donald S. McClure, 'Versification and Master Hammon in *The Shoemakers' Holiday*', *Studies in the Humanities*, 1 (1969), 50–4. On Hammon's role, see also Michael Manheim's 'The Construction of *The Shoemakers' Holiday*' (cited above).

[47] Kaplan, p. 104, citing Harry Levin 'in conversation'.

[48] The point is made by Kaplan, p. 110. Also concerned with the festival aspects of the play are Harold E. Toliver, '*The Shoemakers' Holiday*: Theme and Image', *Boston University Studies in English*, 5 (1961), 208–18, and Arthur F. Kinney, 'Thomas Dekker's Twelfth Night' (cited above). Professor Kinney's belief that Dekker wrote with particular reference to the Christmas festivities is unacceptably restricting, but his essay still has valuable points to make on the play's general holiday mood.

[49] For a discussion of the punctuation and significance of the play's title, see Appendix B.

[50] *The Magnificent Entertainment*, ll. 1419, 1423 (speech at 'the Conduit in Fleet-streete'; Bowers, II.297).

[51] In his *Shakespeare's Festive Comedy* (Princeton, 1962), C. L. Barber sees Shakespeare's comedies in the context of the exuberance and ritual of holiday-keeping in Elizabethan society, providing, in his phrase, a way 'through release to clarification' of the social order they temporarily overthrow. *The Shoemaker's Holiday* belongs in the same tradition.

[52] 'The Discovery-space in Shakespeare's Globe', *Sh.S.*, 12 (1959), 35–46 (p. 41).

[53] Trudy West, *The Timber-frame House in England* (Newton Abbot, n.d.), p. 46.

[54] 'Three Times Ho and a Brace of Widows', in *The Elizabethan Theatre III*, edited by David Galloway (Toronto and London, 1973), pp. 14–32 (p. 29).

[55] J. S. Manifold, *The Music in English Drama* (London, 1956), p. 8; Arthur F. Kinney, 'Thomas Dekker's Twelfth Night' (cited above).

[56] 'Dramaticus', 'The Players who Acted in *The Shoemaker's Holiday*', *Shakespeare Society Papers*, 4 (1849), 110–22; *Henslowe's Diary*, edited by W. W. Greg, 2 vols (London, 1904–08), II.203; Chambers, *E.S.*, II.292; Fredson Bowers, 'Thomas Dekker, Robert Wilson, and *The Shoemakers' Holiday*', *M.L.N.*, 64 (1949), 517–19.

[57] Unidentified newspaper clipping, 2 May 1898, Harvard Theatre Collection.

[58] 'An Elizabethan Revival', *M.L.N.*, 21 (1906), 167.

[59] Unidentified newspaper clipping, 2 February 1913, Harvard Theatre Collection.

[60] Bankside Edition, p. 88.

[61] *The Stage*, 5 June 1919.

[62] *Ibid.*

[63] *Christian Science Monitor*, 24 May 1920.

[64] '*The Shoemaker's Holiday*', *T.P.'s Weekly*, 17 December 1927, pp. 303–4.

[65] *Observer*, 28 March 1926.

[66] *Brief Chronicles* (London, 1943), p. 70.

[67] Agate, p. 70.

[68] Agate misquotes.

[69] *Boston Transcript*, 2 December 1932.

[70] 'H.M.', in the *Observer*, 28 June 1936.

[71] For a study of this performance with emphasis on its relation to contemporary social attitudes, see Richard France, '*The Shoemaker's Holiday* at the Mercury Theatre', *Theatre Survey*, 16 (1975), 150–64.

[72] *The Times*, 3 January 1938.

[73] Richard Lockridge, *New York Sun*, 3 January 1938.

[74] *New York Post*, 3 January 1938.

[75] Jones-Davies, II, 317.

[76] Eric Shorter, *Daily Telegraph*, 5 February 1962.

[77] Alan Brien, *Sunday Telegraph*, 2 August 1964.

[78] Olga Kerensky, *Guardian*, 26 August 1971.

[79] The Enthoven Collection at the Victoria and Albert Museum includes records of the following performances in addition to those mentioned above: 29 March 1948, Kilburn Empire; 11 August 1953, New Lindsey; 11 June 1954, Unity; 5 February 1963, Nottingham Playhouse.

[80] A. W. Pollard and G. R. Redgrave, *A Short-title Catalogue of Books . . . 1475–1640* (London, 1926), No. 6253; W. W. Greg, *A Bibliography of the English Printed Drama to the Restoration*, 4 vols (London, 1939–56), I.282 (no. 175(a)).

[81] E. A. J. Honigmann points to instances in which the cast-lists of Shakespeare plays supply information not provided in the texts, suggesting that they may belong 'to the early, perhaps "prehistoric" phase' of the plays (*The Stability of Shakespeare's Text* (London, 1965), p. 45).

[82] Edward Arber, *A Transcript of the Registers of the Company of Stationers of London, 1554–1640*, 5 vols (London, 1875–94), III.156.

[83] G. E. Bentley, *The Profession of Dramatist in Shakespeare's Time, 1590–1642* (Princeton, N.J., 1971), chapter 10. E. A. J. Honigmann suggests that Dekker may have taken 'energetic measures' to get his plays into print, even against the wishes of the companies that performed them (*The Stability of Shakespeare's Text*, p. 182).

[84] Paul G. Morrison, *Index of Printers, Publishers, and Booksellers . . . 1475 . . . 1640* (Charlottesville, Virginia, 1950); W. Craig Ferguson, *Valentine Simmes, Stationer* (Charlottesville, Virginia, 1968).

[85] *Bibliography of the English Printed Drama*, I.282–5.

[86] W. Craig Ferguson, 'The Compositors of *Henry IV, Part 2, Much Ado about Nothing, The Shoemakers' Holiday*, and *The First Part of the Contention*', S.B., 13 (1960), 19–29; incorporated in his *Valentine Simmes, Stationer*.

[87] In this section, place of publication is London unless otherwise stated.

[88] Textual deficiencies in Steane's edition are pointed out by G. R. Hibbard in his review in *N.&.Q.*, New Series 13 (1966), 315–16.

[89] In phrases such as 'my lord' the noun is normally capitalised only when followed by a proper name (e.g. 'My Lord of Lincoln', i.51) and when it refers to the King without naming him (e.g. 'his Grace', i.46).

THE
SHOMAKERS
Holiday.
OR
The Gentle Craft.

With the humorous life of Simon
Eyre, ſhoomaker, and Lord Maior
of London.

As it was acted before the Queenes moſt excellent Ma-
ieſtie on New-yeares day at night laſt, by the right
honourable the Earle of Notingham, Lord high Ad-
mirall of England, his ſeruants.

Printed by Valentine Sims dwelling at the foote of Adling
hill, neere Bainards Caſtle, at the ſigne of the White
Swanne, and are there to be ſold.
1 6 0 0.

THE SHOEMAKER'S HOLIDAY

A pleasant comedy of the gentle craft

[DRAMATIS PERSONAE]

THE KING OF ENGLAND.

The courtiers:
SIR HUGH LACY, EARL OF LINCOLN.
ROWLAND LACY, *Lincoln's nephew; afterwards disguised as*
HANS MEULTER.
ASKEW, *Lacy's cousin.*
CORNWALL.   5

DRAMATIS PERSONAE] *first given by Fritsche; modified by later editors.*

   DRAMATIS PERSONAE] To the characters he takes over from Deloney Dekker adds others who are invented or derived from history. For W. K. Chandler's suggestion that Dekker deliberately sought out names current during the historical period in which the play is set, see Introduction, pp. 23–4. (Further references to Chandler in the notes on the *Dramatis Personae* are to the article there cited.)

   1. THE KING OF ENGLAND] Historically, Henry VI was king during Eyre's period of civic office. Dekker does not specifically identify the King of the play. For the possibility that he wishes to draw on the associations which Henry V, the victor of Agincourt (fought on the feast of St Crispin), would have had for his audience, see Intrdíntrction, p. 24; see also notes to i.49; viii.8–10; xxi. 25, 85, 141–2.

   2. SIR HUGH LACY, EARL OF LINCOLN] There was no Earl of Lincoln during the period, 1359–1467 (Chandler, p. 178). Dekker may have been influenced in his choice of name by Stow's reference (II.90) to the building of Lincoln's Inn by '*Henry Lacy* Earle of Lincolne . . . [who] deceased in this house in the yeare 1310'. The Lacys were a prominent family in the reigns of Henry V and VI (Chandler, p. 179). The name Hugh is given to Lincoln only in the Epistle (l. 8); the play's frequent allusions to St Hugh mean that the choice of this Christian name could easily be fortuitous. The Earl of Lincoln at the time the play was written was a highly unpopular figure; this might have influenced Dekker's choice of title for this unsympathetic nobleman. (Lincoln's unpopularity is discussed and documented in chapter 3 of C. L. Barber's *Shakespeare's Festive Comedy*, Princeton, N.J., 1959.)

   3. ROWLAND LACY] The name given to the character derived from the Crispine of Deloney's story is found by Chandler (p. 178) among the contemporaries of Eyre, but the surname can be otherwise accounted for (see note on Lincoln, above) and the Christian name was probably chosen for its appropriately romantic ring.

   HANS MEULTER] Hans is a standard name for a stage Dutchman in this period (see, e.g., Sugden, s.v. 'Dutch'). *Meulter* is probably a corruption of the Dutch 'Mulder', meaning 'miller'.

   4. ASKEW] The character corresponds roughly to Deloney's Crispianus; Chandler (p. 178) points to an Askew who fought at Agincourt, but Dekker's choice of the name may well be coincidental.

   5. CORNWALL] Editors usually list him as 'Earl of Cornwall', but the text makes no mention of the title and Chandler (p. 181) suggests that Sir John Cornwall, Lord

LOVELL.

DODGER, a 'parasite' of the Earl of Lincoln.

The citizens:
SIR ROGER OATLEY, Lord Mayor of London.
ROSE, Oatley's daughter.
SYBIL, Rose's maid.   10
MASTER HAMMON, a City gentleman.

Fanhope, prominent in the chronicle accounts of the reigns of Henry V and VI, is intended. Dekker may simply have thought the name appropriate for an attendant courtier, as he does in *Old Fortunatus*.

6. LOVELL] He enters as a messenger at i.50 and is sometimes listed by editors as a 'servant' of the King. But a courtier is probably intended. Chandler (p. 181) identifies him as a member of the noble family, one of whom appears in Stow (II. 90, alongside Henry Lacy, Earl of Lincoln) as the rebuilder of Lincoln's Inn who placed 'thereon aswell the *Lacies* armes as his owne'.

7. DODGER, a 'parasite' of the Earl of Lincoln] The role has no source in Deloney, and even Chandler finds no historical precedent. Lacy describes Dodger at i.197 as 'mine uncle's parasite', apparently using the term in the sense it bears in Greek New Comedy and in Roman comedy, where the parasite is a stock character. His characteristic features are 'importunity, love of sensual pleasures, and above all the desire of getting a good dinner without paying for it' (William Smith, *Dictionary of Greek and Roman Antiquities*, 2 vols, London, 1890, s.v. 'Parasiti'). But Dodger displays none of these characteristics. Lacy (i.197–201) describes his qualities with a vividness that arouses expectations that are not fulfilled. The role becomes little more than that of a messenger, though Dodger's self-important ineffectiveness has provided a cue for comic interpretations (see *The play on the stage*, pp. 51, 52). Dekker may have intended more than he wrote into the role. Dodger's social status is uncertain. He is treated with contempt by Lacy, but addressed several times as 'Master Dodger' by Oatley, who also calls him a 'gentleman' (sc. ix). A degree of affectation may be implied by Firk's 'Monsieur Dodger' (xviii.180). *O.E.D.* defines 'dodger' as 'one who dodges, . . . *esp.* a haggler; later, *esp.* one who practises artful shifts or dodges'. Its illustrations up to 1611 are in the sense of 'haggler', but the use of the verb meaning 'to baffle or parry by shifts and pretexts' goes back to 1573.

8. SIR ROGER OATLEY] Dekker identifies the anonymous Lord Mayor in Deloney's story of Eyre (Appendix A, pp. 210–16). '*Robert Oteley*, Grocer' is listed in Stow (II.173) as Lord Mayor in 1434, alongside Eyre as Sheriff. Dekker's change of Christian name may be only a slip, though Chandler (p. 177) says 'there is authority for both Roger and Robert'. The surname is variously spelled; the pun at xiii.34 influences our choice of spelling. On the possibility of a connection between Oatley and an Elizabethan Lord Mayor of London, see Introduction, pp. 25–6.

9. ROSE] The renaming of Ursula in the Crispine story in *The Gentle Craft* may possibly have been suggested by Deloney's description of Crispine going to meet 'his Rose cheeked Lady' (p. 125).

11–13. MASTER HAMMON . . . MASTER WARNER . . . MASTER SCOTT] These are all names which Chandler (p. 180) traces to historical sources (in particular

MASTER WARNER, *Hammon's brother-in-law*.
MASTER SCOTT, *a friend of Oatley's*.

The shoemakers:
SIMON EYRE.
MARGERY, *Eyre's wife*.   15
HODGE (*nickname of* ROGER), *Eyre's foreman*.
RALPH DAMPORT, *a journeyman of Eyre's*.
JANE, *Ralph's wife*.
FIRK, *a journeyman of Eyre's*.

Stow), though they are common enough, and Dekker might well have chosen them at random. The title 'Master', used frequently in the play of each of them, clearly implies a degree of social and civic dignity. (Both Dekker and Deloney show Eyre, through his acquisition of wealth, arriving somewhat self-consciously at this title (see ix.74–5, and Appendix A, p. 212).) All three roles are Dekker's additions to his sources. On the significance of that of Hammon (a variant of 'Hammond', a spelling which occurs in Q1), see Introduction, pp. 34–7; on the name Scott, see ii.22–3, n.

12. brother-in-law] Hammon addresses Warner as 'Cousin' at v.1, but claims him as a 'brother-in-law' at vi.51. 'Cousin' was often loosely used for a close relative (see note to i.5).

14. SIMON EYRE] The historical Eyre was Sheriff of London in 1434, Lord Mayor in 1445, and died in 1458. He was remembered chiefly for his part in the building of Leadenhall (see xxi.130–4, n.), though Stow (I.154) records many lavish benefactions to London. Dekker follows Deloney for the main outlines of Eyre's career, but ignores Deloney's statement (Appendix A, p. 217) that after serving as Sheriff Eyre changed his trade from shoemaker to draper. According to Stow he was a draper throughout his career (Stow, II. 173–4; I.154; for further biographical information on Eyre (including correction of the date of death given by Stow), see Merritt E. Lawlis, 'Another look at Simon Eyre's will', *N.&Q.*, 199 (1954), 13–16).

15. MARGERY] In Deloney Eyre's wife is nameless. Dekker transforms Deloney's statement that Eyre married 'a Maiden that was a neere neighbor vnto him' (Appendix A, p. 206) into Eyre's boast that he has taken Madgy 'from selling tripes in Eastcheap' (vii.69–70).

16. HODGE] The character is not in Deloney. The name is a familiar form of Roger, used 'As a typical name for the English rustic' (*O.E.D.*). This suggests how the role might be played.

17. RALPH DAMPORT] The character is not in Deloney. The name is regularly spelled 'Rafe' in Q1, reflecting normal Elizabethan (and the approved modern) pronunciation, as reflected in the pun at i.177–8. *Damport* is a form of 'Davenport'.

journeyman] one who has served his apprenticeship and can work at his trade for daily wages.

19. FIRK] Firk is a lively and highly individualised descendant of the amoral type-character of the Vice, common in earlier English drama—though Dekker abandons the tradition of the Vice's idleness by making Firk whole-heartedly involved in Eyre's working community. He has no equivalent in Deloney. Though

A Dutch Skipper.   20
A Boy, *working for Eyre.*
A Boy, *with the hunters.*
A Prentice, *working for Oatley.*

Noblemen, Soldiers, Huntsmen, Shoemakers, Apprentices,
     Servants.]   25

---

he is described as a journeyman at i.133 and iv.68, Eyre's remark at xx.8–9 implies
(perhaps as a slip on Dekker's part) that he is still an apprentice. He is certainly
young, and probably best played as a cheeky adolescent (see also xiii.16, n.).
Characteristically of a type-character (cf. Dodger), his name is meaningful: as a noun
firk could signify, for instance, a trick, dodge, or prank; as a verb, to cheat, to rob, to
move quickly, to beat, to trounce, and to copulate. Comic exploitation of 'the
euphemistic pronunciation of *fuck*' (Partridge) seems to underlie most occurrences
of the word in the play (see i.132, 230; vii.44; xiii.28; xvi.100; xviii.78).

20. *Dutch Skipper*] In Deloney the ship has a Greek captain who speaks no English
but is able to converse with Eyre's French workman, John (Appendix A, p. 207).
Dekker simplifies.

21–3. *Boy . . . Boy . . . Prentice*] all tiny parts which might be played by one actor.
Eyre's Boy speaks in sc. iv and sc. vii, is named in the opening stage direction of sc.
xiii, and could be included among the company of shoemakers in other scenes; the
Boy with the hunters appears in sc. v and sc. vi; and the Prentice in sc. xv, where the
designation *Prentice* is probably fortuitous, and Oatley addresses him as 'sir boy'.

[The Epistle]

To all good fellows, professors of the Gentle Craft, of what degree soever.

Kind gentlemen and honest boon companions, I present you here with a merry conceited comedy called *The Shoemaker's Holiday*, acted by my Lord Admiral's Players this present Christmas before the Queen's most excellent Majesty; for the mirth and pleasant matter by her Highness graciously accepted, being indeed no way offensive. The argument of the play I will set down in this epistle: Sir Hugh Lacy, Earl of Lincoln, had a young gentleman of his

---

Epistle] See Introduction, p. 54.

0.1–2. *fellows . . . Gentle . . . degree*] On the play's concern with class-consciousness, see Introduction, pp. 32–7, and *passim*.

0. *professors*] members of the profession.

the Gentle Craft] a stock phrase: Tilley, C801, citing first Robert Wilson, *The Cobbler's Prophecy* (*c.* 1590). The title-page of the first surviving edition (1627) of Deloney's *The Gentle Craft* advertises its 'declaring the cause why it is called the gentle craft', and chapter 3 tells how Saint Hugh, having worked as a shoemaker for a year, and then being imprisoned, 'the Iourneyman Shoomakers neuer left him, but yeelded him great reliefe continually, so that hee wanted nothing that was necessary for him; in requitall of which kindnesse he called them *Gentlemen of the Gentle Craft*' and wrote a song celebrating their kindness to their fellows (pp. 105–8). In *George-à-Greene* the title of 'the Gentle Craft' is granted as a favour by King Edward.

2. *conceited*] witty, ingenious.

The Shoemaker's Holiday] For the significance (and form) of the title, see Appendix B, pp. 219ff. The line 'Then Shoomakers made Holiday' occurs in the song at the end of chapter 9 of Deloney (p. 139).

3. *my Lord Admiral's Players*] See *The play on the stage*, p. 46.

3–4. *this present Christmas*] i.e., the Christmas season of 1599–1600; see *The play on the stage*, p. 47.

6. *no way offensive*] a disclaimer of offence commonly accompanies Elizabethan authors' assertions that their works are entertaining. Thus, the title-page of the second part of Deloney's *The Gentle Craft* claims that it is 'not altogether vnprofitable nor any way hurtfull' (first surviving edition, 1639). Playwrights often felt a particular need to guard against accusations of personal satire.

7. *argument*] subject-matter, plot-summary.

own name, his near kinsman, that loved the Lord Mayor's
daughter of London; to prevent and cross which love the   10
Earl caused his kinsman to be sent colonel of a company
into France, who resigned his place to another gentleman
his friend, and came disguised like a Dutch shoemaker to
the house of Simon Eyre in Tower Street, who served the
Mayor and his household with shoes: the merriments that   15
passed in Eyre's house, his coming to be Mayor of London,
Lacy's getting his love, and other accidents; with two
merry three-man's songs. Take all in good worth that is
well intended, for nothing is purposed but mirth. Mirth
lengtheneth long life, which with all other blessings I hear-   20
tily wish you.

                          Farewell.

---

14. *Tower Street*] Deloney does not specifically locate Eyre's shop in this street
(running east from the Tower to Eastcheap), though he mentions it more than once.
It is one of the few London place-names derived by Dekker from his source. At xiv.1
we learn that the shop is marked by 'the Sign of the Last'.

17. *accidents*] happenings.

18. *three-man's songs*] songs for three male voices, often used as worksongs in
Elizabethan times. An example that is still sometimes heard is 'We be soldiers three'.
Deloney's shoemakers frequently sing, and specifically demand that a journeyman
must be able to 'beare his part in a three mans Song' (p. 115).

Take . . . in good worth] take in good part, be content with.

19-20. *Mirth lengtheneth long life*] not directly proverbial, but cf. *Ralph Roister
Doister*, Prologue, l. 8: 'Mirth prolongeth life, and causeth health'; Tilley, C82: 'Care
brings grey hair', varied in *Tw.N.* as 'Care's an enemy to life' (I.iii.2); Dekker's
Epistle to *The Wonderful Year*: 'mirth is both physical and wholesome against the
plague' (Pendry, p. 27); *2H4*: 'A merry heart lives long-a!' (V.iii.48); and *K.B.P.*: 'tis
nought but mirth, / That keepes the body from the earth' (V.342-3).

The First Three-Man's Song

O the month of May, the merry month of May,
  So frolic, so gay, and so green, so green, so green;
O and then did I unto my true love say,
  'Sweet Peg, thou shalt be my summer's queen'.

Now the nightingale, the pretty nightingale,   5
  The sweetest singer in all the forest's choir,
Entreats thee, sweet Peggy, to hear thy true love's tale—
  Lo, yonder she sitteth, her breast against a briar.

The Songs] No early music for either song has survived. William Chappell records
a tune called 'The Cobbler's Jigg' which first appeared in England in 1686. It had
been published in Holland as an English song-tune in 1622 and in 1626, where it was
entitled 'Cobbeler, of: Het Engelsch Lapperken'. Chappell adapts the Second Song
in *The Shoemaker's Holiday* to this tune (*Popular Music of the Olden Time*, 2 vols,
London [1855–9]; repr. New York, 1965; I.277–8). J. S. Manifold suggests that the
tune could be used in performance both for this song and as a repeated motif in
incidental music (*The Music in English Drama*, London, 1956). The most important
problem in relation to the songs is at what points of the play they should be sung. As
is suggested in the Introduction (p. 55), they may well be late additions to the text,
necessitating adjustments in the dialogue; it is not possible to assign a place to them
with any confidence. Like many editors we therefore follow Q1 in printing them
before the text of the play. Other editors, plausibly but not entirely convincingly,
select points at which to insert them, mostly following Rhys's placing of the first
after xi.25 and the second after xx.32. Harrison prints the first song after vii.27;
Halliday and Koszul after xi.75. Harrison opens sc. xiii with the second song;
Lawrence exceptionally places it 'at the latter end' of the entire play, but it has none
of the characteristics of an epilogue.

  2. *frolic*] joyous.

  4. *summer's queen*] an allusion to the custom of electing a Lord and Lady, or King
and Queen, of May; cf. Spenser, *The Shepheardes Calender*, May Eclogue, ll. 27–31:

> Tho to the greene Wood they speeden hem all,
> To fetchen home May with their musicall;
> And home they bringen in a royall throne,
> Crowned as king: and his Queene attone
> Was Lady Flora . . .

  8. *breast . . . briar*] E. A. Armstrong describes this common superstition (Tilley,
N183) as a 'curious literary conceit' which 'has never become folklore' and has no
scientific basis (*The Folklore of Birds*, London, 1958, pp. 188–9). *O.D.E.P.* gives
references from 1510 onwards; Bartlett Jere Whiting, *Proverbs, Sentences, and
Proverbial Phrases in English Writings mainly before 1500* (Cambridge, Mass., 1968), p.
430, cites examples from 1449.

But O, I spy the cuckoo, the cuckoo, the cuckoo;
  See where she sitteth—come away, my joy.   10
Come away, I prithee, I do not like the cuckoo
  Should sing where my Peggy and I kiss and toy.

O the month of May, the merry month of May,
  So frolic, so gay, and so green, so green, so green;
And then did I unto my true love say,   15
  'Sweet Peg, thou shalt be my summer's queen'.

The Second Three-Man's Song
(This is to be sung at the latter end.)

Cold's the wind, and wet's the rain,
  Saint Hugh be our good speed.
Ill is the weather that bringeth no gain,
  Nor helps good hearts in need.

---

9. *cuckoo*] 'O word of fear, / Unpleasing to a married ear' *(L.L.L.,* V. ii.888–9); the symbol of cuckoldry.
  12. *toy*] dally.

Second song: 0.2. This . . . latter end] The meaning of this direction is uncertain, and its provenance obscure. The phrase *the latter end* was regularly used of the conclusion, the very end, the final moments *(O.E.D.)* and is so used by Bottom in *M.N.D.* of a song in a play: 'I will sing it in the latter end of a play, before the Duke' (IV.i.18–19). It might mean that the song is to be sung after the last words of the play have been spoken (as Lawrence decides); towards the end of the play; or, possibly, at (or towards) the end of a scene unspecified in the cryptic form of this direction.
  1. *Cold's . . . rain*] This inevitably reminds a modern reader of the refrain of Feste's song at the end of *Tw.N.:* 'With hey, ho, the wind and the rain. . . . For the rain it raineth every day'. This recurs in *Lr.* (III.ii.75); perhaps these are all variations on a traditional refrain, otherwise lost.
  2. *Saint Hugh*] the patron saint of shoemakers, and the subject of the first story in Deloney (chapters 1–4). See also iv.49, n.
  speed] 'that which promotes success or prosperity' *(O.E.D.).*
  3. *Ill . . . gain*] fully proverbial by Dekker's time; Tilley, W421. Bad weather is good for shoemakers' business.

Troll the bowl, the jolly nut-brown bowl,   5
    And here, kind mate, to thee.
Let's sing a dirge for Saint Hugh's soul,
    And down it merrily.

Down-a-down, hey down-a-down,
    Hey-derry-derry down-a-down   10
                    (*Close with the tenor boy*)
Ho, well done, to me let come,
    Ring compass, gentle joy.

Troll the bowl, the nut-brown bowl,
    And here, kind *etc.*   (*as often as there be men to drink*)

    At last when all have drunk, this verse:

Cold's the wind, and wet's the rain,   15
    Saint Hugh be our good speed.
Ill is the weather that bringeth no gain,
    Nor helps good hearts in need.

5–6. *Troll . . . thee*] Cf. K.B.P., II. 432: 'troule the blacke bowle to mee'. A song with a similar refrain is printed in Thomas Ravenscroft's *Pammelia* (1609), no. 62. These appear to be different versions of the same traditional drinking song.

5. *Troll*] pass, circulate; cf. xviii.210–11.

nut-brown] (the traditional hue of beer).

9–10. *Down-a-down . . . down-a-down*] These traditional phrases are used in two of the songs in Deloney (pp. 116–17, 127).

10.1. *Close with the tenor boy*] 'Close' is probably the imperative verb: 'sing in unison with the boy with a tenor voice who has been singing solo'. We assume that the first two stanzas are sung solo, and that this direction refers to the two lines which precede it (9 and 10). Sutherland takes the imperative verb as an indication 'that the play was printed off a prompter's copy which had the stage directions interspersed in this way'. He also instances 'Cast up caps' (xviii.220); but there seems no reason why these should not be authorial directions.

12. *Ring compass, gentle joy*] 'A compass is the full range of tones which a voice or instrument is capable of producing. "Ring compass, gentle joy" would therefore mean, "Let joy reach its fullest range, let joy be unconfined" ' (Sutherland).

14.1. *as often . . . drink*] In the ritual of drinking, the refrain is sung while each man drinks.

THE PROLOGUE
as it was pronounced before the Queen's Majesty.

As wretches in a storm, expecting day,
With trembling hands and eyes cast up to heaven
Make prayers the anchor of their conquered hopes,
So we, dear goddess, wonder of all eyes,
Your meanest vassals, through mistrust and fear   5
To sink into the bottom of disgrace
By our imperfect pastimes, prostrate thus
On bended knees our sails of hope do strike,
Dreading the bitter storms of your dislike.

Since, then, unhappy men, our hap is such   10
That to ourselves ourselves no help can bring,
But needs must perish if your saint-like ears,
Locking the temple where all mercy sits,
Refuse the tribute of our begging tongues:
O grant, bright mirror of true chastity,   15
From those life-breathing stars your sun-like eyes
One gracious smile; for your celestial breath
Must send us life, or sentence us to death.

9–10] *undivided, Q1; divided, Koszul.*

The Prologue] The speaker of the Prologue normally wore a long, black cloak
(Chambers, *E.S.*, II.547). This one was obviously written specially for the performance at Court on 1 January 1600. Henslowe (pp. 187, 207, etc.) provides evidence for
this practice. Lines 7–8 suggest that it was spoken by one actor while the rest of the
company knelt before the Queen. Lange says 'As a rule only the epilogue was
spoken "on bended knees" ', but this Prologue, with its prayer for indulgence, fulfils
the function of many epilogues. Editors (except Koszul) follow Q1 in printing the
lines without a break, but they fall clearly into two stanzas, each in blank verse with a
concluding couplet.

3. *anchor*] 'that which gives stability or security' (*O.E.D.*); used here as part of the
sustained sea-imagery.

4. *goddess*] the Queen; cf. l. 12, 'saint-like': characteristic eulogy of Elizabeth I.

5. *vassals*] punning on 'vessels'.

6. *bottom*] used particularly of the hull of a ship.

8. *strike*] lower.

10. *hap*] chance, fortune.

15. *mirror*] exemplar.

THE SHOEMAKER'S HOLIDAY
A PLEASANT COMEDY OF THE GENTLE CRAFT

[SCENE I.]

Enter [Sir ROGER OATLEY, *the*] Lord Mayor, [*and the* Earl of]
LINCOLN.

Lincoln. My Lord Mayor, you have sundry times
    Feasted myself and many courtiers more.
    Seldom or never can we be so kind
    To make requital of your courtesy.
    But leaving this, I hear my cousin Lacy   5
    Is much affected to your daughter Rose.
Oatley. True, my good lord; and she loves him so well
    That I mislike her boldness in the chase.
Lincoln. Why, my Lord Mayor, think you it then
       a shame
    To join a Lacy with an Oatley's name?   10
Oatley. Too mean is my poor girl for his high birth.
    Poor citizens must not with courtiers wed,
    Who will in silks and gay apparel spend
    More in one year than I am worth by far.
    Therefore your honour need not doubt my girl.   15
Lincoln. Take heed, my lord; advise you what you do.

---

0. *Pleasant*] merry, amusing.

2. *Feasted*] The play's first sentence associates the office of Lord Mayor with the giving of feasts, such as the one that is to form the climax of the action. Cf. Introduction, pp. 41 ff.

5. *cousin*] The word could be used of any collateral relation more distant than brother or sister. Lacy is Lincoln's nephew.

6. *affected to*] infatuated with.

8. *in the chase*] in hunting (him).

11. *mean*] low-born.

15. *doubt*] fear, worry about.

16. *advise you*] take care.

A verier unthrift lives not in the world
Than is my cousin; for, I'll tell you what,
'Tis now almost a year since he requested
To travel countries for experience.   20
I furnished him with coin, bills of exchange,
Letters of credit, men to wait on him,
Solicited my friends in Italy
Well to respect him. But to see the end:
Scant had he journeyed through half Germany   25
But all his coin was spent, his men cast off,
His bills embezzled, and my jolly coz,
Ashamed to show his bankrupt presence here,
Became a shoemaker in Wittenberg—
A goodly science for a gentleman   30
Of such descent! Now judge the rest by this:
Suppose your daughter have a thousand pound,
He did consume me more in one half-year;
And make him heir to all the wealth you have,
One twelve-month's rioting will waste it all.   35
Then seek, my lord, some honest citizen
To wed your daughter to.

---

17. *verier unthrift*] more thorough-going spendthrift.

20. *To travel . . . experience*] Many young Elizabethan noblemen travelled for this reason. Cf. the opening of *T.G.V.*

21. *bills of exchange*] promissory notes.

24. *to see*] *O.E.D.* 'to' B2: 'In absolute or independent construction, usually introductory or parenthetic.'

25. *Scant*] hardly, scarcely.

27. *embezzled*] wasted, squandered.

coz] diminutive of 'cousin' (see l. 5, n.).

29. *Wittenberg*] university town on the Elbe, some fifty miles from Berlin, famous for its connection with Martin Luther, who was a professor there. It seems to have had no particular importance as a shoemaking centre. It is even possible that Dekker thought it was in Holland; cf. iii.21.

30. *science*] trade, occupation.

32. *a thousand pound*] (as dowry).

33. *consume*] waste, squander.

me] part of the construction known as the ethic dative, used 'to imply that a person other than the subject or object has an interest in the fact stated' (*O.E.D.*). Here it might be paraphrased as 'at my cost': see Abbott §220, citing *1H4*, III.iii.41–2: 'The sack that thou hast drunk me.' The construction recurs frequently in the play, and is specially associated with Eyre. Later uses are not normally noted.

34. *And make*] i.e., and even if you make.

Oatley.   I thank your lordship.
    [*Aside*] Well, fox, I understand your subtlety.
    [*To Lincoln*] As for your nephew, let your lord-
       ship's eye
    But watch his actions and you need not fear;   40
    For I have sent my daughter far enough.
    And yet your cousin Rowland might do well
    Now he hath learned an occupation.
    [*Aside*] And yet I scorn to call him son-in-law.
Lincoln. Ay, but I have a better trade for him.   45
    I thank his Grace, he hath appointed him
    Chief colonel of all those companies
    Mustered in London and the shires about
    To serve his Highness in those wars of France.
    See where he comes.

            Enter LOVELL, LACY, *and* ASKEW.

                Lovell, what news with you?   50
Lovell. My Lord of Lincoln, 'tis his Highness' will
    That presently your cousin ship for France
    With all his powers. He would not for a million
    But they should land at Dieppe within four days.
Lincoln. Go certify his Grace it shall be done.   55
                      Exit LOVELL.

41 sent] Q2; *not in* Q1.
50 *Enter . . .* ASKEW.] *placed here, Warnke and Proescholdt; after* you? Q1.

---

   38. *fox . . . subtlety*] The craftiness *(subtlety)* of the fox was proverbial (Tilley, F629).
   46. *his Grace*] the King.
   47. *colonel*] (three syllables).
   49. *those wars of France*] Wars against France continued from the accession of Henry V in 1413 to beyond the period of Eyre's mayoralty in 1445. Dekker's references to the war provide no indication of a precise historical setting for the play.
   52. *presently*] immediately.
   53. *powers*] forces, troops.
   53–4. *would not for a million | But*] would give a million pounds to ensure that.
   54. *Dieppe*] 'Deepe' in Q1, reflecting contemporary pronunciation. Its position on the Channel coast would make it a convenient landing place for troops beginning a campaign in northern France.

Now, cousin Lacy, in what forwardness
Are all your companies?
Lacy.   All well prepared.
The men of Hertfordshire lie at Mile End;
Suffolk and Essex train in Tothill Fields;
The Londoners, and those of Middlesex,   60
All gallantly prepared in Finsbury,
With frolic spirits long for their parting hour.
Oatley. They have their imprest, coats, and furniture,
And if it please your cousin Lacy come
To the Guildhall he shall receive his pay,   65
And twenty pounds besides my brethren
Will freely give him to approve our loves
We bear unto my lord your uncle here.
Lacy. I thank your honour.
Lincoln.   Thanks, my good Lord Mayor.
Oatley. At the Guildhall we will expect your coming.   70
                                                    Exit.

Lincoln. To approve your loves to me? No, subtlety!
Nephew, that twenty pound he doth bestow
For joy to rid you from his daughter Rose.

71–2 No, subtlety! / Nephew,] *Spencer;* no subtiltie / Nephew: *Q1;* No subtilty! / Nephew, *Warnke and Proescholdt.*

---

56. *forwardness*] state of preparation.
58. *Mile End*] a hamlet to the north-east of London, a mile from Aldgate, beyond Whitechapel. Mile End Green was a training and mustering ground.
59. *Tothill Fields*] open ground in Westminster, on the left bank of the Thames, used as a military training ground. Q1 spells 'Tuttle', doubtless reflecting contemporary pronunciation.
61. *Finsbury*] an area of fields to the north of Cripplegate, used as a training and mustering ground for troops and also for archery practice (see vii.64 and n.).
62. *frolic*] joyful, cheerful.
63. *imprest*] advance payment.
coats] (of mail or armour).
furniture] equipment, whether of weapons or stores.
65. *Guildhall*] common hall of the City of London, on the north side of Catte (or Catteten) Street, meeting place of the City courts, including that of the Lord Mayor.
66. *brethren*] fellow-aldermen. The metre requires a trisyllabic pronunciation.
67. *approve*] demonstrate.
71. *No, subtlety!*] Editors have interpreted in various ways: see collation. Probably 'No, that is trickery'; or 'No, you trickster!'.

But, cousins both, now here are none but friends,
I would not have you cast an amorous eye   75
Upon so mean a project as the love
Of a gay, wanton, painted citizen.
I know this churl even in the height of scorn
Doth hate the mixture of his blood with thine.
I pray thee, do thou so. Remember, coz,   80
What honourable fortunes wait on thee.
Increase the King's love which so brightly shines
And gilds thy hopes. I have no heir but thee—
And yet not thee if with a wayward spirit
Thou start from the true bias of my love.   85
Lacy. My lord, I will for honour—not desire
Of land or livings, or to be your heir—
So guide my actions in pursuit of France
As shall add glory to the Lacys' name.
Lincoln. Coz, for those words here's thirty portagues;   90
And, nephew Askew, there's a few for you.
Fair honour in her loftiest eminence
Stays in France for you till you fetch her thence.
Then, nephews, clap swift wings on your designs.
Begone, begone; make haste to the Guildhall.   95
There presently I'll meet you. Do not stay.

---

77. *gay, wanton, painted citizen*] The accusation stems from prejudice, though
London women had a reputation for sophistication. Hamlet's outburst (III.i.142 ff.)
reflects the strength of feeling of some Elizabethans against cosmetics.

85. *start from the true bias*] depart from the natural course (*bias* is the natural course
of the bowl in a game of bowls; 'to run against the bias' was a proverbial expression:
Tilley, B339).

88. *in pursuit of France*] The expression is a little odd. Davies says: 'one is strongly
tempted to emend "France" to "Fame". Lincoln's conception of Honour as a lady to
be seized by force . . . would then echo Lacy's remark. Again, "Fame" rhymes with
"name" as "desire" was probably meant to rhyme with "heire". However, it might
be argued that "Fame" and "France" are too dissimilar to admit of orthographical
confusion.' This is fair. The possibilities that Dekker was writing carelessly, and also
that *France* might mean 'King of France', are other deterrents to emendation.

90. *portagues*] Portuguese gold coins, known as great crusadoes. They were worth
up to £5 each. Lincoln's gift is lavish; two-thirds of it is later enough to serve as a
deposit on a ship's rich cargo (vii.23–4).

92–3. *Fair honour . . . fetch her thence*] Cf. Hotspur in *1H4*: 'pluck bright honour . . .
redeem her thence' (I.iii.202–6).

Where honour beckons, shame attends delay.   *Exit.*
Askew. How gladly would your uncle have you gone!
Lacy. True, coz; but I'll o'er-reach his policies.
    I have some serious business for three days,   100
    Which nothing but my presence can dispatch.
    You, therefore, cousin, with the companies,
    Shall haste to Dover. There I'll meet with you,
    Or if I stay past my prefixèd time,
    Away for France; we'll meet in Normandy.   105
    The twenty pounds my Lord Mayor gives to me
    You shall receive, and these ten portagues,
    Part of mine uncle's thirty. Gentle coz,
    Have care to our great charge. I know your
      wisdom
    Hath tried itself in higher consequence.   110
Askew. Coz, all myself am yours. Yet have this care,
    To lodge in London with all secrecy.
    Our uncle Lincoln hath—besides his own—
    Many a jealous eye that in your face
    Stares only to watch means for your disgrace.   115
Lacy. Stay, cousin, who be these?

    Enter SIMON EYRE, [MARGERY] *his wife,* HODGE, FIRK,
        JANE, *and* RALPH *with a piece.*

97 beckons] *conj. Malone;* becomes Q1.

---

    97. *Where . . . delay*] Tilley records a proverb 'It is better to die with honour than to live with shame' (H576); and cf. Falstaff's 'honour pricks me on' (*1H4*, V.i.130).
    beckons] the emendation from 'becomes' (Qq) is Malone's, written in the margin of his copy. It was first adopted by Warnke and Proescholdt. Bowers comments: 'Although *becomes* can be defended, the metre is against it and the generally superior sense of *beckons* is manifest. Possibly the word was written in the ms. as *becōs.* Dekker's spelling is "becon" in line 28 of the *Sir Thomas More* section.'
    99. *o'er-reach*] outdo.
    policies] tricks, politic schemings.
    100. *three days*] a false lead: the interval proves to have no significance. (On the time-scheme, see Introduction, p. 23.)
    105. *Normandy*] scene of much of the fighting in the French wars of both Henry V and Henry VI.
    110. *tried . . . consequence*] been put to the test in more important matters.
    114. *jealous*] watchful, vigilant. This seems to imply that Lincoln has spies out, one of whom may be Dodger; cf. ll. 202–3.
    116.2. piece] firearm (a sign that Ralph has been conscripted).

Eyre. Leave whining, leave whining. Away with this whim-
pering, this puling, these blubbering tears, and these wet
eyes! I'll get thy husband discharged, I warrant thee,
sweet Jane. Go to!   120
Hodge. Master, here be the captains.
Eyre. Peace, Hodge; husht, ye knave, husht.
Firk. Here be the cavaliers and the colonels, master.
Eyre. Peace, Firk; peace, my fine Firk. Stand by, with your
pishery-pashery, away! I am a man of the best presence.   125
I'll speak to them an they were popes. [*To Lacy and
Askew*] Gentlemen, captains, colonels, commanders;
brave men, brave leaders, may it please you to give me
audience. I am Simon Eyre, the mad shoemaker of
Tower Street. This wench with the mealy mouth that   130
will never tire is my wife, I can tell you. Here's Hodge,
my man and my foreman. Here's Firk, my fine firking
journeyman; and this is blubbered Jane. All we come to
be suitors for this honest Ralph. Keep him at home and,

126 popes.] *Q3 (Popes:); Popes, Q1.*

118. *puling*] whining.
119. *discharged*] released from his obligation to serve in the army. At ll. 136–7 Eyre
offers a bribe for this purpose. *2H4*, III.ii dramatizes what was apparently the
common practice of buying oneself out of service; see *Shakespeare's England*, I.113.
122. *husht*] an earlier form of 'hush'.
123. *cavaliers*] horse-soldiers. Firk's suggestion of numbers *(cavaliers and colonels)* is
inappropriate in reference simply to Lacy and Askew. Perhaps it is intended for
comic effect.
125. *pishery-pashery*] nonsense, gibble-gabble. *O.E.D.* cites this as the use of an
'obsolete nonce-word', defining '?Depreciatory talk'. Henley and Farmer, citing
this use, define more appropriately as 'gabble'. The word occurs again at l. 163 and
(of clothes) at xi.43 and xx.57.
best presence] most impressive demeanour or appearance.
129. *mad*] high-spirited, exuberant. A few seconds after his first entrance Eyre uses
the word which will serve as a recurrent motif for him throughout the play (see
Introduction, p. 38).
130. *Tower Street*] See Epistle,14, n.
wench] (implying familiarity, but not necessarily youth; cf. xxi.29, *old wench*).
mealy] 'given to mince matters' *(O.E.D.),* as in 'mealy-mouthed'.
132. *firking*] See *Dram. Per.,* 19, n.
134. *for*] on behalf of.

as ! am a true shoemaker and a gentleman of the Gentle   135
Craft, buy spurs yourself and I'll find ye boots these
seven years.

Margery. Seven years, husband?

Eyre. Peace, midriff, peace, I know what I do. Peace.

Firk. Truly, Master Cormorant, you shall do God good   140
service to let Ralph and his wife stay together. She's a
young, new-married woman. If you take her husband
away from her a night, you undo her; she may beg in
the daytime; for he's as good a workman at a prick and
an awl as any is in our trade.   145

Jane. O, let him stay, else I shall be undone!

Firk. Ay, truly, she shall be laid at one side like a pair of old
shoes else, and be occupied for no use.

Lacy. Truly, my friends, it lies not in my power.
The Londoners are pressed, paid, and set forth   150
By the Lord Mayor. I cannot change a man.

135–6. *Gentle Craft*] See Epistle, o, n.

136. *find*] provide with.

139.] This line should perhaps be spoken aside to Margery.

midriff] one of many allusions to Margery's plumpness.

140. *Cormorant*] Firk's characteristic mistake for 'colonel', which was regularly pronounced with three syllables and often spelt 'coronel'. Steane also suggests a pun on *cormorant* as a predatory bird 'gobbling up others' goods, much as the officer takes good men away from their home, wife and business'.

140–1. *do God good service*] (presumably by relieving Jane of the temptation of desiring a substitute).

143. *a night*] for a single night; or, possibly, *a-night*, at night, during the nights.

143. *beg*] because she is *undone*—i.e., left destitute. This is the beginning of a sequence of bawdy double-meanings.

144–5. *prick . . . awl*] pointed tools in the shoemaker's trade. Deloney (p. 114) writes of 'the pricking Aule'. But bawdy is uppermost in Firk's mind: *prick*, the male organ; *awl* (punning on 'hole'), the female.

146. *undone*] (with a bawdy quibble).

148. *shoes*] Often used with bawdy innuendo in Eliizabethan drama: see Gordon Williams, 'Ophelia's "Show" ', *Trivium*, 4 (1969), 108–11.

occupied] The word had a sexual sense; 'copulated with'; cf. Doll Tearsheet in *2H4*, II.iv.136–40: 'A captain! God's light, these villains will make the word as odious as the word "occupy"; which was an excellent good word before it was ill sorted.'

use] with a secondary sense of 'sexual enjoyment' (Partridge).

150. *pressed*] conscripted.

paid] given their advance payment.

150–1. *set forth | By the Lord Mayor*] The Lord Mayor bore responsibility for recruitment in London. Davies quotes a passage from Stow's *Annals* (1605, p. 1281)

Hodge. Why, then, you were as good be a corporal as a
   colonel, if you cannot discharge one good fellow. And I
   tell you true, I think you do more than you can answer,
   to press a man within a year and a day of his marriage.   155
Eyre. Well said, melancholy Hodge! Gramercy, my fine
   foreman!
Margery. Truly, gentlemen, it were ill done for such as you to
   stand so stiffly against a poor young wife, considering
   her case. She is new-married—but let that pass. I pray,   160
   deal not roughly with her. Her husband is a young man
   and but newly entered—but let that pass.
Eyre. Away with your pishery-pashery, your pols and your

---

illustrating the Lord Mayor's powers of conscription: 'The 9 of Aprill [1596] being
good friday, in the afternoone, the lord maior and aldermen of London being in
Powles church yard, hearing the sermon at Paules crosse, were sodainelie called from
thence, and foorthwith by a precept from her maiestie and counsell, pressed 1000.
men, which was doone by 8. of the clocke the same night . . .' It is clear that Lacy feels
himself unable to exercise the power of exemption which Eyre (l. 119) expects him
to wield and which would have been Lacy's if he had himself conscripted Ralph.

   154–5. *more . . . marriage*] Cf. Deuteronomy, xxiv.5: 'When a man taketh a new
wife, hee shall not goe a warrefare, neither shal bee charged with any businesse: but
shall be free at home one yeare, and reioyce with his wife which he hath taken'; but
this does not appear to have been a statutory ground for exemption (cf. C. G.
Cruickshank, *Elizabeth's Army*, Oxford, 1946; second edition, Oxford, 1966, p. 24).

   156. *melancholy*] Sanna suggests that this means 'riflessivo', and alludes to Hodge's
remembrance of the biblical injunction. This might be supported by *O.E.D.*, 3b,
'pensive, thoughtful; sadly meditative'.

   Gramercy] Thank you very much.

   159. *stand so stiffly*] pursue so harsh a course (with sexual double meaning,
characteristically unconscious on Margery's part).

   160. *case*] (with the secondary meaning of the female organ).

   let that pass] This is to become a catch-phrase of Margery's, perhaps indicative
generally of incoherence and specifically of bemused embarrassment when she finds
she has said something that could be misunderstood—as in her use of it in the
following line. It is always an invitation to look for double meanings, which become
additionally comic since Margery herself shows awareness of them.

   161. *deal not roughly*] (with sexual innuendo).

   162. *entered*] used mainly for its bawdy suggestiveness, but having the ostensible
primary sense of 'entered upon his career'.

   163. *pishery-pashery*] See l. 125, n.

   163–4. *pols . . . edepols*] 'The not unusual collocation of these two interjections is
probably a reminiscence of Lily's *Grammer*, where in the section "Of the Aduerbe"
it is stated that "Some be of Swearing: as Pol, aedepol, hercle, medius fidius" (*Short*

edepols. Peace, midriff; silence, Cicely Bumtrinket. Let
your head speak.   165
Firk. Yea, and the horns too, master.
Eyre. Tawsoone, my fine Firk, tawsoone. Peace, scoundrels.
See you this man, captains? You will not release him?
Well, let him go. He's a proper shot. Let him vanish.
Peace, Jane. Dry up thy tears, they'll make his powder   170
dankish. Take him, brave men. Hector of Troy was an
hackney to him, Hercules and Termagant scoundrels.

164 midriff] *Rhys;* Midasse *Q1.*
167 Tawsoone . . . tawsoone] *conj. George;* Too soone . . . too soone *Q1.*
168 man, captains?] *Bowers;* man? Captaines, *Q1.*

Introduction of Grammar, 1577, C1*v).* The words seem sometimes to mean nonsensi-
cal talk; cf. Dekker, *Shoemaker's Holiday . . .'* (McKerrow, *Nashe,* IV.304–5,
annotating *Have With You to Saffron Walden* (III.7)).

164. *Cicely Bumtrinket*] This seems to be a derogatory nickname for Margery. In
Dekker's *Satiromastix,* it is one of the 'horrible vngodlie' names applied by Tucca to
Mistress Miniver. Dekker later uses it as the name of Margery's maid for the sake of a
bawdy joke (iv.36). It is just possible that she is a silent character, imagined here to be
on the point of speaking on Margery's behalf.
   165. *head*] Simon Eyre (as the *head* or 'master' of the household).
   166. *horns*] the signs of cuckoldry; the jest was so conventional that even from a
man to his master it probably did not seem offensive.
   167. *Tawsoone*] be quiet (from the Welsh). The emendation was proposed by J.
George in *N.&Q.,* 194 (1949), 192: 'The words "too soon" have troubled commen-
tators and some of the interpretations offered are inconsistent with the character of
Eyre's wife . . . and with the relation of confidence and affection, which, after
thirty-six years of married life, underlies Eyre's blustering abuse.' George cites
'Bartley and Richards in the *Welsh Review* (vol. VI, i, pp. 39 ff.)' as remarking that
the Welsh expression 'taw-â-sôn' 'seems to have been a very well-known phrase and
is always used in its proper sense'. He notes that 'Captain Tucca (not a Welshman)
says in *Satiromastix* (V.ii.180, ed. Penniman): "Taw-soone, hold thy peace" ' (ed.
Bowers, V.ii.172; George erroneously reads 'peace' for 'tongue'). Bowers makes the
emendation, and also notes the use of this expression in the Welsh dialect scenes of
Dekker's *Patient Grissil* (III.ii.232). Davies, who also emends, adds another parallel
in Dekker and Webster's *Northward Ho* (IV.i.121). Steane, who claims to follow
Bowers's text, neither emends nor records the suggestion.
   169. *proper shot*] good marksman.
   170. *powder*] gunpowder.
   171. *dankish*] damp.
   172. *hackney*] (figuratively) a horse kept for hire.
   Termagant] 'An imaginary deity held in medieval Christendom to be worshipped
by Mohammedans: in the mystery plays representing a violent overbearing personage' *(O.E.D.).*

Prince Arthur's Round Table, by the Lord of Ludgate,
ne'er fed such a tall, such a dapper swordman. By the life
of Pharaoh, a brave, resolute swordman. Peace, Jane. I   175
say no more, mad knaves.

Firk. See, see, Hodge, how my master raves in commenda-
tion of Ralph.

Hodge. Ralph, thou'rt a gull, by this hand, an thou goest not.

Askew. I am glad, good Master Eyre, it is my hap   180
To meet so resolute a soldier.
Trust me, for your report and love to him
A common, slight regard shall not respect him.

Lacy. Is thy name Ralph?

Ralph.   Yes, sir.

Lacy.   Give me thy hand.
Thou shalt not want, as I am a gentleman.   185

179 not] Q4; *not in* Q1–3.

---

173. *by the Lord of Ludgate*] a favourite oath of Eyre's. Ludgate, one of the old gates
of the City of London at the top of Ludgate Hill, was named after King Lud,
legendary founder of London, who was traditionally supposed to have built the gate
in 66 B.C. Eyre's phrase may allude to the image of Lud, placed on the east side of
Ludgate when it was rebuilt in 1586. Two other possibilities are that it alludes to a
now-forgotten personage, and that it is 'merely one of Eyre's alliterative impromp-
tues' (Lange).

174. *tall*] valiant (cf. xx.25).

dapper] skilful, quick (without the pejorative sense of modern usage; see also
x.166, n.).

174–5. *By . . . Pharaoh*] 'by the life of Pharao, ye shal not goe hence' (Genesis,
xlii.15); a popular oath: cf. Herford and Simpson's note (IX.337) on Jonson's *Every
Man in his Humour* (1601), I.iii.75.

175–6. *I say . . . knaves*] Perhaps Eyre announces that he has come to the end of his
commendations; or perhaps we should punctuate 'Peace, Jane, I say. No more, mad
knaves'.

177–8. *raves . . . Ralph*] (punningly).

179. *gull*] fool (perhaps with an implication of cowardice).

not] first added in Q4, and possibly a sophistication; it is not accepted by all editors.
Bowers comments: 'If we follow Q1–3 and omit it, there is a humorous reversal
later in line [189]. It should be remarked that the Q1 line fills the measure
completely, and under such circumstances a word could be lost. Moreover, if the
reversal is indeed to take place at line [189], it must be motivated; and on the whole it
seems better for Hodge to be won over at line [179] by Eyre's eloquence than in line
[189] by Lacy's.' We concur.

182–3. *for . . . / A common slight regard shall not respect him*] because of . . . he will be
accorded more than the low esteem in which recruits are commonly held. (The
construction *respect him* is unusual; *O.E.D.* affords no parallel.)

[*To Jane*] Woman, be patient. God, no doubt, will
  send
Thy husband safe again; but he must go.
His country's quarrel says it shall be so.

Hodge. Thou'rt a gull, by my stirrup, if thou dost not go. I
  will not have thee strike thy gimlet into these weak   190
  vessels—prick thine enemies, Ralph.

Enter DODGER.

Dodger. [*To Lacy*] My lord, your uncle on the Tower
  Hill
Stays with the Lord Mayor and the Aldermen,
And doth request you with all speed you may
To hasten thither.

Askew.   Cousin, let's go.
                                     195
Lacy. Dodger, run you before. Tell them we come.

                                  Exit DODGER.

This Dodger is mine uncle's parasite,
The arrant'st varlet that e'er breathed on earth.
He sets more discord in a noble house

---

195 let's] Q1; come lets Q2; let vs *Bowers.*
196 *Exit* DODGER.] *as here, Fritsche; printed after* 'thither.', *l. 195, Q1.*

---

    187. *again*] back.
    189. *stirrup*] a leather strap whose function is illustrated in Deloney: 'hee holds it now as fast as the stirrop doth the shooe while we sow it' (p. 157).
    190–1. *strike thy gimlet . . . prick*] (bawdy).
    weak vessels] a traditional joke deriving from I Peter iii.7: 'giving honour unto thy wife as unto the weaker vessel'.
    192. *Tower Hill*] a regular place of assembly in sixteenth-century London, and the scene of many public executions.
    193. *Stays*] waits.
    195. *let's*] emended to *let vs* by Bowers, who comments: 'An extra syllable is doubtless required by the metre.' In this he is presumably influenced by Q2's regularization 'come lets' (wrongly said by Bowers to be 'accepted by all modern editors'). Emendation can be defended, especially in view of the faulty elision in line 189, but is unnecessary. Abbott finds that 'The interval between two speakers sometimes justifies the omission of an accent' (§506) and that an accent is sometimes omitted after a vocative (§507.3).
    197. *parasite*] See *Dram. Per.,* 7, n.
    198. *arrant'st*] most notorious, unmitigated.

By one day's broaching of his pickthank tales   200
    Than can be salved again in twenty years;
    And he, I fear, shall go with us to France
    To pry into our actions.
Askew.   Therefore, coz,
    It shall behove you to be circumspect.
Lacy. Fear not, good cousin. Ralph, hie to your colours.   205

                    [Exeunt LACY *and* ASKEW.]

Ralph. I must, because there is no remedy.
    But, gentle master and my loving dame,
    As you have always been a friend to me,
    So in mine absence think upon my wife.
Jane. Alas, my Ralph.
Margery.   She cannot speak for weeping.   210
Eyre. Peace, you cracked groats, you mustard tokens, disquiet
    not the brave soldier. Go thy ways, Ralph.
Jane. Ay, ay, you bid him go—what shall I do when he is
    gone?
Firk. Why, be doing with me, or my fellow Hodge. Be not   215
    idle.
Eyre. Let me see thy hand, Jane. [*He takes her hand.*] This fine
    hand, this white hand, these pretty fingers must spin,
    must card, must work, work, you bombast-cotton-can-

---

206 there is] Q2; theres Q1.   210] *as verse, Wheeler; as prose, Q1.*

---

    200. *pickthank*] sycophantic.

    201. *salved*] remedied, set right.

    205. *colours*] regimental standard.

    206. *there is*] The expansion of Q1's 'theres' seems demanded by the metre. Bowers correctly states in his collations that Q2 reads 'there is', but his Historical Collation (p. 99) attributes 'theres' to all the early quartos.

    211. *cracked groats*] damaged fourpenny pieces—a jocular insult.

    mustard tokens] substitute coins issued by tradesmen to be exchanged for various commodities, here of little value. Plague sores were also called *tokens* (cf. Dekker, *Plague Pamphlets*, p. 29, 19, and n.), so the insult may be a compound one.

    215. *doing*] (with a pun on the sexual sense).

    219. *card*] prepare wool for spinning by combing it with a card.

    219–20. *bombast-cotton-candle quean*] Bombast is cotton-wool; more expensive candles made of wax or white tallow, instead of kitchen fat, had cotton wicks rather than rush ones (*Shakespeare's England*, II.124); *quean* could mean 'prostitute' but here

dle quean, work for your living, with a pox to you.   220
Hold thee, Ralph, here's five sixpences for thee. Fight
for the honour of the Gentle Craft, for the Gentlemen
Shoemakers, the courageous cordwainers, the flower of
Saint Martin's, the mad knaves of Bedlam, Fleet Street,
Tower Street, and Whitechapel. Crack me the crowns   225
of the French knaves, a pox on them—crack them.
Fight, by the Lord of Ludgate, fight, my fine boy.
Firk. Here, Ralph, here's three twopences. Two, carry into
France; the third shall wash our souls at parting—for
sorrow is dry. For my sake, firk the *baisez-mon-culs.*   230

---

it is no stronger than 'wench', though in line with the other bawdy of the passage.
Eyre coins the expression for its associations of softness, whiteness, and refinement;
thus it seems more of a compliment than an insult.

220. *work . . . pox*] *work* had a bawdy sense; the joking implication of the whole
passage is that Jane will work as a prostitute in her husband's absence, and thus be in
danger of catching the pox. Cf. xii. 0.1, n. Eyre himself is not necessarily conscious of
the bawdy implications.

223. *cordwainers*] shoemakers. 'Cordwain' was a type of fine Spanish leather,
named from Cordova. *Cordwainers* is still used in the name of the London company
of shoemakers, who are clearly distinguished from mere 'cobblers'.

223–4. *flower of Saint Martin's*] The area around the site of the former church of
Saint Martin's-le-Grand (demolished in 1548), in particular Saint Martin's Lane,
was, by the 1590s, a well-known centre of the footwear trade; it is mentioned as such
by Dekker (*Gull's Hornbook*, Pendry, p. 84) and by Deloney in *The Gentle Craft, Part
Two*, as well as in *Thomas of Reading* (Lawlis, pp. 256 ff. and 293). Stow (I.81) records
the removal of 'the Shoomakers . . . of Cordwayner Streete . . . to Saint *Martins Le
Grand*'.

224. *Bedlam*] Bethlehem Hospital, just outside Bishopsgate, London's principal
lunatic asylum (though the primary sense of Eyre's *mad* is, as usual, no more than
'carefree' 'energetic', etc.). Presumably the area around the hospital was one where
shoemakers could be found.

Fleet Street] Running west from Ludgate Hill, and noted especially for its taverns
(and later for its tobacconists' shops), Fleet Street seems also to have been an area of
shoemakers: in *The Gentle Craft, Part Two*, Deloney tells a story of Peachey 'the
famous Shoomaker of Fleet-street' (pp. 213 ff.).

225. *Whitechapel*] a London parish to the east of Aldgate, noted for butchers' and
shoemakers' shops.

225–6. *crowns . . . French . . . pox*] There is probably an underlying pun, as 'French
crown' alludes to the baldness produced by the 'French' (venereal) disease.

228. *twopences*] Silver twopenny pieces were in circulation.

229. *wash our souls*] (euphemistically) buy us a drink.

230. *sorrow is dry*] The proverbial phrase (Tilley, S656) occurs in *The Gentle Craft,
Part Two* (p. 205).

firk] beat (see *Dram. Per.*, 19, n.).

Hodge. Ralph, I am heavy at parting, but here's a shilling for
          thee. God send thee to cram thy slops with French
          crowns, and thy enemies' bellies with bullets.
Ralph. I thank you, master; and I thank you all.
          Now, gentle wife, my loving, lovely Jane,   235
          Rich men at parting give their wives rich gifts,
          Jewels, and rings to grace their lily hands.
          Thou know'st our trade makes rings for women's
          heels.
          Here, take this pair of shoes cut out by Hodge,
          Stitched by my fellow, Firk, seamed by myself,   240
          Made up and pinked with letters for thy name.
          Wear them, my dear Jane, for thy husband's sake,
          And every morning, when thou pull'st them on,
          Remember me, and pray for my return.
          Make much of them, for I have made them so   245
          That I can know them from a thousand moe.

Sound drum. Enter [Sir ROGER OATLEY, *the*] *Lord Mayor,* [*the* Earl of]
LINCOLN, LACY, ASKEW, DODGER, *and soldiers. They pass over the
stage.* RALPH *falls in amongst them.* FIRK *and the rest cry 'Farewell', etc.,
and so exeunt.*

---

230. baisez-mon-culs] (spelt 'Basamon cues' in Q1) 'kiss-my-arses'; a way of
referring to the French.

231. *heavy*] sad.

232. *send thee to*] grant that you may.

slops] baggy breeches.

232–3. *French crowns*] (as booty. See also ll. 225–6, n.).

237–8. *rings . . . heels*] Cf. *The Gentle Craft, Part Two:* 'Sir (quoth he) I am a
Goldsmith that makes rings for womens heeles. . . . I am (quoth *Tom*) of the Gentle
Craft, vulgarly called a Shoomaker' (p. 221). The expression seems to be an attempt
to elevate shoemakers to the level of goldsmiths.

241. *pinked . . . name*] decorated by having your initials pricked in them.

245–6.] These lines offer an obvious pointer to what is to happen. The rhyme
emphasises the statement and also serves, as often in Elizabethan drama, to mark the
end of the scene.

246. *moe*] more (the old form, preserved for the rhyme).

246.2–3. *pass over the stage*] This expression (which recurs at the opening of sc.
xix) had a technical sense which is of uncertain meaning. Allardyce Nicoll has
argued that it applies to 'a movement from yard to platform to yard again' (*Sh.S.* 12,
53); he is supported by Richard Southern in *The Staging of Plays before Shakespeare*
(London, 1973, pp. 584–91). This would be an effective way of staging this episode.

[SCENE II.]
Enter ROSE *alone, making a garland.*

[*Rose.*] Here sit thou down upon this flow'ry bank,
 And make a garland for thy Lacy's head.
 These pinks, these roses, and these violets,
 These blushing gilliflowers, these marigolds,
 The fair embroidery of his coronet,   5
 Carry not half such beauty in their cheeks
 As the sweet countenance of my Lacy doth.
 O, my most unkind father! O, my stars,
 Why loured you so at my nativity
 To make me love, yet live robbed of my love? 10
 Here as a thief am I imprisonèd
 For my dear Lacy's sake within those walls
 Which by my father's cost were builded up
 For better purposes. Here must I languish
 For him that doth as much lament, I know,   15
 Mine absence as for him I pine in woe.

Enter SYBIL.

Sybil. Good morrow, young mistress. I am sure you make
 that garland for me, against I shall be Lady of the
 Harvest.
Rose. Sybil, what news at London?   20
Sybil. None but good. My Lord Mayor your father, and

16.1 *Enter* SYBIL.] *as here, Fritsche; at end of l. 15, Q1.*

Sc.ii.] The setting moves to Old Ford (l. 31).
 1. *Here sit . . . bank*] The wording is remarkably close to *M.N.D.*, IV. i.1: 'Come,
sit thee down upon this flow'ry bed'.
 4. *gilliflowers*] wallflowers.
 16.1.] Q1 places the direction at the end of l.15, perhaps indicating an intention to
allow Rose to *languish* for some moments before Sybil addresses her.
 18. *against*] ready for the time when.
 18–19. *Lady of the Harvest*] queen of the harvest; 'a young woman chosen from the
reapers, to whom was given a post of honour at the harvest home' (*O.E.D.*, s.v.
'harvest-queen').

Master Philpot your uncle, and Master Scott your cousin, and Mistress Frigbottom, by Doctors' Commons,
do all, by my troth, send you most hearty commenda-
tions.   25
Rose. Did Lacy send kind greetings to his love?
Sybil. O yes, out of cry. By my troth, I scant knew him—
here 'a wore a scarf, and here a scarf, here a bunch of
feathers, and here precious stones and jewels, and a pair
of garters—O, monstrous!—like one of our yellow silk   30
curtains at home here in Old Ford House, here in Master
Bellymount's chamber. I stood at our door in Cornhill,
looked at him, he at me indeed; spake to him, but he not

28 wore a scarf] *Q3;* wore scarffe *Q1.*

22–3. *Philpot . . . Scott . . . Frigbottom*] The first and last names are so clearly meant
to be bawdily comic that it may not be far-fetched to suggest that *Scott* puns on
'scut', meaning 'short tail . . . hence, posteriors or pudend' (Partridge); though, of
course, Scott, unlike the others, appears in the play (sc. ix).

23. *Frigbottom*] Dekker's compound. *Frig* is first recorded in 1598, meaning
'wriggle' or 'tickle'; the fully sexual meaning seems to be a later development (see
O.E.D., 1972 Supplement). O.E.D. first records *bottom* as 'posteriors' in 1794, but
clearly it has a related sense here.

by] i.e., who lives by.

Doctors' Commons] lodging-house for the College of Doctors of the Law at the
corner of Saint Bennett's Hill and Knightrider Street. Formerly the town house of
the Blounts, Lords Mountjoy, it was established as *Doctors' Commons* only in the first
years of Elizabeth's reign.

27. *out of cry*] beyond all measure.

28. *scarf*] 'a broad band of silk or other material, worn (chiefly by soldiers or other
officials) either diagonally across the body from shoulder to the opposite hip, or
round the waist' *(O.E.D.).* This and the other objects mentioned in this speech may
be favours presented by girls to a soldier, and thus a reason why Sybil thinks that
Lacy does not love Rose (ll. 44–5).

28–9. *bunch of feathers*] cockade.

29. *jewels*] ornaments; or, more specifically, stones in a setting.

30–1. *like . . . curtains*] The expression seems designed partly to stress where the
scene is set, perhaps also to suggest that Lacy wore a pair of garters whose bright
colouring showed that they had come from a fashionably dressed woman.

31. *Old Ford*] a village three-and-a-half miles north-east of Saint Paul's, beyond
Stratford Bow. Sugden suggests that 'an old mansion there, sometimes called King
John's Palace, . . . is probably the Old Ford House' of the play. Davies rightly points
out that at ll. 12–13 Rose implies that Oatley built the house.

31–2. *Master Bellymount*] another bawdily comic name.

32. *Cornhill*] a street running east from the Poultry, the location of Oatley's town
house (see also xiii.63).

to me, not a word. 'Marry gup,' thought I, 'with a
wanion!' He passed by me as proud—'marry, foh, are   35
you grown humorous?' thought I—and so shut the
door, and in I came.

Rose. O Sybil, how dost thou my Lacy wrong!
My Rowland is as gentle as a lamb;
No dove was ever half so mild as he.   40

Sybil. Mild?—yea, as a bushel of stamped crabs. He looked
upon me as sour as verjuice. 'Go thy ways,' thought I,
'thou mayst be much in my gaskins, but nothing in my
netherstocks.' This is your fault, mistress, to love him
that loves not you. He thinks scorn to do as he's done to;   45
but if I were as you, I'ld cry 'Go by, Jeronimo, go by!'
I'ld set mine old debts against my new driblets
And the hare's foot against the goose giblets;

47–50] *as verse, Q6; as prose, Q1.*

---

34. *Marry gup*] not recorded elsewhere; but obviously related to 'marry come up',
an Elizabethanism 'used to express indignant or amused surprise or contempt:
="hoity-toity" ' (*O.E.D.;* cf. vi.29).

34–5. *with a wanion*] with a plague, with a vengeance.

36. *humorous*] moody.

39. *gentle as a lamb*] proverbial (Tilley, L34).

40. *dove . . . mild*] proverbial (Tilley, D573).

41. *stamped crabs*] crab-apples that have been crushed to extract the (very sour)
juice.

42. *as sour as verjuice*] proverbial: Tilley cites this as his first instance (V32). *Verjuice*
is the juice of unripe, sour fruit, formerly used in cooking.

43–4. *thou . . . netherstocks*] *gaskins:* breeches or hose; *netherstocks:* stockings. As
Davies says, this is not recorded as proverbial, but seems to be so, meaning 'we may
be acquainted, but we are far from being intimate friends'.

44. *your fault*] i.e., a fault in you.

45. *thinks scorn*] disdains.
do as he's done to] biblical (Matthew, vii. 12) and proverbial (Tilley, D395).

46. *'Go by, Jeronimo, go by!'*] be off!, 'on your way!' The phrase derives from
Thomas Kyd's *The Spanish Tragedy* (*c.* 1587–92): 'Not I. Hieronimo, beware: go by,
go by' (Revels Plays, ed. Edwards, III. xii. 31). F. S. Boas says: 'Perhaps no single
passage in Elizabethan drama became so notorious as this. It is quoted over and over
again as the stock phrase to imply impatience of anything disagreeable, incon-
venient, or old-fashioned' (Kyd, *Works,* ed. Boas, Oxford, 1901, p. 406). Dekker
uses the phrase again in *Satiromastix,* I. ii. 372.

47–8. *I'ld set . . . giblets*] proverbial expressions (Tilley, H161); the second is often
used alone, but as Lange points out, the two are associated in Harington's *Orlando
Furioso* (1591): 'Yet will I do to thee no further wrong / But pardon thee, and thou

> For if ever I sigh when sleep I should take,
> Pray God I may lose my maidenhead when I
>   wake.   50

Rose. Will my love leave me then, and go to France?

Sybil. I know not that, but I am sure I see him stalk before the
> soldiers. By my troth, he is a proper man—but he is
> proper that proper doth. Let him go snick up, young
> mistress.   55

Rose. Get thee to London, and learn perfectly
> Whether my Lacy go to France or no.
> Do this, and I will give thee for thy pains
> My cambric apron, and my Romish gloves,
> My purple stockings, and a stomacher.   60
> Say, wilt thou do this, Sybil, for my sake?

Sybil. Will I, quoth 'a! At whose suit?—by my troth, yes, I'll
> go—a cambric apron, gloves, a pair of purple stockings,
> and a stomacher!—I'll sweat in purple, mistress, for you;
> I'll take anything that comes a' God's name—O rich, a   65

---

shalt me forgive / And quite each other all old debts and driblets / And set the hares
head against the goose gyblets' (Book 43, st. 136; ed. Robert McNulty, Oxford,
1972, p. 507). Sutherland comments: 'Sybil is suggesting that though the love of
Lacy would be a fine thing for Rose to have, it must be set off against the
unpleasantness of his possible neglect of her.' This interpretation is, in the light of the
following two lines, preferable to Lange's 'off with the old love, on with the new'.
    47. *driblets*] small or petty debts.

    49. *sigh*] (for unrequited love).
    52. *see*] (dialectal for 'saw').
    53. *proper*] handsome.
    53–4. *he is proper that proper doth*] proverbial (Tilley, C586).
    54. *go snick up*] go hang.
    59. *cambric*] fine linen; expensive and thus to be coveted.
    Romish] made of Italian leather.
    60. *stomacher*] 'an ornamental covering for the chest (often covered with jewels)
formerly worn by women under the lacing of the bodice' (*O.E.D.*).
    62. *quoth 'a!*] says she!
    At whose suit?] i.e., why bother to ask?
    64. *sweat in purple*] work hard in rich clothes; possibly, as Sutherland suggests,
punning on *purple* as a disease producing purplish spots.
    65. *a' God's name*] free, for nothing. Cf. Middleton and Rowley, *The Changeling:*
'If you could buy a gale amongst the witches, / They could not serve you such a
lucky pennyworth / As comes a' God's name' (Revels Plays, ed. Bawcutt, I. i.
17–19).

cambric apron! Faith, then, have at uptails all, I'll go
jiggy-joggy to London and be here in a trice, young
mistress.   *Exit.*

Rose. Do so, good Sybil. Meantime wretched I
   Will sit and sigh for his lost company.   70
                                                             Exit.

[SCENE III.]
Enter ROWLAND LACY *like a Dutch shoemaker.*

Lacy. How many shapes have gods and kings devised
   Thereby to compass their desirèd loves!
   It is no shame for Rowland Lacy then
   To clothe his cunning with the Gentle Craft
   That, thus disguised, I may unknown possess   5

---

66. *have at uptails all*] an expression of high spirits and of the intention to get
moving. 'Uptails all' was the name of a song, used in a wide variety of contexts; cf.
Dekker's *Satiromastix*, IV. iii. 149, 'feele my light-vptailes all', where it refers to a
sword. Henley and Farmer's definitions include 'riot, high jinks', 'boon companions', and 'wantonness, and spec. the act of kind'.
   67. *jiggy-joggy*] (slang) with a jolting motion. O.E.D. cites this as its only use,
deriving it from 'jig-a-jog', first recorded in Dekker's *Satiromastix* (III. i. 222), where
the phrase 'thou shalt ryde Iagga-Iogge' implies sudden and unwonted prosperity, as
here. In Marston's *The Dutch Courtesan* Cocledemoy says, 'I bid my selfe most
hartily welcome to your merry nuptials, and wanton Jigga-joggies' (ed. P. Davison,
Fountainwell Drama Texts, 1968, V. iii. 155–7). This suggests a bawdy sense more
appropriate to the expression's later use at xiii.33.

   Sc. iii.] The action moves back to London.
   0.1. like a Dutch shoemaker] The phrase sounds authorial. According to Sugden,
stage Dutchmen characteristically wore 'baggy slops or breeches, short doublets,
and large felt hats'. The Dutch had a high reputation as shoemakers, and Lacy would
be identified as one by carrying 'St Hugh's bones' (iv.49). Foreign artisans were a
regular feature of Tudor London.
   1. *How many . . . devised*] In Deloney, Crispine, disguised as a shoemaker, says 'The
necessity of these times makes many Noble personages to maske in simple habite, as
Iupiter did in a shepheards weed . . .' (p. 133). The Ovidian reference to disguised
gods is common in episodes in which men of rank wear humble disguise for
romantic reasons; cf. e.g. Chapman, *May-Day*, ed. Parrott, II.i.494–5, where
Lorenzo is to disguise himself as a chimney-sweeper.
   shapes] disguises.
   4. *cunning*] wit, intelligence (a rather strained use, mainly for the sake of the pun on
Craft).

The only happy presence of my Rose.
For her have I forsook my charge in France,
Incurred the King's displeasure, and stirred up
Rough hatred in mine uncle Lincoln's breast.
O love, how powerful art thou, that canst change   10
High birth to bareness, and a noble mind
To the mean semblance of a shoemaker!
But thus it must be; for her cruel father,
Hating the single union of our souls,
Hath secretly conveyed my Rose from London   15
To bar me of her presence; but I trust
Fortune and this disguise will further me
Once more to view her beauty, gain her sight.
Here in Tower Street with Eyre the shoemaker
Mean I a while to work. I know the trade;   20
I learnt it when I was in Wittenberg.
Then cheer thy drooping sprites; be not dismayed!
Thou canst not want—do Fortune what she can,
The Gentle Craft is living for a man!   *Exit.*

11 bareness] *Q1;* baseness *Q4.*   22 drooping] *This ed.;* hoping *Q1.*

---

6. *only happy presence*] i.e., here whose presence alone makes me happy.

11. *bareness*] Many editors follow Q4 and emend to 'baseness'. Bowers retains the original reading, citing xxi. 109–10: 'your nephew . . . did stoop / To bare necessity.' Davies disagrees: 'I think the high–low, or noble–mean antithesis is more characteristically Dekkerian than the clothed–unclothed antithesis.' But *O.E.D.* records *bareness* as 'Destitution', citing Hollyband's *Dictionary of the French Tongue* (1580), defining *Pouvreté* as 'barenesse, want'.

14. *single*] perhaps 'involving celibacy' (*O.E.D.* II.8.b) or 'absolute' (*O.E.D.* I.4).

20. *I know the trade*] Cf. i.29–31 and Introduction, p. 33.

21. *Wittenberg*] See i.29, n.

22. *drooping*] Although no objection has been made to Q1's 'hoping', it is poor sense. We propose *drooping* as a far more likely reading: cf. *1H6* V.ii.1: 'These news, my lords, may cheer our drooping spirits'; and Robert Wilson, *The Coblers Prophecie* (1594), Malone Society Reprints, l. 988, 'Now hast thou cheard my 'drooping thoughts'.

sprites] spirits (the old form retained for the sake of the metre).

24. *The Gentle Craft is living for a man*] See Introduction, p. 38, and cf. Deloney, dedicatory verses: 'And neuer yet did any know, a shoemaker a begging goe' (p. 91).

[SCENE IV.]
Enter EYRE, *making himself ready.*

Eyre. Where be these boys, these girls, these drabs, these
scoundrels? They wallow in the fat brewis of my
bounty, and lick up the crumbs of my table, yet will not
rise to see my walks cleansed. Come out, you powder-
beef queans! What, Nan! What, Madge Mumblecrust!   5
Come out, you fat midriff-swag-belly whores, and
sweep me these kennels, that the noisome stench offend
not the nose of my neighbours. What, Firk, I say! What,
Hodge! Open my shop windows! What, Firk, I say!

Enter FIRK.

Firk. O, master, is't you that speak bandog and bedlam this   10
morning? I was in a dream, and mused what madman
was got into the street so early. Have you drunk this
morning, that your throat is so clear?

6 midriff-swag-belly whores] *Q2;* Midriffe-swag, belly-whores *Q1.*
8 nose] *Q1;* noses *Q3.*

Sc. iv.] This scene is based on a brief passage of Deloney (Appendix A, p. 206).
   0.1. making himself ready] completing his dressing. This is an early-morning
scene in front of Eyre's workshop.
   1. *drabs*] slatternly women.
   2. *brewis*] broth (or bread soaked in broth).
   4. *rise to*] get up in time to.
   walks] paths and passages.
   4–5. *powder-beef*] beef salted to preserve it—used insultingly of the age and state of
preservation of Eyre's female servants.
   5. *queans*] properly, prostitutes; here, a general insult.
   Madge Mumblecrust] To *mumble* meant at this period 'to chew toothlessly', but
probably all that Eyre's wife has done to deserve this insult is to have the same first
name as the Madge Mumblecrust who figures in Udall's *Ralph Roister Doister* (*c.*
1553). Cf. Dekker's *Satiromastix*: 'dost loue that mother Mumble-crust, dost thou?
dost long for that whim-wham?' (III.i.139–40).
   6. *midriff-swag-belly*] *Swag-belly,* 'person having a pendulous abdomen', is first
recorded by O.E.D. in 1611, but this compound is quoted under *midriff,* 'applied as a
term of contempt'.
   7. *kennels*] surface drains in streets; gutters.
   10. *speak bandog and bedlam*] speak ferociously (a *bandog* is a savage dog kept tied
up; a *bedlam* is a madman).

Eyre. Ah, well said, Firk; well said, Firk—to work, my fine
    knave, to work! Wash thy face, and thou'lt be more   15
    blessed.

Firk. Let them wash my face that will eat it. Good master,
    send for a souse-wife if you'll have my face cleaner.

Enter HODGE.

Eyre. Away, sloven! Avaunt, scoundrel! Good morrow,
    Hodge; good morrow, my fine foreman.   20

Hodge. O master, good morrow. You're an early stirrer.
    Here's a fair morning. Good morrow, Firk. I could have
    slept this hour. Here's a brave day towards.

Eyre. O, haste to work, my fine foreman, haste to work.

Firk. Master, I am dry as dust to hear my fellow Roger talk of   25
    fair weather. Let us pray for good leather, and let clowns
    and ploughboys, and those that work in the fields, pray
    for brave days. We work in a dry shop—what care I if it
    rain?

Enter [MARGERY,] *Eyre's wife.*

Eyre. How now, Dame Margery, can you see to rise? Trip   30
    and go, call up the drabs your maids.

Margery. See to rise! I hope 'tis time enough; 'tis early enough

---

15–16. *Wash . . . blessed*] Firk is just out of bed. The expression sounds proverbial,
and may be a variant of 'A fair face must have good conditions' (Tilley, F5): *and*
should perhaps be understood as 'an', meaning 'if'.

18. *souse-wife*] one who prepared pigs' heads, ears, trotters, etc., for eating by
washing and pickling them. (Perhaps her function of pickling reminds Firk of his
thirst.)

23. *brave*] fine.

towards] before us.

25. *dry as dust*] proverbial (Tilley, D647); one of Firk's series of references to his
thirst.

26. *clowns*] peasants.

28–9.] This accords with the sentiment of the second three-man's song.

30. *can you see to rise?*] sarcastic: 'is it light enough for you to get up?'.

30–1. *Trip and go*] the name of a morris-dance, also used to mean 'act quickly'; cf.
xvii.27 and xx.56. (The background of the phrase is explored in the note to IV.ii.139
of *L.L.L.*, ed. R. David (new Arden edition, 1951).)

32–5. *early . . . noon*] Dekker writes satirically in *The Gull's Horn-Book* that 'noon
. . . is the most healthful hour to be stirring. . . . At what time do lords and ladies use

for any woman to be seen abroad. I marvel how many
wives in Tower Street are up so soon. God's me, 'tis not
noon! Here's a yawling.   35
Eyre. Peace, Margery, peace. Where's Cicely Bumtrinket,
your maid? She has a privy fault: she farts in her sleep.
Call the quean up. If my men want shoethread, I'll
swinge her in a stirrup.
Firk. Yet that's but a dry beating. Here's still a sign of   40
drought.

Enter LACY [*as* HANS], *singing.*

Lacy [*as Hans*]. *Der was een bore van Gelderland,*
    Frolick sie byen;
He was als dronck he could niet stand,
    Upsee al sie byen;   45

42–7] *as six lines, Fritsche; as three lines, Q1.*
45 *Upsee al sie*] *conj. Lange;* vpsolce se *Q1.*

---

to rise but then? Your simpering merchants' wives are the fairest liers in the world,
and is not eleven o'clock their common hour?' (Pendry, p. 82).

33. *marvel*] wonder.

35. *yawling*] yelling, bawling.

36. *Cicely Bumtrinket*] See i.164, n.

37. *privy fault*] Cf. Thomas Lodge and Robert Greene, *A Looking Glass for London
and England* (1594): 'thy wiues priuy fault . . . she . . . doth vse to breake winde in her
sleepe' (Malone Society Reprints, 1932, ll. 640–3). Eyre's intimate knowledge of his
wife's maid has been used to create amusement in modern productions, though it
was not uncommon for a maid to sleep in her mistress's bedroom.

privy] (punningly) secret.

38. *want*] lack (through Cicely's negligence).

39. *swinge*] beat, thrash.

stirrup] See i.189, n.; *in* probably means 'with'.

40. *dry beating*] literally, a thrashing that does not draw blood. Firk draws
attention to his thirst.

42–7. *Der . . . mannekin*] 'There was a boor from Gelderland, merry they are. He
was so drunk he could not stand, drunk they all are. Fill up the cannikin, drink, fine
mannikin.' 'Boor' could mean simply a peasant or countryman, particularly a Dutch
or German one, but also already had a derogatory sense, i.e. 'country clown' or
'rude, ill-bred fellow' (*O.E.D.* 3b). On the treatment of Lacy's pseudo-Dutch in this
text, see Introduction, p. 62. Lacy's entry with a drinking song reflects the reputation
of the Dutch as heavy drinkers.

45. *Upsee al sie*] Lange comments that Q1's 'vpsolce' is 'Very likely only a
misprint; i.e. "ol"="al" was transposed or inserted by the compositor, who was
doubtless not familiar with Dutch, into what was intended for "upsee". What
Dekker wrote was probably: "Upsee al se byen".' Bowers, freed by his editorial

Tap eens de canneken,
Drincke, schone mannekin.

Firk. Master, for my life, yonder's a brother of the Gentle
    Craft! If he bear not Saint Hugh's bones, I'll forfeit my
    bones. He's some uplandish workman. Hire him, good   50
    master, that I may learn some gibble-gabble. 'Twill
    make us work the faster.

Eyre. Peace, Firk. A hard world; let him pass, let him vanish.
    We have journeymen enough. Peace, my fine Firk.

Margery. Nay, nay, you're best follow your man's counsel.   55
    You shall see what will come on't. We have not men
    enough but we must entertain every butter-box—but
    let that pass.

Hodge. Dame, fore God, if my master follow your counsel

---

47 *schone*] *Shepherd;* schoue *Q1.*

---

method from the need to explain what he prints, does not comment. Davies 'inclines
to agree' with Lange, but does not emend. Sanna also cites Lange with respect.
'Upsee' is common in drinking phrases; cf. 'upsy Friese', *The Gull's Horn-Book*
(Pendry, p. 74), and Nashe, *Piers Penniless* (McKerrow, I.205), with the note 'i.e. in
the Frisian manner (from Dutch *op zijn Friesch*) . . . but the uses of this and the similar
"vpsee-Dutch" and "vpsee-English" are somewhat puzzling'. In the circumstances
the most honest editorial procedure seems to be to emend while admitting that
obscurity remains.

49. *Saint Hugh's bones*] The story of how shoemakers' tools came to have this
name is told by Deloney (pp. 112–15). Sir Hugh, who became a shoemaker for love
of Winifred, suffered martyrdom with her, leaving his bones 'to all the kind
Yeomen of the *Gentle Craft*'. A company of journeymen shoemakers found his body
hanging up and picked clean of flesh. They took the bones, and, in order to 'turne
them to profit, and auoyd suspition', made various tools with them, 'which euer
since were called Saint *Hughes* bones'. Firk's speech closely parallels a passage in
Deloney's story of Eyre (Appendix A, p. 206).

50. *uplandish*] normally used to refer to high-lying land, or land inward from the
sea; but here seems to mean 'foreign' (cf. 'outlandish'), with perhaps a joking,
implied allusion to the Low Countries.

51. *gibble-gabble*] unintelligible chatter (Firk's way of referring to a foreign
language).

55–8.] This speech seems self-contradictory. It can only be explained by the
assumption that Margery is supporting her husband by sarcastically appearing to
agree to Firk's request.

57. *butter-box*] a nickname for a Dutchman; cf. vii.148, xiii.57, xvi.42. In *The
Wonderful Year*, Dekker says that the Low Countries 'are built upon butter-firkins
and Holland cheese' (Pendry, p. 51), and he uses the term 'butter-box' in *The Gull's
Horn-Book*, chapter 3 (Pendry, p. 87).

he'll consume little beef. He shall be glad of men an he   60
can catch them.

Firk. Ay, that he shall.

Hodge. Fore God, a proper man and, I warrant, a fine workman. Master, farewell. Dame, adieu. If such a man as he
cannot find work, Hodge is not for you.   65

Offer to go.

Eyre. Stay, my fine Hodge.

Firk. Faith, an your foreman go, dame, you must take a
journey to seek a new journeyman. If Roger remove,
Firk follows. If Saint Hugh's bones shall not be set
a-work, I may prick mine awl in the walls, and go play.   70
Fare ye well, master. Goodbye, dame.

Eyre. Tarry, my fine Hodge, my brisk foreman. Stay, Firk.
Peace, pudding-broth. By the Lord of Ludgate, I love
my men as my life. Peace, you gallimaufry. Hodge, if he
want work, I'll hire him. One of you to him—stay, he   75
comes to us.

Lacy [as Hans]. Goeden dach, meester, end you fro, auch.

Firk. 'Nails, if I should speak after him without drinking, I
should choke! And you, friend Auch, are you of the
Gentle Craft?   80

Lacy [as Hans]. Yaw, yaw; ik bin den skomawker.

---

60. *consume little beef*] i.e., not prosper.

60–1. *He shall . . . them*] i.e., he ought to be pleased to hire men when he has the chance.

64–5. *adieu . . . for you*] the rhyme, though in a prose speech, suggests a parting couplet.

65.1 Offer] make as if (a common formula for instructions for incompleted actions in Elizabethan dramatic texts).

70. *prick mine awl . . . play*] i.e., 'down tools'.

prick] stick.

73, 74. *Peace*] Presumably Margery is fretting and fuming.

73. *pudding-broth*] literally, the liquid, doubtless fatty, in which *pudding*—a kind of sausage—had been boiled; here applied derogatorily to Margery.

74. *gallimaufry*] literally, a hash of odds and ends of food, applied to Margery again.

77. Goeden . . . auch] 'Good-day, master, and you, goodwife, too.'

78. *'Nails*] God's nails! This oath referring to the nails of the Cross had weakened into a common, mild expletive. Dekker reserves it for Firk, who uses it frequently.

after] like.

79. *friend Auch*] Firk—perhaps mockingly—takes *auch* (also) as a name.

81. 'Yaw . . . skomawker'] 'Yes, yes, I am a shoemaker.'

Firk. '*Den skomawker*', quoth 'a; and hark you, skomawker,
    have you all your tools—a good rubbing-pin, a good
    stopper, a good dresser, your four sorts of awls, and
    your two balls of wax, your paring-knife, your hand-   85
    and thumb-leathers, and good Saint Hugh's bones to
    smooth up your work?

Lacy [*as Hans*]. *Yaw, yaw, be niet vorveard. Ik hab all de dingen
    voour mack skoes groot end klene.*

Firk. Ha, ha! Good master, hire him. He'll make me laugh so   90
    that I shall work more in mirth than I can in earnest.

Eyre. Hear ye, friend: have ye any skill in the mystery of
    cordwainers?

Lacy [*as Hans*]. *Ik weet niet wat you seg; ik verstaw you niet.*

Firk. Why thus, man! [*He mimes the actions of a shoemaker.*] 'Ik   95
    verste you niet', quoth 'a.

Lacy [*as Hans*]. *Yaw, yaw, yaw; ik can dat wel doen.*

Firk. '*Yaw, yaw*'—he speaks yawing like a jackdaw, that
    gapes to be fed with cheese curds. O, he'll give a
    villainous pull at a can of double beer. But Hodge and I   100
    have the vantage; we must drink first, because we are
    the eldest journeymen.

Eyre. What is thy name?

---

94 *verstaw*] Q2; vestaw Q1.

83–6. *tools . . . thumb-leathers*] A similar, though not identical, list of shoemaker's
tools is given in Deloney (p. 114). Some items are self-explanatory. A *stopper* was a
'stopping-stick', perhaps used for filling crevices (*O.E.D.* cites only Deloney and
Dekker). A *dresser* was presumably an implement for trimming or polishing (*O.E.D.*
defines only as 'A shoemaker's tool', citing Deloney). *Awls* were used for piercing
holes in leather; the *four sorts* are presumably of different sizes. *Wax* is defined by
O.E.D. as 'A thick resinous composition used by shoemakers for rubbing their
thread'; the first use cited is in Dekker and Massinger's *The Virgin Martyr*, there
dated 1622.

88–9. Yaw . . . klene] 'Yes, yes, do not be afraid. I have everything to make shoes
large and small.'

92. *mystery*] craft, art.

93. *cordwainers*] See i.223, n.

94. Ik . . . niet] 'I do not know what you say; I do not understand you.'

97. Yaw . . . doen] 'Yes, yes, yes; I can do that well.'

98. *yawing*] (dialectal) with his mouth wide open, yawningly.

jackdaw] (often kept in captivity and taught to talk).

100. *double*] extra-strong.

Lacy [*as Hans*]. Hans; Hans Meulter.

Eyre. Give me thy hand, thou'rt welcome. Hodge, entertain   105
    him. Firk, bid him welcome. Come, Hans. Run, wife;
    bid your maids, your trullibubs, make ready my fine
    men's breakfasts. To him, Hodge.

Hodge. Hans, thou'rt welcome. Use thyself friendly, for we
    are good fellows; if not, thou shalt be fought with, wert   110
    thou bigger than a giant.

Firk. Yea, and drunk with, wert thou Gargantua. My master
    keeps no cowards, I tell thee. Ho, boy, bring him an
    heelblock. Here's a new journeyman.

Enter Boy.

Lacy [*as Hans*]. O, ik verstaw you. Ik moet een halve dossen cans   115
    betaelen. Here, boy, *nempt dis skilling, tap eens freelick.*

                                                    Exit Boy.

Eyre. Quick, snipper-snapper, away! Firk, scour thy throat;
    thou shalt wash it with Castilian liquor. Come, my last
    of the fives,

Enter Boy.

117 away!] *Warnke and Proescholdt;* away Q1.

---

   107. *trullibubs*] a variant of 'trillibubs', meaning 'entrails, the inwards of an animal'. *O.E.D.* cites this as the first instance of the term 'applied to a person'; it became a jeering name for a fat person.

   109. *Use thyself friendly*] behave in a friendly manner.

   112. *Gargantua*] a giant of French folklore, represented by Rabelais as a voracious eater and drinker. References of about the same date as Dekker's include Jonson, *Every Man in his Humour* (1598: I.iv.130) and *A.Y.L.I.*, III.ii.221.

   114. *heelblock*] a block used in fastening a heel to a shoe. But in this context it seems to act as a hint that Hans should buy a round of drinks.

   115–16. *O . . . freelick*] 'O, I understand. I am to pay for half a dozen cans. Here, boy, take this shilling; fill up merrily.'

   117. *snipper-snapper*] whipper-snapper, cheeky young fellow.

   118. *Castilian*] Eyre uses the adjective from Castile (the Spanish province) instead of 'Castalian', from Castalia, a spring on Mount Parnassus sacred to the Muses. This may be Dekker's deliberate malapropism. 'Castalian' is used by the Host in *M.W.W.* (II.iii.30) in a similarly grandiloquent passage of uncertain meaning.

   118–19. *last of the fives*] usually explained as a last for a small, size-five foot, in allusion to the boy's small stature. Cf. 'A Love Sonnet', in *The Poetry of George Wither*: 'Her waist exceeding small, / The fives did fit her shoe' (ed. F. Sidgwick, 2 vols, London, 1902, I.150).

give me a can. Have to thee, Hans! Here, Hodge; here,
Firk: drink, you mad Greeks, and work like true Tro-
jans, and pray for Simon Eyre the shoemaker. Here,
Hans; and thou'rt welcome.

Firk. Lo, dame, you would have lost a good fellow that will
teach us to laugh.—This beer came hopping in well.   125

Margery. Simon, it is almost seven.

Eyre. Is't so, Dame Clapperdudgeon? Is't seven o'clock and
my men's breakfast not ready? Trip and go, you soused
conger, away. Come, you mad Hyperboreans. Follow
me, Hodge; follow me, Hans; come after, my fine Firk: 130
to work, to work a while, and then to breakfast.   *Exit.*

Firk. Soft, yaw, yaw, good Hans. Though my master have
no more wit but to call you afore me, I am not so foolish
to go behind you, I being the elder journeyman.   *Exeunt.*

---

120. *Have to thee*] Here's to you!

121. *mad Greeks*] a familiar phrase (Tilley, M901, 'a merry Greek'), meaning
'boon companions', 'lively fellows'. (See Terence Spencer, *Fair Greece, Sad Relic,*
London, 1954, pp. 35 ff.)

121–2. *work like true Trojans*] 'To work like a Trojan' is not listed in Tilley or
O.D.E.P., and is first given in O.E.D. in 1846; but this seems a clear instance.
However, *Trojan* could also have the same sense as *Greek*: O.E.D. defines 'a merry or
roystering fellow; a boon companion . . . a good fellow (often with the alliterative
epithet *true* or *trusty)'*.

126. *seven*] Breakfast was normally served at 6.30 a.m. (*Shakespeare's England,*
II.134).

127. *Dame Clapperdudgeon*] another of Eyre's terms of affectionate abuse. 'A
clapperdudgeon is in English a "beggar born"' (Dekker, *English Villainies Discovered
by Lantern and Candlelight,* third edition, 1612; in Pendry, p. 295). The derivation is
uncertain, but 'if a clapper-dudgeon is one who beats his clap-dish (a wooden dish
with a lid carried by lepers and beggars), Eyre probably means to allude to the
incessant "clapping" of his wife's tongue' (Sutherland).

128–9. *soused conger*] pickled eel. Doll Tearsheet calls Falstaff a 'muddy conger'
(*2H4,* II.iv.52). Eyre may allude again to his wife's tongue.

129. *Hyperboreans*] rather sound than sense. Hyperboreans were in Greek legend a
people who lived idyllically beyond the North wind.

132–4.] Firk's assertion of status makes a comically effective end to the scene.

[SCENE V.]

Holloaing within. Enter WARNER *and* HAMMON, *like hunters.*

Hammon. Cousin, beat every brake. The game's not far.
　　This way with wingèd feet he fled from death
　　Whilst the pursuing hounds, scenting his steps,
　　Find out his highway to destruction.
　　Besides, the miller's boy told me even now   5
　　He saw him take soil, and he holloaed him,
　　Affirming him so embossed
　　That long he could not hold.
Warner.　　　　　　　　　　If it be so,
　　'Tis best we trace these meadows by Old Ford.

A noise of hunters within. Enter a Boy.

Hammon. How now, boy, where's the deer? Speak, sawst
　　thou him?   10
Boy. O yea, I saw him leap through a hedge, and then over a
　　ditch, then at my Lord Mayor's pale. Over he skipped
　　me and in he went me, and 'Holloa' the hunters cried,
　　and 'There, boy, there, boy'—but there he is, 'a mine
　　honesty.   15

---

6 soil] Q2; saile Q1.
7 him so] Q1; him to have been so *Warnke and Proescholdt.*

Sc. v.] The scene moves back to Old Ford.
　1. *brake*] thicket.
　game] quarry (of any kind).
　4. *Find*] (historic present).
　6. *soil*] refuge (as in a 'soil', a muddy place or pool, in an attempt to throw hounds off the scent).
　7. *him so*] usually emended to 'him to have been so'; but 'it is simpler to regard the line as irregularly short' (Bowers).
　embossed] driven to extremity, exhausted (a hunting term; cf. G. Turbervile, *The Noble Art of Venery*: 'When he (the hart) is foamy at the mouth, we saye that he is *embost*', 1576; repr. Oxford, 1908, p. 244).
　9. *trace*] search.
　9.1. *Boy*] (presumably the *miller's boy*, l. 5).
　12. *pale*] fence.
　12–13. *skipped me . . . went me*] the ethic dative; cf. i.33, n. Here, *me* is 'used expletively in narrative' (*O.E.D.*, 2c).

Hammon. Boy, godamercy. Cousin, let's away.
   I hope we shall find better sport today.   *Exeunt.*

[SCENE VI.]
Hunting within. Enter ROSE *and* SYBIL.

Rose. Why, Sybil, wilt thou prove a forester?
Sybil. Upon some, no! Forester, go by. No, faith, mistress,
   the deer came running into the barn through the
   orchard, and over the pale. I wot well I looked as pale as
   a new cheese to see him, but 'Whip!' says Goodman   5
   Pinclose, up with his flail, and our Nick with a prong,
   and down he fell, and they upon him, and I upon them.
   By my troth, we had such sport; and in the end we
   ended him; his throat we cut, flayed him, unhorned
   him, and my Lord Mayor shall eat of him anon when he   10
   comes.

Horns sound within.

Rose. Hark, hark, the hunters come. You're best take heed.
   They'll have a saying to you for this deed.

---

16. *godamercy*] thank you.
17. *better sport*] (in the Lord Mayor's house, to which the deer now leads him).

0.1. Hunting within] i.e., make the sounds of hunting offstage.
1. *prove*] become.
forester] officer having charge of a forest; also 'huntsman'.
2. *Upon some*] This asseveration serves as a catch-phrase for Sybil in this scene (see
also ll. 17 and 29). It appears to have no more than an intensive function, Sybil
always using it along with 'no' and Warner (l. 18) jokingly turning it against her
with 'ay'.
go by] cf. ii.46, and n.
4–5. *pale as a new cheese*] (proverbial in tone, but not recorded by Tilley or in
O.D.E.P.).
5. *Whip!*] used as an exclamation expressive of haste or the need for speed:
'Quick!'
5–6. *Goodman Pinclose*] *Goodman* was used in a number of senses, including 'head
of a household', 'husband', and 'yeoman'. *Pinclose* seems like another of Dekker's
vaguely comic names, perhaps analogous to 'pinfold', a pound.
9. *flayed*] skinned.
13. *have a saying to you*] presumably 'give you a talking to', 'rebuke you'.

Enter HAMMON, WARNER, Huntsmen, *and* Boy.

Hammon. God save you, fair ladies.

Sybil.   'Ladies'! O, gross!

Warner. Came not a buck this way?

Rose.   No, but two does.   15

Hammon. And which way went they? Faith, we'll hunt at
     those.

Sybil. At those? Upon some, no! When, can you tell?

Warner. Upon some, ay!

Sybil.   Good Lord!

Warner.   'Wounds, then farewell.

Hammon. Boy, which way went he?

Boy.   This way, sir, he ran.

Hammon. This way he ran indeed. Fair Mistress Rose,   20
     Our game was lately in your orchard seen.

Warner. Can you advise which way he took his flight?

Sybil. Follow your nose, his horns will guide you right.

Warner. Thou'rt a mad wench.

Sybil.   O rich!

Rose.   Trust me, not I.
     It is not like the wild forest deer   25
     Would come so near to places of resort.
     You are deceived. He fled some other way.

Warner. Which way, my sugar candy—can you show?

Sybil. Come up, good honey-sops: upon some, no!

Rose. Why do you stay, and not pursue your game?   30

25 *like the*] Q1; *like that the* Q2.

---

14. *gross*] stupid (because only Rose is a lady); or perhaps (as Davies suggests) 'lady'
could have a derogatory sense.

15. *does*] i.e., herself and Sybil.

17. *When, can you tell?*] a phrase of defiance (Tilley, T88).

18. *'Wounds*] God's wounds.

23. *Follow your nose*] proverbial (Tilley, N230).

horns] (the common joke on cuckoldry, suggesting that one horned beast will
attract another).

24. *mad*] (appreciative, as often in this play) lively, humorous.

25.] an irregular line; Q2's regularisation, followed by Warnke and Proescholdt
and other editors, is unnecessary; *wild* may have been 'so emphasized as to dispense
with an unaccented syllable' (Abbott, §484).

29. *Come up*] an expression of contempt or indignation.

honey-sops] bread sops soaked in honey (a pert response to *sugar candy*).

Sybil. I'll hold my life their hunting nags be lame.
Hammon. A deer more dear is found within this place.
Rose. But not the deer, sir, which you had in chase.
Hammon. I chased the deer; but this dear chaseth me.
Rose. The strangest hunting that ever I see.　　　　　　35
　　　But where's your park?　　　　　　*She offers to go away.*
Hammon.　　　　　　'Tis here. O, stay!
Rose. Impale me, and then I will not stray.
Warner. They wrangle, wench. We are more kind than they.
Sybil. What kind of hart is that dear hart you seek?
Warner. A heart, dear heart.
Sybil.　　　　　　Whoever saw the like?　　　　40
Rose. To lose your hart? Is't possible you can?
Hammon. My heart is lost.
Rose.　　　　　　Alack, good gentleman.
Hammon. This poor lost heart would I wish you might find.
Rose. You by such luck might prove your hart a hind.
Hammon. Why, luck had horns, so have I heard some say.　　　45
Rose. Now God an't be His will send luck into your way.

32–40 deer . . . dear . . . deer . . . deer . . . dear . . . dear . . . dear] *Rhys;* deere . . . deere
. . . deere . . . deere . . . deere . . . deere . . . deare Q1.
39–44 hart . . . hart . . . heart . . . heart . . . hart . . . heart . . . heart . . . hart] *This ed.;* hart
. . . hart . . . hart . . . hart . . . heart . . . heart . . . hart . . . hart Q1.

32–40. *deer . . . dear . . . deer . . . deer . . . dear . . . dear*] Given the flexibility of
Elizabethan spelling, and the freedom taken by compositors, it is impossible to be
certain what word-play is intended, but here, as later with *hart* (ll. 39–44), the men
clearly intend the romantic sense whenever possible.

35. *see*] dialectal for 'saw', as at ii.52; here for the sake of the rhyme.

37. *Impale*] Literally (*a*) enclose with pales or stakes (but implying 'embrace'); (*b*)
thrust a pointed stake through (with bawdy implications).

38. *kind*] affectionate.

39–44. *hart . . . hart . . . heart . . . heart . . . hart . . . heart . . . heart . . . hart*] Cf. ll. 32–40,
n. We take it that in ll. 39 and 41, the girls pretend an innocent meaning, and that the
men reply with a romantic interpretation which Rose finally acknowledges by her
pun in l. 44.

44. *prove . . . hind*] i.e., if Rose found his *heart* (within herself) his *hart* (male deer)
would turn out to be a *hind* (female deer).

45. *luck . . . say*] In this wit-combat, meanings become strained. *Luck had horns*: i.e.,
was a *hart*, not a *hind*; the expression is not recorded as a proverb: it could be an
allusion to the cornucopia of Fortune.

46. *send . . . way*] Rose delicately insults Hammon by wishing he may become a
cuckold.

Enter [Sir ROGER OATLEY, *the*] Lord Mayor, *and* Servants.

Oatley. What, Master Hammon—welcome to Old Ford!
Sybil. God's pitikins, hands off, sir!—Here's my lord.
Oatley. I hear you had ill luck, and lost your game.
Hammon. 'Tis true, my lord.
Oatley.   I am sorry for the same.   50
      What gentleman is this?
Hammon.   My brother-in-law.
Oatley. You're welcome, both. Sith Fortune offers you
      Into my hands, you shall not part from hence
      Until you have refreshed your wearied limbs.
      Go, Sybil: cover the board. You shall be guest   55
      To no good cheer, but even a hunters' feast.
Hammon. I thank your lordship. [*Aside to Warner*]
                                    Cousin, on my life,
      For our lost venison, I shall find a wife.
Oatley. In, gentlemen. I'll not be absent long.
                                    Exeunt [*all except* OATLEY].
      This Hammon is a proper gentleman,   60
      A citizen by birth, fairly allied.
      How fit an husband were he for my girl!
      Well, I will in, and do the best I can
      To match my daughter to this gentleman.
                                                      Exit.

59 *Exeunt* . . . OATLEY]] *as here, Harrison; after l. 58, Q1.*

---

48. *God's pitikins*] (a mild oath) by God's pity. O.E.D. cites this as its first use of the phrase.
   hands off] presumably Warner is embracing her (cf. l. 38).
   55. *cover the board*] lay the table.
   56. *even a hunters' feast*] Cf. l. 10; apparently an apology for a hastily prepared meal: cf. 'pot-luck' (first recorded 1592). G. Turbervile, *The Noble Art of Venery*, describes how, after a hart has been killed, it is cut up and the huntsmen give to the 'Prince or chiefe personage in field, some fine sauce' so that tender morsels can be cooked and eaten on the spot (1576; repr. Oxford, 1908, p. 128).
   60. *proper*] The word had a wide range of senses. Oatley here uses it to mean that Hammon entirely conforms to his notion of what a gentleman should be.

[SCENE VII.]
Enter LACY [*as* HANS], Skipper, HODGE, *and* FIRK.

Skipper. Ik sal you wat seggen, Hans; dis skip dat comen from
Candy is al fol, by Got's sacrament, van sugar, civet,
almonds, cambric, end alle dingen—tousand tousand ding.
Nempt it, Hans, nempt it vor your meester. Daer be de bils
van laden. Your meester Simon Eyre sal hae good copen. Wat   5
seggen you, Hans?
Firk. Wat seggen de reggen de copen, slopen—laugh, Hodge,
laugh!
Lacy [*as* Hans]. *Mine liever broder Firk, bringt Meester Eyre tot*
den signe van swannekin. Daer sal you find dis skipper end   10
me. Wat seggen you, broder Firk? Doot it, Hodge! Come,
skipper!
Exeunt [LACY *as* HANS *and* Skipper].

---

9 *tot*] Warnke and Proescholdt; lot Q1.   10 *van*] Steane; vn Q1.

Sc. vii.] The scene moves back to London.

1–6. Ik . . . Hans?] 'I shall tell you what, Hans: this ship that came from Candy
[Crete] is absolutely full, by God's sacrament, of sugar, civet, almonds, cambric, and
all things—a thousand thousand things. Take it, Hans, take it for your master. There
are the bills of lading. Your master, Simon Eyre, shall have a good bargain. What do
you say, Hans?'

1–3. dis skip . . . tousand ding] 'it chanced that a Ship of the Ile of *Candy* was driuen
vpon our Coast, laden with all kind of Lawnes and Cambrickes, and other linnen
cloth . . .' (Deloney, Appendix A, p. 206).

2. civet] an animal substance used in perfumery.

4–5. bils van laden] Properly, bills of lading are given by the master to the
consigner as a receipt. Dekker seems to be using the term for its air of nautical
authenticity rather than in a precise sense.

7. Wat . . . slopen] meaningless: Firk imitates the Skipper.

9–11. Mine . . . Hodge!] 'My dear brother Firk, bring Master Eyre to the Sign of
the Swan. There you shall find this skipper and me. What do you say, brother Firk?
Do it, Hodge!'

10. signe van swannekin] The tavern-sign of a swan (cf. l. 99 below) was common
in Elizabethan London. The most famous was probably the Swan in Crooked Lane
(off New Fish Street, near London Bridge). Stow (I.219) mentions it as 'the most
ancient house in this lane . . . now called the Swan . . . possessed of strangers, and
selling of Rhenish wine'. Further from Eyre's shop in Tower Street, but closer to the
river wharfs, and, in particular, to the Steelyard (see l. 18, n.), was the Swan in
Dowgate, off Thames Street. Both these inns are mentioned by John Taylor the
Water-Poet as houses that sell Rhenish wine and are 'inhabited by onely Dutchmen'
(*Taylors Travels . . . through . . . London and Westminster*, 1636, sig. D7). Dekker may,
however, have picked up the name from Deloney (cf. Appendix A, p. 216).

Firk. 'Bring him,' quoth you? Here's no knavery, to bring
my master to buy a ship worth the lading of two or
three hundred thousand pounds. Alas, that's nothing—a   15
trifle, a bauble, Hodge.

Hodge. The truth is, Firk, that the merchant owner of the ship
dares not show his head, and therefore this skipper, that
deals for him, for the love he bears to Hans offers my
master Eyre a bargain in the commodities. He shall have   20
a reasonable day of payment. He may sell the wares by
that time, and be an huge gainer himself.

Firk. Yea, but can my fellow Hans lend my master twenty
porpentines as an earnest-penny?

Hodge. 'Portagues' thou wouldst say—here they be, Firk: 25
hark, they jingle in my pocket like Saint Mary Overy's
bells.

---

14. *worth the lading of*] of which the cargo is worth (again, suggestive of nautical
jargon).

14–15. *two or three hundred thousand pounds*] An absurdly large sum considering the
nature of the ship's cargo; the richest Spanish treasure-ship captured by Elizabeth's
navy was worth only £141,000 (J. E. Neale, *Queen Elizabeth I*, 1934; Harmondsworth, 1960, p. 331). In Deloney £3,000 is necessary to secure the cargo, which can
later be sold for 'three and three thousand pounds profit' (Appendix A, p. 208).
Dekker's figures are intended to be impressive, but it is possible that he originally
wrote 'two or three hundred' and substituted 'thousand' for 'hundred', but that the
printer reproduced both. See also ix.70 and n.

18. *dares . . . head*] No explanation is offered. Sutherland says 'Dekker may have
been indebted to a contemporary event, the closing of the Stilliard or Steelyard, the
headquarters of the Hanseatic traders in London. In 1597 Elizabeth withdrew all the
privileges that the Hanse had enjoyed, and expelled the merchants from the country.
Those who lingered on to wind up their affairs were naturally afraid to "show their
heads", and, if they had any cargoes to dispose of, would gladly seize any chance to
get rid of them, even at a serious loss. In Deloney's narrative the ship that enriches
Eyre has been wrecked on the coast.' Cf. l. 146 and n. (By a curious coincidence the
Steelyard soon joined the Swan (see l. 10, n.) as a resort of Dutchmen, noted for its
Rhenish wine (Sugden), and a scene in Dekker and Webster's *Westward Ho* (II.iii)
takes place there, with wine served by Hans ('Butterbox'), a Dutchman.)

20. *commodities*] merchandise.

24. *porpentines*] porcupines; Firk's mistake for 'portagues'; see i.90, n.
earnest-penny] down-payment.

26–7. *Saint Mary Overy's bells*] The church of Saint Mary Overy, in Southwark,
near London Bridge, so called because it was 'over' the river from London (Sugden).
The large bell-tower was not erected until the sixteenth century.

27.] Harrison places the first three-man's song here. Certainly Firk sings something (cf. l. 32), but there is no cue for a formal song.

Enter EYRE *and* [MARGERY] *his wife* [*and a* Boy].

Firk. Mum, here comes my dame and my master. She'll
scold, on my life, for loitering this Monday. But all's
one. Let them all say what they can, Monday's our   30
holiday.

Margery. You sing, Sir Sauce, but I beshrew your heart,
I fear for this your singing we shall smart.

Firk. Smart for me, dame? Why, dame, why?

Hodge. Master, I hope you'll not suffer my dame to take   35
down your journeymen.

Firk. If she take me down, I'll take her up—yea, and take her
down, too, a buttonhole lower.

Eyre. Peace, Firk. Not I, Hodge. By the life of Pharaoh, by
the Lord of Ludgate, by this beard, every hair whereof I   40
value at a king's ransom, she shall not meddle with you.

27.1. *Boy*] Q1 provides no entry for him: his only function in this scene is to fetch
beer (ll. 76 ff.). His entry might be delayed till he has been given this duty (cf. iv.114),
or he might be brought on at the beginning of the scene (cf. xiii.0.2). Here, as in sc.
iv, Dekker has not fully worked out the mechanics of the staging, which might have
been adjusted in performance.

30–1. *Monday's our holiday*] Monday was a traditional holiday for shoemakers,
giving rise to the phrase 'Cobbler's Monday' recorded in *Dialect Dict.* Cf. Dekker's
The Honest Whore: 'would I had bin created a Shoomaker; for all the gentle craft are
gentlemen euery Monday by their Copy, and scorne (then) to worke one true stitch'
(IV.i.2–4). There may be some connection with the Monday market day (see
xxi.158–9, 161–2 n.), perhaps because workmen were given the day off while
employers attended the market.

32. *Sir Sauce*] a common way of addressing an impudent person, also used by
Eyre's wife in Deloney (Appendix A, p. 215); cf. *K.B.P.*, III. 525.

beshrew] curse, blame greatly.

33. *singing . . . smart*] In the light of what follows, this may have bawdy
implications. *Sing* could mean 'to coït with' (Partridge), whence *smart* could allude
to the pains of venereal disease.

35–6. *take down*] rebuke, humiliate (with a bawdy quibble).

37. *take . . . up*] reprove.

37–8. *take . . . lower*] proverbial (Tilley, P181, 'I will take you a peg (buttonhole,
hole) lower', modern 'take down a peg or two'); here with bawdy implications in
'buttonhole'.

39–40. *life . . . Ludgate*] Cf. i.173–5, and n.

40–1. *every . . . ransom*] repeated at xxi. 21–3.

41. *meddle*] (with a bawdy quibble).

Peace, you bombast-cotton-candle quean, away, Queen
of Clubs, quarrel not with me and my men, with me
and my fine Firk. I'll firk you if you do.

Margery. Yea, yea, man, you may use me as you please—but   45
let that pass.

Eyre. Let it pass, let it vanish away. Peace, am I not Simon
Eyre? Are not these my brave men, brave shoemakers,
all gentlemen of the Gentle Craft? Prince am I none, yet
am I nobly born, as being the sole son of a shoemaker.   50
Away, rubbish. Vanish, melt, melt like kitchen-stuff.

Margery. Yea, yea, 'tis well. I must be called rubbish, kitchen-
stuff, for a sort of knaves.

Firk. Nay, dame, you shall not weep and wail in woe for me.
Master, I'll stay no longer. Here's a venentory of my   55
shop tools. Adieu, master. Hodge, farewell.

Hodge. Nay, stay, Firk, thou shalt not go alone.

Margery. I pray, let them go. There be more maids than

---

47 Let it pass, let it vanish away] *Q1;* Let it pass? Let it vanish away! *Palmer.*

---

42. *bombast-cotton-candle quean*] Cf. i.219–20.

42–3. *Queen of Clubs*] another of Eyre's jovial insults, combining associations with
card-games, clubs as weapons, and 'Clubs!' as the apprentices' rallying-cry; cf. xviii.
31–2, and n.

44. *firk*] See note to *Dram. Per.*, 19.

45. *use*] (with sexual innuendo).

47. Palmer's interpretation ('Let it pass? Let it vanish away!') is attractive,
particularly because it is in keeping with Eyre's usual habit of contradicting his wife.

49–50. *Prince . . . born*] For Dekker's use of Eyre's motto, see Introduction, pp. 17
and 39. His immediate source is Deloney. W. F. McNeir attributes 'the precise
phrasing of the idea' to Greene's *Orlando Furioso*: 'I am no king, yet am I princely
born' (I.i.93) ('The Source of Simon Eyre's Catch-phrase', *M.L.N.*, 53 (1938),
275–6).

50. *sole*] (punningly).

51. *kitchen-stuff*] kitchen-refuse. Cf. *The Gentle Craft, Part Two*: 'fie how hee
stinkes of Kitchin stuffe' (p. 253) and Dekker's *The Wonderful Year*, 'more greasy
than a kitchen-stuff wife's basket' (Pendry, p. 61).

53. *sort*] gang.

54. *wail in woe*] Firk may allude to the ballad 'I waile in wo, I plunge in pain'
(printed in Clement Robinson's *A Handful of Pleasant Delights* (1584), ed. H. E.
Rollins, Cambridge, Mass., 1924, pp. 65–8), also mentioned in *Eastward Ho* (Jonson,
Chapman, and Marston, ed. C. G. Petter, New Mermaids, London, 1973, V.v.40).

55. *venentory*] Firk's mistake for 'inventory'.

58–9. *more . . . Malkin*] This proverbial expression, well established by Dekker's

Malkin, more men than Hodge, and more fools than
Firk.   60

Firk. Fools? 'Nails, if I tarry now, I would my guts might be
turned to shoe-thread.

Hodge. And if I stay, I pray God I may be turned to a Turk
and set in Finsbury for boys to shoot at. Come, Firk.

Eyre. Stay, my fine knaves, you arms of my trade, you pillars   65
of my profession. What, shall a tittle-tattle's words
make you forsake Simon Eyre? Avaunt, kitchen-stuff;
rip, you brown-bread Tannikin, out of my sight! Move
me not. Have not I ta'en you from selling tripes in
Eastcheap, and set you in my shop, and made you   70
hail-fellow with Simon Eyre the shoemaker? And now
do you deal thus with my journeymen? Look, you
powder-beef quean, on the face of Hodge. Here's a face
for a lord.

Firk. And here's a face for any lady in Christendom.   75

Eyre. Rip, you chitterling, avaunt! Boy, bid the tapster of the

---

76 chitterling, avaunt! Boy,] *Warnke and Proescholdt;* chitterling, auaunt boy, *Q1.*

---

time (Tilley, M39), occurs in *The Gentle Craft, Part Two,* chapter iii (p. 195). Malkin,
or Mawkin, was common as a girl's name.

61. *'Nails*] See iv.78, n.

61–2. *I would . . . shoe-thread*] a variant on the proverb 'To make garters of a man's
guts' (recorded in *O.D.E.P.* from *c.* 1591; not in Tilley).

63–4. *Turk . . . Finsbury*] Representations of Turks were used as targets for archery.
A parish account of the period has 'Item, making a Turk for shott, boards, nails and
making xviiid.' (quoted in *Shakespeare's England,* II.384). Finsbury was a training
ground for archery (see i.61, n.).

68. *rip*] run away (cf. xx.11).

brown-bread Tannikin] Brown bread was coarser than white. *Tannikin,* a familiar
form of Anne, or Anna, was normally a colloquial name for a Dutchwoman, as in
Dekker's *Patient Grissil* (III.ii.243).

Move] anger.

70. *Eastcheap*] a London street to the west of, and running into, Tower Street.
(Eyre's courting apparently took place close to home, as it does in Deloney: '*Simon
. . .* fell in loue with a Maiden that was a neere neighbor vnto him' (Appendix A, p.
206).) Stow (I.216) describes Eastcheap as 'a flesh Market of Butchers . . . on both
sides of the streete'.

73. *powder-beef quean*] Cf. iv.4–5, and n.

76. *chitterling*] pig's intestines fried for food.

Boar's Head fill me a dozen cans of beer for my journeymen.

Firk. A dozen cans! O brave, Hodge—now I'll stay!

Eyre. [*Aside to the Boy*] An the knave fills any more than two,   80
he pays for them.   [*Exit.* Boy.]
[*Aloud*] A dozen cans of beer for my journeymen!

[*Enter the* Boy *with two cans, and exit.*]

Here, you mad Mesopotamians, wash your livers with
this liquor. Where be the odd ten? No more, Madge; no
more. Well said, drink and to work. What work dost   85
thou, Hodge? What work?

Hodge. I am a-making a pair of shoes for my Lord Mayor's
daughter, Mistress Rose.

Firk. And I a pair of shoes for Sybil, my Lord's maid. I deal
with her.   90

Eyre. Sybil? Fie, defile not thy fine, workmanly fingers with
the feet of kitchen-stuff and basting-ladles. Ladies of the
Court, fine ladies, my lads, commit their feet to our
apparelling. Put gross work to Hans. Yerk and seam,
yerk and seam.   95

Firk. For yerking and seaming let me alone, an I come to't.

Hodge. Well, master, all this is from the bias. Do you

---

77. *Boar's Head*] The most famous of several London inns of this name, and the
nearest to Eyre's shop in Tower Street, was the Boar's Head near Saint Michael's
Lane in Eastcheap, the setting for several scenes in Shakespeare's *H4*. No definite
record of an inn here exists before 1537. Though Eastcheap adjoined Tower Street,
the speed of the boy's return shows scant regard for credibility.

83. *Mesopotamians*] of no obvious significance; probably just one of Eyre's
grandiloquent terms of address.

84. *Where . . . ten*] (He pretends to call for the drinks he has not ordered.)

84–5. *No more . . . more*] Presumably he silences Margery; though this could refer
to the fact that he does not intend to order more beer.

85. *Well said*] (commonly used to mean 'Well done').

89. *deal*] (with sexual innuendo).

92. *basting-ladles*] (seems to be used as a vague term of abuse for the servant).

94. *Yerk*] sew (leather). Firk characteristically sees bawdy possibilities (cf. xiii. 28).

96. *let . . . to't*] trust me to do it thoroughly, if I'm put to the test.

97. *from the bias*] off the point (a commonplace metaphor from bowls; cf. i.85).

remember the ship my fellow Hans told you of? The
skipper and he are both drinking at the Swan. Here be
the portagues to give earnest. If you go through with it,   100
you cannot choose but be a lord at least.

Firk. Nay, dame, if my master prove not a lord, and you a
lady, hang me.

Margery. Yea, like enough, if you may loiter and tipple thus.

Firk. Tipple, dame? No, we have been bargaining with   105
Skellum-Skanderbag-can-you-Dutch-spreaken for a
ship of silk cypress, laden with sugar candy.

> *Enter the* Boy *with a velvet coat and an Alderman's gown.*
> Eyre *puts it on.*

Eyre. Peace, Firk. Silence, tittle-tattle. Hodge, I'll go through
with it. Here's a seal ring, and I have sent for a guarded

106 Skellum-Skanderbag-can-you-Dutch-spreaken] *cf. Lange;* Skellum Skanderbag: can you Dutch spreaken *Q1.*

---

100. *give earnest*] put down as an advance.

102–3. *if . . . lady*] In Deloney, this is Eyre's motive for buying the ship's cargo:
'Beleeue me wife, quoth he, I was studying how to make my selfe Lord Maior, and
thee a Lady' (Appendix A, p. 207).

106. *Skellum-Skanderbag-can-you-Dutch-spreaken*] Lange does not hyphenate, but
is clearly right to interpret this as Firk's composite name for the Skipper. *Skellum* was
a word for a rogue. *Skanderbag* is a corruption of Iskander Bey, the Turkish name for
an Albanian, George Castriota, a Christian hero who expelled the Turks from
Albania in the fifteenth century. *The historie of George Castriot, surnamed Scanderbeg,
King of Albania,* by Jacques de la Vardin, had been published in translation in 1596.
Here, the name is simply derisory.

spreaken] speak. The inversion, *Dutch spreaken,* suggests that Firk is imitating
Lacy's pseudo-Dutch.

107. *ship . . . candy*] Firk is characteristically confused. The ship came from *Candy,*
and was laden with cambric and sugar (cf. ll. 1–2).

cypress] a fabric, originally from Cyprus.

107. 1–2.] This direction shows Dekker both giving a practical stage-direction
(*Enter the* Boy) and anticipating future action (*Eyre puts it on*). For practical purposes,
the Boy must enter at some point before 'See where it comes' (l. 110), and Eyre must
begin to put on the gown at 'Help me, Firk' (l. 111). (The slight vagueness reflects
the fact that the play was printed from authorial copy that had not been fully
prepared for the theatre; see Introduction, p. 55.) On Dekker's adaptation of
Deloney's account of Eyre's disguise, see Introduction, p. 21.

109–10. *seal ring . . . guarded gown . . . damask cassock*] The details are from Deloney;
cf. Appendix A, p. 210.

109. *guarded*] ornamented, braided.

gown and a damask cassock. See where it comes. Look   110
here, Madgy. Help me, Firk. Apparel me, Hodge. Silk
and satin, you mad Philistines, silk and satin!

Firk. Ha, ha! My master will be as proud as a dog in a doublet,
all in beaten damask and velvet.

Eyre. Softly, Firk, for rearing of the nap and wearing thread-   115
bare my garments. How dost thou like me, Firk? How
do I look, my fine Hodge?

Hodge. Why, now you look like yourself, master. I warrant
you there's few in the City but will give you the wall,
and come upon you with the 'Right Worshipful'.   120

Firk. 'Nails, my master looks like a threadbare cloak new
turned and dressed. Lord, Lord, to see what good rai-
ment doth. Dame, dame, are you not enamoured?

Eyre. How sayst thou, Madgy; am I not brisk? Am I not fine?

Margery. Fine? By my troth, sweetheart, very fine. By my   125
troth, I never liked thee so well in my life, sweetheart—
but let that pass. I warrant there be many women in the
City have not such handsome husbands, but only for
their apparel—but let that pass, too.

Enter [LACY *as*] HANS *and* Skipper.

129.1 *Lacy* [as Hans]] *From this point to the end of the play, Q1 uses 'Hans' as the speech-prefix for Lacy.*

---

112. *mad Philistines*] another of Eyre's mouth-filling phrases, of no precise significance, though *Philistine* was later used for a drunkard: cf. Henley and Farmer, and F.
Grose, *A Classical Dictionary of the Vulgar Tongue* (1796), ed. E. Partridge (1963).

113. *as proud . . . doublet*] proverbial (Tilley, D452).

114. *beaten*] embroidered.

115. *Softly*] 'Take it easy.'

for rearing of] so as not to raise. Firk is behaving exuberantly.

119. *give you the wall*] give you precedence (i.e., when passing you in the street,
allow you to be nearest to the wall in the interests of both cleanliness and security
from attack).

120. *come upon you with*] address you as.

'*Right Worshipful*'] (the proper form of address for an alderman).

122. *dressed*] adorned.

124. *brisk*] spruce.

128. *but only for*] except merely in.(Margery's syntax is awkward; her husband's
new apparel seems to have awakened in her a fresh appreciation of his intrinsic
qualities.)

Lacy [*as Hans*]. *Godden day, meester; dis be de skipper dat heb de*   130
skip van marchandice. De commodity ben good. Nempt it,
meester; nempt it.

Eyre. Godamercy, Hans. Welcome, skipper. Where lies this
ship of merchandise?

Skipper. De skip ben in revere. Dor be van sugar, civet, almonds,   135
cambric, end a tousand tousand tings, Got's sacrament!
Nempt it, meester; you sal heb good copen.

Firk. To him, master. O sweet master! O sweet wares!
Prunes, almonds, sugar candy, carrot-roots, turnips—O, brave fatting meat! Let not a man buy a   140
nutmeg but yourself.

Eyre. Peace, Firk. Come, skipper, I'll go aboard with you.
Hans, have you made him drink?

Skipper. Yaw, yaw. Ik heb veale gedrunck.

Eyre. Come, Hans; follow me. Skipper, thou shalt have my   145
countenance in the City.

                    Exeunt [EYRE, Skipper, *and* LACY *as* HANS].

135 *revere*] *Warnke and Proescholdt; rouere Q1.*
142 *aboard*] *Q3; abroade Q1.*

130–32. Godden . . . meester; nempt it] 'Good-day, master; this is the skipper who
owns the ship of merchandise. The commodity is good. Take it, master: take it.'

133. Godamercy] thank you.

135–7. De . . . copen] 'The ship is in the river. There are sugar, civet, almonds,
cambric, and a thousand thousand things, by God's sacrament! Take it, master; you
shall have a good bargain.'

139–40. carrot-roots, turnips] Steane, followed by Davies, links these with the rest
of the list with the claim that they were 'still exotic vegetables'. But according to
Shakespeare's England (II.138), carrots, like radishes, cost 2d a bunch; and Anne Page
imagines the fate of being 'set quick i' the garden, / And bowled to death with
turnips' (*M.W.W.*, III.iv.90–1). The explanation surely is that Firk, who has already
confused 'Candy' and *sugar candy* (l. 107), now mistakes 'cambric' as *carrots*, and adds
turnips by association.

140. brave fatting meat] fine, fattening food.

141. nutmeg] i.e., 'even so small a thing as a nutmeg'.

142. aboard] J. C. Maxwell, reviewing Palmer's edition (*N. & Q.*, New Series 23
(1976), 259) defends Q1's 'abroade' on the grounds that Eyre's next remark ('countenance in the City') 'suggests a walk "abroad" as plausible'. But the probable
implication of *countenance* makes this unlikely.

143. made him drink] perhaps no more than hospitality; but perhaps with an
ulterior motive.

144. Yaw . . . gedrunck] 'Yes, yes. I have drunk a lot.'

146. countenance] support, patronage; Eyre seems to promise protection against the
danger alluded to earlier; cf. l. 18 and n.

Firk. '*Yaw heb veale gedrunck*', quotha! They may well be
called butter-boxes when they drink fat veal, and thick
beer too. But come, dame; I hope you'll chide us no
more.   150

Margery. No, faith, Firk. No, perdie, Hodge. I do feel honour
creep upon me, and, which is more, a certain rising in
my flesh—but let that pass.

Firk. Rising in your flesh do you feel, say you? Ay, you may
be with child; but why should not my master feel a   155
rising in his flesh, having a gown and a gold ring on! But
you are such a shrew, you'll soon pull him down.

Margery. Ha, ha! Prithee, peace, thou makest my worship
laugh—but let that pass. Come, I'll go in. Hodge,
prithee, go before me. Firk, follow me!   160

Firk. Firk doth follow. Hodge, pass out in state!

Exeunt.

[SCENE VIII.]
Enter [*the* Earl of] LINCOLN *and* DODGER.

Lincoln. How now, good Dodger, what's the news in France?

Dodger. My lord, upon the eighteen day of May

---

147. *quotha!*] says he!, indeed!

148. *butter-boxes*] Cf. iv.57.

veal] The pun occurs in *L.L.L.*, V.ii.247: ' "Veal" quoth the Dutchman. Is not
"veal" a calf?'

thick] extra-strong; cf. iv.100. The Dutch were proverbially heavy drinkers.

151. *perdie*] (a mild oath) by God, indeed.

152–3 *rising . . . pass*] As often, Margery catches herself out in a subconscious
double-meaning. Her intended meaning seems to be 'elevation of status'.

154–5. *you . . . child*] not to be taken too seriously; but cf. xxi.29–32.

155–6. *why . . . ring on*] with bawdy innuendo: the gown and ring are marks of a
bridegroom as well as of an alderman.

157. *pull him down*] (a) humble him; (b) (in a sexual sense).

158. *my worship*] (comic affectation of the status of an alderman's wife).

159–60. *Hodge . . . before me*] She makes a stately exit, preceded by her husband's
foreman. Lange compares Massinger, *The City Madam*: 'this usher / Succeeded in the
eldest 'prentice's place / To walk before you' (ed. Cyrus Hoy, Regents Renaissance
Drama Series, London, 1964, IV.iv.98–100).

2–10.] The circumstantial account of the battle creates a sense of authenticity,
reinforced by the echo of *H5* in ll. 8–10, but it has no historical basis.

2. *eighteen*] eighteenth.

The French and English were prepared to fight.
Each side with eager fury gave the sign
Of a most hot encounter. Five long hours   5
Both armies fought together. At the length
The lot of victory fell on our sides.
Twelve thousand of the Frenchmen that day died,
Four thousand English, and no man of name
But Captain Hyam and young Ardington.   10

Lincoln. Two gallant gentlemen; I knew them well.
But, Dodger, prithee tell me, in this fight
How did my cousin Lacy bear himself?

Dodger. My lord, your cousin Lacy was not there.

Lincoln. Not there?

Dodger.   No, my good lord.

Lincoln.   Sure, thou mistakest.   15
I saw him shipped, and a thousand eyes beside
Were witnesses of the farewells which he gave
When I with weeping eyes bid him adieu.
Dodger, take heed.

Dodger.   My lord, I am advised
That what I spake is true. To prove it so,   20
His cousin Askew, that supplied his place,
Sent me for him from France that secretly

---

11 *This line is attributed to Dodger in Qq. The emendation was made by Sutherland.*

8–10. *Twelve thousand . . . Ardington*] Cf. Shakespeare's adaptation of Holinshed's account of the battle of Agincourt (*H5*, IV.viii.78–104), especially ll. 102–4: 'Sir Richard Kikely, Davy Gam, Esquire; / None else of name; and of all other men / But five and twenty.'

10. *Hyam . . . Ardington*] Chandler finds historical bearers of these names during Eyre's period (cf. notes on *Dram. Per.*), but they do not occur in Elizabethan historical accounts of the French wars of the fifteenth century, and their presence in a passage of invented circumstantial detail needs no external explanation.

17. *witnesses*] Q3's alteration, 'witness', improves the metre but is unnecessary because the plurals of nouns ending in *s* were frequently pronounced without the additional syllable (Abbott, §471, quoting, *inter alia, Cor.*, III.iii.124: 'As the dead carcasses of unburied men').

19. *advised*] sure.

22. *Sent me for him from France*] i.e., sent me from France to fetch him. Considering what Lacy has told him at i.196–202, Askew's choice of messenger seems unwise.

> He might convey himself thither.
>
> *Lincoln.*   Is't even so?
> Dares he so carelessly venture his life
> Upon the indignation of a king?   25
> Hath he despised my love, and spurned those favours
> Which I with prodigal hand poured on his head?
> He shall repent his rashness with his soul.
> Since of my love he makes no estimate,
> I'll make him wish he had not known my hate.   30
> Thou hast no other news?
>
> *Dodger.*   None else, my lord.
>
> *Lincoln.* None worse I know thou hast. Procure the King
> To crown his giddy brows with ample honours,
> Send him chief colonel, and all my hope
> Thus to be dashed?—but 'tis in vain to grieve.   35
> One evil cannot a worse relieve.
> Upon my life, I have found out his plot.
> That old dog love that fawned upon him so,
> Love to that puling girl, his fair-cheeked Rose,
> The Lord Mayor's daughter, hath distracted him,   40
> And in the fire of that love's lunacy
> Hath he burnt up himself, consumed his credit,
> Lost the King's love, yea and, I fear, his life,
> Only to get a wanton to his wife.
> Dodger, it is so.

23 thither] *Fritsche;* hither *Q1.*

---

   23. *thither*] The emendation seems necessary. Askew has sent Dodger to recall
Lacy back to his duties (cf. i.100–5). Early editors (e.g. Warnke and Proescholdt,
Rhys, Sutherland) emend. Lange, who emends, says that Q's 'hither' 'may be
defended on the ground that Dodger is reporting Askew's message'. This seems
strained. Spencer prints *hither* but glosses 'i.e., thither', without justification.
Modern editors, following Bowers, neither emend nor discuss, with the exception
of Sanna who accepts Lange's explanation of *hither.*
   29. *of . . . estimate*] he puts no value on my love.
   32. *Procure*] i.e., 'to think that I prevailed upon . . .'.
   33. *giddy*] frivolous.
   34. *colonel*] (three syllables).
   36. *One evil cannot a worse relieve*] (not recorded as proverbial).
   39. *puling*] whining.
   42. *credit*] reputation (as well as 'financial resources').
   43. *his life*] (because the punishment for desertion would be execution).
   44. *to his*] as his.

Dodger.   I fear so, my good lord.   45
Lincoln. It is so.—Nay, sure it cannot be.
   I am at my wits' end. Dodger—
Dodger.   Yea, my lord?
Lincoln. Thou art acquainted with my nephew's haunts.
   Spend this gold for thy pains. Go seek him out.
   Watch at my Lord Mayor's. There if he live,   50
   Dodger, thou shalt be sure to meet with him.
   Prithee, be diligent. Lacy, thy name
   Lived once in honour, now dead in shame!
   Be circumspect.   *Exit.*
Dodger.   I warrant you, my lord.   *Exit.*

[SCENE IX.]
Enter [Sir ROGER OATLEY, *the*] Lord Mayor, *and* Master SCOTT.

Oatley. Good Master Scott, I have been bold with you
   To be a witness to a wedding knot
   Betwixt young Master Hammon and my daughter.
   O, stand aside. See where the lovers come.

Enter HAMMON *and* ROSE.

Rose. Can it be possible you love me so?   5
   No, no; within those eyeballs I espy
   Apparent likelihoods of flattery.
   Pray now, let go my hand.
Hammon.   Sweet Mistress Rose,
   Misconstrue not my words, nor misconceive

47 end. Dodger—] *Warnke and Proescholdt (end. Dodger!);* end Dodger. *Q1.*
53 now dead] *Q1;* [is] now dead *Fritsche;* now 'tis dead *Warnke and Proescholdt.*

---

   47. *at my wits' end*] already a standard expression (Tilley, W 575); it occurs again at
xx.13.
   50. *There . . . live*] i.e., if he is staying there (not 'if he is still alive'). Lincoln's
opinion that Oatley is hiding Lacy is corrected at xvi.6–11.
   2. *witness . . . knot*] Scott has been called as formal witness to a betrothal ceremony.
(On the custom, see, e.g., E. Schanzer, 'The Marriage-Contracts in *Measure for
Measure*', *Sh.S.* 13, 1960, 81–9.) This would be legally binding, and would be
marked by the joining of hands. This solemn moment is shattered by Hammon's and
Rose's last-minute withdrawal (l. 29).
   9. *Misconstrue*] (accented on the second syllable).

    Of my affection, whose devoted soul   10
    Swears that I love thee dearer than my heart.
Rose. As dear as your own heart? I judge it right:
    Men love their hearts best when they're out of sight.
Hammon. I love you, by this hand.
Rose.   Yet hands off, now.
    If flesh be frail, how weak and frail's your vow!   15
Hammon. Then by my life I swear.
Rose.   Then do not brawl.
    One quarrel loseth wife and life and all.
    Is not your meaning thus?
Hammon.   In faith, you jest.
Rose. Love loves to sport; therefore leave love, you're best.
Oatley. What, square they, Master Scott?
Scott.   Sir, never doubt.   20
    Lovers are quickly in and quickly out.
Hammon. Sweet Rose, be not so strange in fancying me.
    Nay, never turn aside. Shun not my sight.
    I am not grown so fond to fond my love
    On any that shall quit it with disdain.   25
    If you will love me, so. If not, farewell.
Oatley. Why, how now, lovers; are you both agreed?
Hammon. Yes, faith, my lord.
Oatley.   'Tis well. Give me your hand;

28–30] *as verse, Fritsche; as prose, Q1.*

---

    11. *Swears*] Rose's objections to the subjects of Hammon's oaths (*heart . . . hand . . . life*) may recall Juliet's similar objections (*R.&J.*, II.ii) in a scene also echoed in sc. xii (see xii.o, n.). Another parallel occurs in *R3*, IV.iv.373 ff.
    15. *If . . . frail*] Matthew xxvi.41: 'The flesh is weak'; and Tilley, F363, 'Flesh is frail'.
    16. *brawl*] wrangle, squabble (presumably Hammon is losing his patience).
    19. *sport*] (*a*) jest; (*b*) toy.
    therefore] i.e., since you object to jesting.
    20. *square*] wrangle.
    22. *strange in fancying*] an odd expression: 'reluctant to love'; or, perhaps, 'strained, perverse in the expression of your love'.
    24. *so fond to fond*] *so fond*, so foolish; *to fond* is probably a variant, for the sake of word-play, of 'to found', i.e., to establish.
    25. *quit*] requite, respond to.

Give me yours, daughter. How now—both pull back!
What means this, girl?
Rose.   I mean to live a maid.   30
Hammon. (Aside) But not to die one. Pause ere that be said.
Oatley. Will you still cross me, still be obstinate?
Hammon. Nay, chide her not, my lord, for doing well.
     If she can live an happy virgin's life,
     'Tis far more blessèd than to be a wife.   35
Rose. Say, sir, I cannot. I have made a vow:
     Whoever be my husband, 'tis not you.
Oatley. Your tongue is quick. But, Master Hammon, know
     I bade you welcome to another end.
Hammon. What, would you have me pule, and pine, and
          pray,   40
     With 'lovely lady', 'mistress of my heart',
     'Pardon your servant', and the rhymer play,
          Railing on Cupid and his tyrant's dart?
     Or shall I undertake some martial spoil,
     Wearing your glove at tourney and at tilt,   45
     And tell how many gallants I unhorsed?
     Sweet, will this pleasure you?
Rose.   Yea; when wilt begin?
     What, love-rhymes, man? Fie on that deadly sin!
Oatley. If you will have her, I'll make her agree.
Hammon. Enforcèd love is worse than hate to me.   50
     [*Aside*] There is a wench keeps shop in the Old Change.

---

     32. *still*] continually, persistently.

     34–5. *If . . . wife*] a commonplace sentiment (cf. *M.N.D.*, I.i.74–5), ultimately
deriving from I Corinthians, vii.8: 'I say therfore to the vnmaried and widowes, it is
good for them if they abide euen as I.'

     37. *you*] Rhyme seems to require 'thou', which may have been the reading of the
manuscript, but Rose has addressed Hammon as *you* throughout the scene.

     39. *to another end*] with something else in mind.

     40. *pule*] whine.

     42. *rhymer*] versifier (*O.E.D.* first records in 1639); perhaps with the sense of 'one
who uses verse for deceitful purposes'.

     44. *spoil*] expedition.

     45. *glove*] (as a favour).

     48. *deadly sin*] (mischievous hyperbole).

     51. *wench*] (Jane (see xii.1), though this is the first we have heard of Hammon's
interest in her).

To her will I. It is not wealth I seek.
I have enough, and will prefer her love
Before the world. [*To Oatley*] My good Lord Mayor,
    adieu.
[*Aside*] Old love for me—I have no luck with new.   55
                                                           Exit.

Oatley. [*To Rose*] Now, mammet, you have well behaved
    yourself.
But you shall curse your coyness, if I live.
—Who's within, there? See you convey your mistress
Straight to th'Old Ford. [*To Rose*] I'll keep you strait
    enough.
—Fore God, I would have sworn the puling girl   60
Would willingly accepted Hammon's love.
But banish him, my thoughts.—Go, minion, in.   *Exit* ROSE.
Now tell me, Master Scott, would you have thought
That Master Simon Eyre, the shoemaker,
Had been of wealth to buy such merchandise?   65

Old Change] a street in London running between Knightrider Street and West
Cheap, and so called after 1566 when Sir Thomas Gresham's new (Royal) Exchange
was opened. By Dekker's time the latter was clearly a more notable location for
haberdashers' and milliners' shops (the trade in which Jane is engaged in sc. xii), and
the women who kept them seem to have been of doubtful reputation (see xii.0.1, n.).

55. *Old love*] The implication of earlier acquaintance between Hammon and Jane
need not be taken seriously; Dekker uses the simplest means of moving Hammon
from one plot to the next, but reinforces the suggestion at xii.3. (On the interaction
of plots and time-scheme, see Introduction, p. 23.)

56. *mammet*] doll, puppet; a term of abuse derived from 'Mahomet'. The word
occurs (with *puling*, cf. ll. 40 and 60) in a passage of similar import in *R.&J.*, where
Capulet berates Juliet:

> And then to have a wretched puling fool,
> A whining mammet, in her fortune's tender,
> To answer 'I'll not wed, I cannot love'. (III.v.184–6)

57. *coyness*] reluctance.
58. *within*] Either Oatley calls to someone who remains offstage, or a servant
enters to *convey* Rose.
59. *Straight . . . strait*] immediately . . . strictly.
61. *Would willingly accepted*] (an ellipsis for the metre).
62. *minion*] hussy (also used by Capulet in a similar situation; *R.&J.*, III.v.151).

Scott. 'Twas well, my lord, your honour and myself
    Grew partners with him; for your bills of lading
    Show that Eyre's gains in one commodity
    Rise at the least to full three thousand pound,
    Besides like gain in other merchandise.   70
Oatley. Well, he shall spend some of his thousands now,
    For I have sent for him to the Guildhall.

Enter EYRE.

    See where he comes. Good morrow, Master Eyre.
Eyre. Poor Simon Eyre, my lord, your shoemaker.
Oatley. Well, well, it likes yourself to term you so.   75

Enter DODGER.

    Now, Master Dodger, what's the news with you?
Dodger. I'ld gladly speak in private to your honour.
Oatley. You shall, you shall. Master Eyre, and Master Scott,
    I have some business with this gentleman.
    I pray, let me entreat you to walk before   80
    To the Guildhall. I'll follow presently.
    Master Eyre, I hope ere noon to call you sheriff.
Eyre. I would not care, my lord, if you might call me King of
    Spain. Come, Master Scott.   [*Exeunt* EYRE *and* SCOTT.]

67 him; . . . lading] Q3 (him, . . . lading); him . . . lading, Q1.
75.1 *Enter* DODGER] *as here, Fritsche; after l. 76, Q1.*

66–7. *your honour . . . him*] Again, submerged narrative based on Deloney is
implied (Appendix A, p. 213).

67. *bills of lading*] Cf. vii.4–5, n.

70. *like . . . merchandise*] This appears to be related to Deloney's statement that the
ship's cargo would raise 'three and three thousand pounds profit' (Appendix A, p.
208). But cf. vii.14–15, and n.

73. *Master*] The title implies distinction. The Lord Mayor's use of it to Eyre is a
landmark in Deloney's story, too (Appendix A, p. 212).

75. *likes*] pleases.

so] i.e., *Poor*, whereas they know him to be wealthy.

82. *sheriff*] In Deloney, Eyre shows himself well aware of both the high status and
the responsibilities of the office (Appendix A, pp. 213–14). The Corporation
annually elected two sheriffs; they exercised considerable legal authority. The lists in
Stow's *Survey* show that Eyre was one of several sheriffs who later became Lord Mayor.

83–4. *I . . . Spain*] probably flippant: 'you are as likely to call me King of Spain'.
(Its regular treasure-ships from the New World gave Spain a reputation for great
wealth at this time.)

Oatley. Now, Master Dodger, what's the news you bring?   85
Dodger. The Earl of Lincoln by me greets your lordship
          And earnestly requests you, if you can,
          Inform him where his nephew Lacy keeps.
Oatley. Is not his nephew Lacy now in France?
Dodger. No, I assure your lordship, but disguised   90
          Lurks here in London.
Oatley.   London? Is't even so?
          It may be, but, upon my faith and soul,
          I know not where he lives, or whether he lives.
          So tell my Lord of Lincoln.—Lurch in London?
          Well, Master Dodger, you perhaps may start him.   95
          Be but the means to rid him into France,
          I'll give you a dozen angels for your pains,
          So much I love his honour, hate his nephew;
          And, prithee, so inform thy lord from me.
Dodger. I take my leave.   *Exit* DODGER.
Oatley.   Farewell, good Master Dodger.   100
          Lacy in London? I dare pawn my life
          My daughter knows thereof, and for that cause
          Denied young Master Hammon in his love.
          Well, I am glad I sent her to Old Ford.
          God's Lord, 'tis late; to Guildhall I must hie.   105
          I know my brethren stay my company.   *Exit.*

---

86. *lordship*] (an irregular form of address to the Lord Mayor, who would normally be called 'your worship').

88. *keeps*] is living at present.

93. *whether*] (one syllable: 'whe'er').

94. *Lurch*] a variant of *lurk* (l. 91). 'Lurcher' as a dog for hunting (especially for hunting hares) is not recorded in *O.E.D.* before 1668, but the metaphor of *start* in the following line rouses the suspicion that the variant form is used for the sake of word-play.

95. *start*] (figurative) force an animal from its lair (used especially of the hare, and thus perhaps implying Lincoln's contempt for his nephew).

96. *rid*] remove.

97. *angels*] gold coins with a representation of the Archangel Michael on one side, worth ten shillings in Elizabethan currency.

105. *God's Lord*] a recorded oath; *O.E.D.* 'god', 14a; and cf. Chapman, *An Humorous Day's Mirth* (ed. Parrott, sc. xiv.13).

106. *stay*] await.

[SCENE X.]

Enter FIRK, [MARGERY,] *Eyre's wife,* [LACY *as*] HANS, *and*
ROGER.

Margery. Thou goest too fast for me, Roger. O, Firk.

Firk. Ay, forsooth.

Margery. I pray thee, run—do you hear—run to Guildhall,
and learn if my husband, Master Eyre, will take that
worshipful vocation of Master Sheriff upon him. Hie   5
thee, good Firk.

Firk. Take it? Well, I go. An he should not take it, Firk swears
to forswear him.—Yes, forsooth, I go to Guildhall.

Margery. Nay, when! Thou art too compendious and tedious.

Firk. O rare. Your excellence is full of eloquence. [*Aside*]   10
How like a new cartwheel my dame speaks; and she
looks like an old musty ale-bottle going to scalding.

Margery. Nay, when! Thou wilt make me melancholy.

Firk. God forbid your worship should fall into that humour. I
run.   15

Exit.

Margery. Let me see now, Roger and Hans.

Hodge. Ay, forsooth, dame—mistress, I should say, but the

1 O, Firk.] *Q3; not in Q1.*

---

1. *O, Firk*] Q3's addition, though unauthoritative, seems necessary.

3. *Guildhall*] See i.65, n. Deloney also places Eyre's election as sheriff at the
Guildhall and describes Eyre's wife sending a servant for news of the election
(Appendix A, p. 214). On Dekker's changes to the episode in Deloney, and to the
practice of shrieval elections in Elizabethan London, see Introduction, p. 21.

4–5. *Master . . . Master*] Cf. ix. 73, n.

8. *forswear*] renounce.

9. *Nay, when!*] Well, but when!

compendious] concise; a wrong use, mocked in the following speech.

11. *like . . . cartwheel*] i.e., squeakily; Margery is speaking in an affected manner.

12. *to scalding*] to be scalded. Ale-bottles were made of leather, and this was the
method of cleaning them.

13–14. *melancholy . . . humour*] Melancholy was one of the four *humours*, the relative
proportions of which in the blood were thought to govern mood, disposition, and
character.

17. *dame—mistress*] By the end of the sixteenth century, *dame* as a form of address
was coming to be used only for women of lower rank (*O.E.D.*). Hodge corrects his
customary form of address to that corresponding to the dignity recently conferred
on Eyre; see ix.73, n.

old term so sticks to the roof of my mouth, I can hardly
lick it off.

Margery. Even what thou wilt, good Roger. Dame is a fair   20
name for any honest Christian—but let that pass. How
dost thou, Hans?

Lacy [*as Hans*]. *Me tank you, fro.*

Margery. Well, Hans and Roger, you see God hath blessed
your master; and, perdie, if ever he comes to be Master   25
Sheriff of London—as we are all mortal—you shall see I
will have some odd thing or other in a corner for you. I
will not be your back friend—but let that pass. Hans,
pray thee, tie my shoe.

Lacy [*as Hans*]. *Yaw, ik sal, fro.*   30

Margery. Roger, thou knowest the length of my foot. As it is
none of the biggest, so I thank God it is handsome
enough. Prithee, let me have a pair of shoes made; cork,
good Roger; wooden heel, too.

Hodge. You shall.   35

Margery. Art thou acquainted with never a farthingale-
maker, nor a French-hood-maker? I must enlarge my

---

21. *honest*] possibly (in view of the usually apologetic *let that pass*) with a play on
the sense 'chaste', 'virtuous'.

23. Me . . . fro] 'I thank you, madam.'

25. *perdie*] (a mild oath) by God, indeed.

26. *we . . . mortal*] proverbial (Tilley, M502) and deliberately inappropriate to
what Margery is saying.

27. *odd . . . you*] (probably with bawdy overtones).

28. *back friend*] false friend.

30. Yaw . . . fro] 'Yes, I will, madam.'

31. *knowest . . . foot*] (*a*) literally, as for shoemaking; (*b*) a proverbial expression
(Tilley, L202) meaning 'know how to win my love'; or, more generally, 'take my
measure'. Doubtless Margery is putting her foot in it again.

33–61.] This passage is in the nature of a satirical set-piece on vanities of Dekker's
(rather than Simon Eyre's) time.

33–4, *cork . . . wooden heel*] 'combining in one request the elevating features of two
kinds of ladies' shoes, i.e., the corked shoe or slipper with a pad of cork inside rising
towards the heel, and the shoe with a high wooden heel' (Lange). The fashion for
high shoes is mockingly associated with citizens' wives in Edward Sharpham's *The
Fleire* (1607), Act II (sigs. C4*v*, D1*v*).

36. *farthingale*] a hooped petticoat.

37. *French-hood*] pleated hood with round front, worn over the back of the head
and forming a frame for the face (cf. l. 40). Formerly fashionable at court, by the end

bum. Ha, ha! How shall I look in a hood, I wonder?
Perdie, oddly, I think.

Hodge. [*Aside*] As a cat out of a pillory. [*To Margery*] Very   40
well, I warrant you, mistress.

Margery. Indeed, all flesh is grass. And Roger, canst thou tell
where I may buy a good hair?

Hodge. Yes, forsooth; at the poulterer's in Gracious Street.

Margery. Thou art an ungracious wag. Perdie, I mean a false   45
hair for my periwig.

Hodge. Why, mistress, the next time I cut my beard you shall
have the shavings of it; but they are all true hairs.

Margery. It is very hot. I must get me a fan, or else a mask.

Hodge. [*Aside*] So you had need, to hide your wicked face.   50

40 Hodge.] *From this point to the end of the scene, Q1 uses 'Roger' as the speech prefix for*
Hodge.

---

of the sixteenth century it was, like the high shoes at l. 34, particularly associated
with citizens' wives (Linthicum, p. 233).

37–8. *I . . . bum*] There was a garment known as a 'bumroll', a kind of farthingale,
which extended a dress at the back.

40. *cat . . . pillory*] whore (*cat*) looking out of the *pillory* (in which she is undergoing
punishment).

42. *all flesh is grass*] proverbial (Tilley, F359), biblical (I Peter i.24), and, again,
deliberately malapropos.

43. *hair*] (not recorded by *O.E.D.* in this sense) hair-piece.

44. *poulterer's in Gracious Street*] *Gracious* (Grass, Grace, or (the modern form)
Gracechurch) *Street*, running from Cornhill south to Eastcheap, had, according to
Stow (I.81), only recently become an area for poulterers who 'of late remooued out
of the Poultrie . . . into Grasse streete'.

45. *ungracious*] (punningly).

46. *periwig*] (worn by women of fashion. It is not clear whether Margery wants
false hair as—i.e., for—her *periwig*, or in order to repair or supplement it.)

48. *true hairs*] (probably with a pun on 'heirs').

49. *fan . . . mask*] other appurtenances of a fashionable woman, of the time of
Elizabeth rather than the historical Simon Eyre (*Shakespeare's England*, II.97). The
mask was used to avoid sunburn.

50. *wicked*] In his first edition, Bowers emended to 'wrinkld', while printing a
note admitting to a temptation to emend but countering it with a parallel from
Dekker's *The Honest Whore, Part One*, IV.i.83–5 and the assumption that Dekker
'had in mind a forced pun involving *wicks*, i.e., lips'. The emendation is not made in
the reprints of Bowers's edition. Davies adduces a pertinent parallel in *The Gull's
Horn-Book*: 'a head all hid in hair gives even to a most wicked face a sweet proportion
and looks like a meadow newly married to the spring' (Pendry, p. 86).

Margery. Fie upon it, how costly this world's calling is!
    Perdie, but that it is one of the wonderful works of God,
    I would not deal with it. Is not Firk come yet? Hans, be
    not so sad. Let it pass and vanish, as my husband's
    worship says.   55
Lacy [as Hans]. Ik bin frolick; lot see you so.
Hodge. Mistress, will you drink a pipe of tobacco?
Margery. O, fie upon it, Roger! Perdie, these filthy tobacco
    pipes are the most idle, slavering baubles that ever I felt.
    Out upon it, God bless us; men look not like men that   60
    use them.

                        Enter RALPH, *being lame.*

Hodge. What, fellow Ralph! Mistress, look here—Jane's hus-
    band! Why, how now—lame? Hans, make much of
    him. He's a brother of our trade, a good workman, and
    a tall soldier.   65
Lacy [as Hans]. You be welcome, broder.
Margery. Perdie, I knew him not. How dost thou, good
    Ralph? I am glad to see thee well.
Ralph. I would God you saw me, dame, as well

63 how now] *Q1 (corr.);* how *Q1 (uncorr.).*

---

    51. *this world's calling*] the 'vocation' of worldliness (manifestly not *one of the
wonderful works of God*).
    52. *the wonderful . . . God*] Acts, ii.11.
    54–5. *as . . . says*] Margery shows consciousness of a catch-phrase of her husband's
(cf. iv.53, vii.47); *vanish* is one of his favourite words throughout the play.
    56. *Ik . . . so*] 'I am cheerful. Let's see you so.'
    57. *drink*] the normal term for 'smoke'.
    tobacco] There was much controversy, public and private, about the use of
tobacco: cf., e.g., Chapman, *Monsieur D'Olive*, II.ii. Margery's outburst represents a
conventional prejudice.
    59. *idle*]useless.
    baubles] playthings (also used for the penis (Partridge); there are more *double-
entendres* in this speech).
    61.1 *being lame*] On the effect of Ralph's entrance, see Introduction pp. 30 ff. He
must be on crutches, and has apparently lost most of his left leg; see ll. 71–5, 86, and
118.
    65. *tall*] brave.
    66. *broder*] 'brother'.
    69. ff.] Ralph consistently speaks verse in a scene full of the excited prose of other
characters. The physical contrast created by his lameness is thus matched stylistitcally.
    69.] The line is short. Perhaps we should read 'would to God'.

As when I went from London into France.   70
Margery. Trust me, I am sorry, Ralph, to see thee impotent.
   Lord, how the wars have made him sunburnt! The left
   leg is not well. 'Twas a fair gift of God the infirmity
   took not hold a little higher, considering thou camest
   from France—but let that pass.   75
Ralph. I am glad to see you well, and I rejoice
   To hear that God hath blessed my master so
   Since my departure.
Margery. Yea, truly, Ralph, I thank my maker—but let that
   pass.   80
Hodge. And, sirrah Ralph, what news, what news in
   France?
Ralph. Tell me, good Roger, first, what news in England?
   How does my Jane? When didst thou see my wife?
   Where lives my poor heart? She'll be poor indeed   85
   Now I want limbs to get whereon to feed.
Hodge. Limbs? Hast thou not hands, man? Thou shalt never
   see a shoemaker want bread, though he have but three
   fingers on a hand.
Ralph. Yet all this while I hear not of my Jane.   90
Margery. O Ralph, your wife! Perdie, we know not what's
   become of her. She was here a while, and because she
   was married grew more stately than became her. I
   checked her, and so forth. Away she flung, never
   returned, nor said bye nor bah. And, Ralph, you know: 95
   'ka me, ka thee'. And so as I tell ye—Roger, is not Firk
   come yet?
Hodge. No, forsooth.

---

71. *impotent*] weak, enfeebled. The sexual sense is also present in Margery's mind.

72. *sunburnt*] The word had a sense of 'infected with venereal disease'.

73–5. *the infirmity . . . France*] The 'malady of France' was a name for venereal
disease. Margery denies the suggestion implicit in *sunburnt*.

87–8. *never . . . bread*] an allusion to the proverbial camaraderie of shoemakers.
'Shoomakers will not see one another lacke' (*The Gentle Craft, Part Two*, p. 222).

93. *stately*] proud, arrogant.

95. *bye nor bah*] O.E.D., not commenting on *bye*, cites this use as 'an exclamation
expressive of contempt'.

96. *ka me, ka thee*] Tilley, K1; 'help me and I'll help you': i.e., 'Do as you would be
done by', 'tit for tat'.

Margery. And so, indeed, we heard not of her; but I hear she
  lives in London—but let that pass. If she had wanted, she   100
  might have opened her case to me or my husband or to
  any of my men; I am sure there's not any of them,
  perdie, but would have done her good to his power.
  Hans, look if Firk be come.

Lacy [as Hans]. Yaw, ik sal, fro.   105

                                   Exit [LACY as] HANS.

Margery. And so as I said. But Ralph, why dost thou weep?
  Thou knowest that naked we came out of our mother's
  womb, and naked we must return; and therefore thank
  God for all things.

Hodge. No, faith, Jane is a stranger here. But, Ralph, pull up a 110
  good heart—I know thou hast one. Thy wife, man, is in
  London. One told me he saw her a while ago very brave
  and neat. We'll ferret her out, an London hold her.

Margery. Alas, poor soul, he's overcome with sorrow. He
  does but as I do, weep for the loss of any good thing.   115
  But, Ralph, get thee in. Call for some meat and drink.
  Thou shalt find me worshipful towards thee.

Ralph. I thank you, dame. Since I want limbs and lands,
  I'll to God, my good friends, and to these my hands.   *Exit.*

---

105 *Exit . . .* HANS.] *As here, Fritsche; after l. 104, Q1.*   105 *ik*] *Fritsche; it Q1.*
119 I'll to] *Q1; Ile trust to Q3.* 119 these] *Q1; not in Q3.*

---

101. *opened her case*] discussed her problems (with bawdy innuendo).

103. *to his power*] to the best of his capacity (bawdy again).

105. *Yaw . . . fro*] 'Yes, I shall, mistress.'

107–9. *naked . . . things*] 'naked came I out of my mothers wombe, and naked shall
I turne thither againe: the Lorde gaue, and the Lord hath taken away, blessed bee the
name of the Lord' (Job, i.21). Cf. also Luke, ii.20, 'praysing God for all the things',
and Ephesians, v.20, 'Giving thanks alwaies for al things'.

110. *pull up*] pluck up, rouse up.

112. *brave*] smart, fine-looking.

115. *thing*] (perhaps with an overtone of 'maidenhead').

117. *worshipful*] honourable (probably with a comic consciousness of her dignity).

118–19. *Since . . . hands*] based on a proverb: 'Help, hands, for I have no lands'
(Tilley, H116). See Introduction, pp. 31, 39.

119. *I'll . . . hands*] probably an elliptical construction, explained by Q3's revision,
'I'll trust to God, my good friends, and to my hands'. Fritsche and Warnke and
Proescholdt regularised the metre to 'I'll trust to God, my good friends, and my
hands', and were followed by Rhys and other editors.

Enter [LACY *as*] HANS, *and* FIRK, *running.*

Firk. Run, good Hans. O, Hodge, O, mistress! Hodge, heave   120
up thine ears. Mistress, smug up your looks, on with
your best apparel. My master is chosen, my master is
called, nay, condemned, by the cry of the country to be
sheriff of the City for this famous year now to come and
time now being. A great many men in black gowns   125
were asked for their voices and their hands, and my
master had all their fists about his ears presently, and
they cried 'Ay, ay, ay, ay'; and so I came away.
Wherefore without all other grieve
I do salute you, Mistress Shrieve.   130
Lacy [*as Hans*]. *Yaw, my meester is de groot man, de shrieve.*
Hodge. Did not I tell you, mistress? Now I may boldly say
'Good morrow to your worship'.
Margery. Good morrow, good Roger. I thank you, my good
people all. Firk, hold up thy hand. Here's a threepenny   135
piece for thy tidings.

124–5 come and time now being.] *Bowers* (*come*, . . . *being:*); comȩ: and time now
being, *Q1*.
129–30] *as verse, Fritsche; as prose, Q1.*

---

120. *Run, good.Hans*] Firk's excitement recalls Mistress Quickly's transmission of
Falstaff's call for Doll Tearsheet: 'O, run Doll, run, run, good Doll' (*2H4*, II.iv.376).
121. *smug*] smarten.
123. *condemned*] probably a comical misuse, though possibly alluding to the fact
that civic offices were sometimes thrust upon unwilling recipients.
    cry of the country] general voice, acclamation.
124–5. *this . . . being*] Firk adopts a mock-proclamatory tone to announce his
master's appointment to civic office. Steane sees *this famous year* as a possible allusion
in 1599 to the first year of the coming century.
126. *voices*] expressions of opinion, votes.
127. *fists . . . ears*] hands raised in acclaim.
    presently] immediately.
129–30. *grieve . . . Shrieve*] Firk's doggerel couplet creates a sense that he is, with
conscious comedy, elevating the situation by employing this claptrap theatrical
device.
130. *salute*] (often used for 'kiss': probably he should embrace her).
131. *Yaw . . . shrieve*] 'Yes, yes, my master is the great man, the sheriff.'
135. *people*] almost in the sense of 'subjects'.
135–8. *threepenny piece . . . three halfpence . . . rose*] This is confused as well as

Firk. 'Tis but three halfpence, I think.—Yes, 'tis threepence. I
smell the rose.

Hodge. But, mistress, be ruled by me, and do not speak so
pulingly.   140

Firk. 'Tis her worship speaks so, and not she. No, faith,
mistress, speak me in the old key. 'To it, Firk', 'There,
good Firk', 'Ply your business, Hodge'—'Hodge', with
a full mouth—'I'll fill your bellies with good cheer till
they cry twang'.   145

Enter SIMON EYRE *wearing a gold chain.*

Lacy [as Hans]. See, myn liever broder, heer compt my meester.

Margery. Welcome home, Master Shrieve. I pray God continue you in health and wealth.

Eyre. See here, my Madgy, a chain, a gold chain for Simon
Eyre! I shall make thee a lady. Here's a French hood for   150
thee. On with it, on with it. Dress thy brows with this
flap of a shoulder of mutton, to make thee look lovely.
Where be my fine men? Roger, I'll make over my shop
and tools to thee. Firk, thou shalt be the foreman. Hans,
thou shalt have an hundred for twenty. Be as mad   155

---

anachronistic. Some Elizabethan silver coins, including the threepenny piece and the
three-halfpenny piece, had a rose embossed behind the Queen's head so as to
distinguish them from others of similar size but different value. But the rose was not
a distinguishing mark between the coins mentioned here. Lange says that the
threepenny coin was not in general circulation, but 'was Maundy money, and Mrs
Eyre is here affecting the attitude of almoner to the sovereign'. But threepenny
pieces were coined from 1561 to 1582, and it is likely that they were still circulating.

138. *smell*] (jocularly) discern.

140. *pulingly*] normally 'whiningly'; here seems to mean 'affectedly'.

143–4. *'Hodge', with a full mouth*] (as opposed to the more mealy-mouthed *Roger*
which she has used in l. 134 and earlier).

145. *twang*] 'A vocal imitation of the resonant sound produced when a tense string
is sharply plucked or suddenly released' (*O.E.D.*, citing this passage)—implying full
satisfaction, and more.

146. See . . . meester] 'See, my dear brother, here comes my master.'

150. *French hood*] See l. 37, n.

152. *flap . . . mutton*] Literal explanation seems unnecessary: this is only Eyre's
typically bombastic periphrasis for a woollen hood.

155. *twenty*] i.e., twenty portagues (cf. vii.24).

knaves as your master Sim Eyre hath been, and you shall
live to be sheriffs of London. How dost thou like me,
Margery? Prince am I none, yet am I princely born!
Firk, Hodge, and Hans!

All three. Ay, forsooth; what says your worship Master   160
Sheriff?

Eyre. Worship and honour, you Babylonian knaves, for the
Gentle Craft! But I forgot myself. I am bidden by my
Lord Mayor to dinner to Old Ford. He's gone before, I
must after. Come, Madge, on with your trinkets. Now,   165
my true Trojans, my fine Firk, my dapper Hodge, my
honest Hans, some device, some odd crotchets, some
morris or suchlike for the honour of the gentle shoemakers. Meet me at Old Ford. You know my mind.
Come, Madge, away;   170
Shut up the shop, knaves, and make holiday.

Exeunt [EYRE *and* MARGERY]

Firk. O, rare! O, brave! Come, Hodge. Follow me, Hans;
We'll be with them for a morris dance.   *Exeunt.*

---

160 Master] Q6; mistris Q1.
163 forgot] Q1; forget Bowers.
168 gentle] Q1; gentlemen Q5 (gentleman Q3).
170 1 *as two lines of verse,* Schelling; *as one line of verse,* Lawrence; *as prose,* Q1.

---

158. *Prince . . . born*] See vii. 49–50, n.
160. *Master*] Q1's 'mistris' probably derives from mistaken expansion of a
contraction. But Sutherland retains 'Mistress', noting 'it is just possible that the three
men turn to Margery at this point—her opinion has just been sought by her
husband—and, with mock deference, ask her opinion again'.
162. *Babylonian*] another of Eyre's mouth-filling terms. Sugden gives many
references to it in the sense of 'papist' (from the identification of the Roman Catholic
Church with the Whore of Babylon), and says 'thence it came to mean anti-Puritan,
a jolly good fellow'; but this line provides his only example.
163. *forgot*] have forgotten. Bowers emends to *forget,* which seems unnecessary.
166. *Trojans*] Cf. iv. 121–2, n.
dapper] smart, spruce.
167. *device*] entertainment.
crotchets] (*a*) notes of music; (*b*) fanciful entertainments.
168. *gentle*] The later quartos' emendation to 'gentlemen' (cf. xviii.205) was
adopted by Warnke and Proescholdt and some later editors.

[SCENE XI.]

Enter [Sir ROGER OATLEY, *the*] Lord Mayor, EYRE,
[MARGERY] *his wife in a French hood,* [ROSE],
SYBIL, *and other* Servants.

Oatley. [*To Eyre and Margery*] Trust me, you are as welcome
    to Old Ford
    As I myself.
Margery.   Truly, I thank your lordship.
Oatley. Would our bad cheer were worth the thanks you
    give.
Eyre. Good cheer, my Lord Mayor, fine cheer; a fine house,
    fine walls, all fine and neat.   5
Oatley. Now, by my troth, I'll tell thee, Master Eyre,
    It does me good, and all my brethren,
    That such a madcap fellow as thyself
    Is entered into our society.
Margery. Ay, but, my lord, he must learn now to put on   10
    gravity.
Eyre. Peace, Madgy; a fig for gravity. When I go to Guildhall
    in my scarlet gown I'll look as demurely as a saint, and
    speak as gravely as a Justice of Peace; but now I am here
    at Old Ford, at my good Lord Mayor's house, let it go   15
    by, vanish, Madgy; I'll be merry. Away with flip-flap,
    these fooleries, these gulleries. What, honey—prince
    am I none, yet am I princely born! What says my Lord
    Mayor?

0.2 *wife in a French hood*] Q3; *wife, Sibill in a French hood Q1.*
2] *as verse, Wheeler; as prose,* Q1.

  0.2. wife in a French hood] Bowers (p. 10) plausibly attributes Q1's error to a
misinterpreted interlineation.
  7. brethren] The metre requires the trisyllabic pronunciation, as at i.66.
  8. madcap] The word carries the usual connotations of 'madness' in this play; cf.
i.129, n.
  12. a fig for] already commonplace (Tilley, F210).
  13. scarlet gown] worn by the Lord Mayor and Corporation on ceremonial
occasions (Stow, I.231 and II.193). Dekker refers to the colour of the mayoral gown
in his pageant *Troia-Nova Triumphans* (l. 552; Bowers, III.246).
  16. flip-flap] probably a reference to the French hood in which Margery is
flaunting herself (cf. x.152, n.).
  17. gulleries] frauds, deceptions.

Oatley. Ha, ha, ha! I had rather than a thousand pound   20
      I had an heart but half so light as yours.
Eyre. Why, what should I do, my lord? A pound of care pays
      not a dram of debt. Hum, let's be merry whiles we are
      young. Old age, sack, and sugar will steal upon us ere
      we be aware.   25
Oatley. It's well done. Mistress Eyre, pray give good counsel
      to my daughter.
Margery. I hope Mistress Rose will have the grace to take
      nothing that's bad.
Oatley. Pray God she do; for i' faith, Mistress Eyre,   30
      I would bestow upon that peevish girl
      A thousand marks more than I mean to give her
      Upon condition she'ld be ruled by me.
      The ape still crosseth me. There came of late
      A proper gentleman of fair revenues   35
      Whom gladly I would call son-in-law.
      But my fine cockney would have none of him.
      You'll prove a coxcomb for it ere you die.

26 done.] *Q3* (done,); done *Q1.*
36 call son-in-law] *Q1;* call [my] son-in-law *Fritsche;* call [a] son-in-law *Wheeler.*

22–3. *A pound . . . debt*] proverbial (Tilley, P518); and cf. Deloney, p. 122: 'the
maried sort, that for a dram of delight haue a pound of paine'.
24. *sack, and sugar*] The mixture seems to have been associated with old age. Cf.
Lyly, *Mother Bombie,* ed. Bond, II.v.52: 'without wine and sugar his veins wold
waxe colde', and Falstaff's nickname, 'Sir John Sack and Sugar' (*1H4,* I.ii.109–10).
25.] Rhys, followed by many editors, inserts the first three-man's song after this
line, making Oatley's *It's well done* a comment upon the performance.
31. *peevish*] (another of Capulet's epithets for Juliet, *R.&J.,* IV.ii.14; cf. ix.56, n.)
32. *mark*] (13s 4d).
34. *ape*] fool, 'monkey'.
still] continually.
crosseth] annoys, opposes.
35. *proper*] See vi.60, n.
36.] The line appears short. Lange's suggestion that *gladly* should have three
syllables (glad(e)ly) can be supported by Abbott, §477. Bowers exaggerates in saying
'Editors have been unable to resist Fritsche's smoothing the metre of Qq to read *call
my sonne in law*'. Neither Warnke and Proescholdt, Rhys, nor Lange emends.
Wheeler (1915) reads '[a] son-in-law', and Halliday and Harrison adopt this reading.
Many later editors, e.g. Sutherland, Spencer, McIlwraith, and Brooke and Paradise
do not emend.
37. *cockney*] spoilt child (as 'Londoner', first recorded in 1600).
38. *prove a coxcomb*] make a fool of yourself.

A courtier or no man must please your eye.

Eyre. Be ruled, sweet Rose; thou'rt ripe for a man. Marry not   40
with a boy that has no more hair on his face than thou
hast on thy cheeks. A courtier—wash, go by! Stand not
upon pishery-pashery. Those silken fellows are but
painted images, outsides, outsides, Rose. Their inner
linings are torn. No, my fine mouse, marry me with a   45
Gentleman Grocer like my Lord Mayor your father. A
grocer is a sweet trade; plums, plums! Had I a son or
daughter should marry out of the generation and blood
of the shoemakers, he should pack. What, the Gentle
Trade is a living for a man through Europe, through the   50
world.

A noise within of a tabor and a pipe.

Oatley. What noise is this?

Eyre. O, my Lord Mayor, a crew of good fellows that, for
love to your honour, are come hither with a morris
dance. Come in, my Mesopotamians, cheerly.   55

Enter HODGE, [LACY *as*] HANS, RALPH, FIRK, *and other*
Shoemakers *in a morris. After a little dancing, the*
Lord Mayor *speaks.*

Oatley. Master Eyre, are all these shoemakers?

Eyre. All cordwainers, my good Lord Mayor.

---

42. *wash, go by*] an expression of contempt. *Wash* has various uncomplimentary
senses, such as 'stale urine', 'kitchen swill', etc. For *go by*, see vi.2 and ii.46, n.

42–3. *Stand . . . pishery-pashery*] *Pishery-pashery*, used at i.125 and 163 of words,
here refers to clothing. In both instances it could be generally defined as 'trash'. Here,
the phrase means 'Put no trust in mere finery'.

44–5. *Their . . . torn*] Eyre uses a neatly appropriate metaphor from shoemaking.
mouse] (a term of endearment).

46. *Gentleman Grocer*] member of the Grocers' Company.

49. *pack*] be off.

49–51 *Gentle . . . world*] Cf. iii.24, and Introduction, p. 38.

51.1. *tabor . . . pipe*] portable drum, and a pipe which could be played by the same
performer, often used to provide music for a morris-dance.

55. *Mesopotamians*] Cf. vii.83.

55.1.] This is another point at which the first three-man's song might be sung,
though no editor has printed it here.

Rose. [*Aside*] How like my Lacy looks yond shoemaker!

Lacy [*as Hans*]. [*Aside*] O, that I durst but speak unto my love!

Oatley. Sybil, go fetch some wine to make these drink.   60
    You are all welcome.

All [*the Shoemakers*]. We thank your lordship.

      ROSE *takes a cup of wine and goes to* [LACY *as*] HANS.

Rose. For his sake whose fair shape thou represent'st,
    Good friend, I drink to thee.

Lacy [*as Hans*]. *Ik be dancke, good frister.*   65

Margery. I see, Mistress Rose, you do not want judgement.
    You have drunk to the properest man I keep.

Firk. Here be some have done their parts to be as proper as he.

Oatley. Well, urgent business calls me back to London.
    Good fellows, first go in and taste our cheer,   70
    And to make merry as you homeward go,
    Spend these two angels in beer at Stratford Bow.

Eyre. To these two, my mad lads, Sim Eyre adds another.
    Then cheerly, Firk, tickle it, Hans, and all for the

---

58. *How . . . shoemaker!*] Conventions of disguise are very flexible in Elizabethan drama. Cf., e.g., *A.Y.L.I.*, V.iii.26, and *R.&J.*, I.v.52, for penetrations of disguise for dramatic convenience.

63. *whose . . . represent'st*] (perhaps an attempt to pierce Lacy's disguise while ostensibly alluding to the character he portrays in the morris-dance; or possibly spoken aside in overt recognition).

65. *Ik . . . frister*] 'I thank you, good maid.' (In modern Dutch, *vrijster* means 'spinster'.)

67. *properest*] handsomest.

68. *done . . . he*] Firk resents Margery's praise of the outsider. As so often in interchanges between Firk and Margery, sexual innuendo might be suggested.

69. *urgent . . . London*] Perhaps Oatley is bored or irritated: or this may be simply a rather clumsy device to get him off the stage. Cf. Introduction, p. 41.

72. *angels*] Cf. ix. 97, n.

Stratford Bow] The tavern at Stratford-at-Bow would be the nearest to Old Ford on the road back to London. It was a well-known stopping place for refreshment: 'Mile-end is no walke without a recreatiō at Stratford Bow with Creame and Cakes' (William Kemp, *Kemps Nine Daies Wonder*, in *A Miscellany of Tracts and Pamphlets*, ed. A. C. Ward (London, 1927), p. 136; sig. A3*v* in quarto of 1600).

74. *tickle it*] 'have a good time', 'have fun'. This is a slang expression which, after this initial usage, Dekker repeats several times (xiii.7, 49, xx.19) in a sense not distinguished by *O.E.D.* It clearly means 'initiate, or sustain, a party atmosphere, a mood of carefree enjoyment'. See also xvi.158.

honour of shoemakers.   75

All [*the* Shoemakers] *go dancing out.*

Oatley. Come, Master Eyre, let's have your company.

Exeunt [OATLEY, EYRE, *and* MARGERY].

Rose. Sybil, what shall I do?

Sybil.   Why, what's the matter?

Rose. That Hans the shoemaker is my love, Lacy,

Disguised in that attire to find me out.

How should I find the means to speak with him?   80

Sybil. What, mistress, never fear. I dare venture my maidenhead to nothing—and that's great odds—that Hans the
Dutchman, when we come to London, shall not only
see and speak with you, but, in spite of all your father's
policies, steal you away and marry you. Will not this   85
please you?

Rose. Do this, and ever be assured of my love.

Sybil. Away, then, and follow your father to London, lest
your absence cause him to suspect something.

Tomorrow, if my counsel be obeyed,   90

I'll bind you prentice to the Gentle Trade.   [*Exeunt.*]

77] *as verse, Wheeler; as prose,* Q1.

75.] Some editors have placed the first three-man's song after this line; cf. The
Songs, n.

82. *and . . . odds*] (We may take this as seriously as we please.)

85. *policies*] precautions, stratagems.

[SCENE XII.]

Enter JANE *in a sempster's shop, working, and* HAMMON, *muffled, at another door. He stands aloof.*

Hammon. Yonder's the shop, and there my fair love sits.
She's fair and lovely, but she is not mine.
O would she were! Thrice have I courted her,
Thrice hath my hand been moistened with her hand
Whilst my poor famished eyes do feed on that   5
Which made them famish. I am infortunate.
I still love one, yet nobody loves me.
I muse in other men what women see
That I so want. Fine Mistress Rose was coy,
And this too curious. O no, she is chaste,   10

Sc. xii.] The basic situation of this scene—that of a man wooing a reluctant woman—resembles that of the first two chapters of *The Gentle Craft, Part One,* in which Sir Hugh woos Winifred, who dedicates herself to a religious life. The situation is so commonplace that the parallel would not be worth noting except for Dekker's known dependence on Deloney, and for the existence of verbal echoes; see notes to ll. 11–12, 46–7, and 122. The scene also has affinities with one of successful wooing, *R.&J.,* II.ii (the 'balcony' scene), though here the resemblances are structural rather than verbal. Both scenes open with a lover addressing his unhearing beloved, who later sees and speaks to him; and both end with a protracted farewell. (For other echoes of *R.&J.* see Introduction, p. 17, and n. 29.)

0.1. in a sempster's shop] The shop is referred to by Hammon at ix.51 (see n.). The doubtful reputation of women who kept Exchange shops is remarked by Sugden, citing evidence from a number of plays, among them Dekker and Webster's *Westward Ho,* where the phrase 'as stale as . . . an Exchange Sempster' occurs (I.ii.95–6). This is the first we have seen of Jane since the opening scene, and her appearance in this vulnerable situation is significant (see l. 29, Introduction, pp. 28, 35, and i.220, n.).

0.1–2. shop . . . another door] See *The play on the stage,* p. 45.

0.1. muffled] 'well wrapped up', and thus disguised. The cold (ll. 15–17) reflects Hammon's *cold heart* (l. 12).

0.2. aloof] i.e., to one side.

1. *fair*] In the B.M.[1] copy, 'true' is written above this word in what appears to be an early hand. Though unauthoritative, it is interesting in view of the repetition of *fair* in the following line.

3. *Thrice . . . courted her*] Cf. ix.55, and n.

5. *do*] The irregular tense emphasises the fervour of his gaze, and perhaps the frequent repetitions of the situation.

7. *still love one*] am always in love with somebody.

10. *curious*] fastidious, 'choosy'.

And, for she thinks me wanton, she denies
To cheer my cold heart with her sunny eyes.
How prettily she works! O pretty hand!
O happy work! It doth me good to stand
Unseen to see her. Thus I oft have stood   15
In frosty evenings, a light burning by her,
Enduring biting cold only to eye her.
One only look hath seemed as rich to me
As a king's crown, such is love's lunacy.
Muffled I'll pass along, and by that try   20
Whether she know me.

Jane.   Sir, what is't you buy?
What is't you lack, sir? Calico, or lawn,
Fine cambric shirts, or bands—what will you buy?

Hammon. [*Aside*] That which thou wilt not sell. Faith, yet I'll
     try.
[*To Jane*] How do you sell this handkercher?

Jane.   Good cheap.   25

Hammon. And how these ruffs?

Jane.   Cheap, too.

Hammon.   And how this band?

Jane. Cheap too.

Hammon.   All cheap. How sell you then this hand?

Jane. My hands are not to be sold.

Hammon.   To be given, then.
     Nay, faith, I come to buy.

Jane.   But none knows when.

28–9 To . . . then. / Nay . . . buy.] *Fritsche; one line in* Q1.

11–12. *she denies . . . eyes*] Cf. Deloney, chapter I: 'Long and tedious hath the
winter of my woes bin, which with nipping care hath blasted the beautie of my
youthfull delight which is like neuer againe to florish except the bright Sun-shine of
thy fauour doe renew the same' (p. 97).

13–14. *works . . . work*] sews . . . needlework.

21–2. *what . . . lack*] standard 'cries' of shopkeepers.

22–3. *Calico . . . lawn . . . cambric*] *Calico* is a general name for cotton cloth; *lawn* and
cambric are kinds of fine white linen.

23. *bands*] hat-ribbons, collars, ruffs, etc.

25. *How*] at what price.
Good cheap] cheaply.

29. *I . . . buy*] See Introduction, p. 35.

Hammon. Good sweet, leave work a little while. Let's play.   30
Jane. I cannot live by keeping holiday.
Hammon. I'll pay you for the time which shall be lost.
Jane. With me you shall not be at so much cost.
Hammon. Look how you wound this cloth, so you wound
       me.
Jane. It may be so.
Hammon.   'Tis so.
Jane.   What remedy?   35
Hammon. Nay, faith; you are too coy.
Jane.   Let go my hand.
Hammon. I will do any task at your command.
       I would let go this beauty, were I not
       Enjoined to disobey you by a power
       That controls kings. I love you.
Jane.   So. Now part.   40
Hammon. With hands I may, but never with my heart.
       In faith, I love you.
Jane.   I believe you do.
Hammon. Shall a true love in me breed hate in you?
Jane. I hate you not.
Hammon.   Then you must love.
Jane.   I do.
       What, are you better now? I love not you.   45
Hammon. All this, I hope, is but a woman's fray,
       That means 'Come to me!' when she cries 'Away!'

39 Enjoined] *George; In mind Q1.*
44–5 I do / . . . not you.] *Fritsche; as one line, Q1.*

---

31. *live*] earn my living. This line is relevant to the play's deepest concerns. See Introduction, pp. 38 ff., and 43.
34. *Look how*] just as.
wound his cloth] Hammon adopts the diction of conventional love poetry.
39. *Enjoined*] George's emendation (see i. 167, n.) seems necessary.
40. *controls*] (accented on the first syllable).
46–7. *a woman's . . . 'Away!'*] proverbial; cf. Tilley, M34, 'Maids say nay and take it', and W660, 'A woman says nay and means aye'. Cf. also Deloney, chapter I: 'Tush *Hugh,* let not a few froward words of a woman dismay thee, for they loue to be intreated, and delight to bee wooed, though they would make the world beleeue otherwise; for their denyals proceed more of nicenesse then nigardlinesse, refusing that they would fainest haue' (p. 93).
46. *fray*] fear, timidity; or 'noise' (i.e., empty words).

In earnest, mistress, I do not jest;
A true chaste love hath entered in my breast.
I love you dearly as I love my life.   50
I love you as a husband loves a wife.
That, and no other love, my love requires.
Thy wealth, I know, is little. My desires
Thirst not for gold. Sweet beauteous Jane, what's mine
Shall, if thou make myself thine, all be thine.   55
Say, judge, what is thy sentence—life or death?
Mercy or cruelty lies in thy breath.
Jane. Good sir, I do believe you love me well.
For 'tis a silly conquest, silly pride,
For one like you—I mean, a gentleman—   60
To boast that by his love tricks he hath brought
Such and such women to his amorous lure.
I think you do not so, yet many do,
And make it even a very trade to woo.
I could be coy, as many women be;   65
Feed you with sunshine smiles and wanton looks.
But I detest witchcraft. Say that I
Do constantly believe you constant have—
Hammon. Why dost thou not believe me?
Jane.   I believe you.

68 believe you constant have—] Bowers; beleeue you, constant haue. Q1; beleeue,
you constant haue—Warnke and Proescholdt.

---

48. mistress] could be trisyllabic; cf. Abbott, §477.
55. make . . . thine] i.e., by agreeing to marry me. The construction is awkward;
'make thyself mine' might have been expected.
57. breath] 'judgement or will expressed in words' (O.E.D., 9).
59. silly . . . silly] unworthy . . . foolish.
61-2. brought . . . lure] i.e., seduced. (A lure is an apparatus used by falconers to
recall their hawks.)
64. very trade] regular profession.
65. coy] 'displaying modest backwardness or shyness (sometimes with emphasis
on the displaying)' (O.E.D., 2a). The parenthesis in O.E.D.'s definition helps to
distinguish this usage from that in ll. 9 and 36.
68. constantly . . . have—] Q1's line is unacceptable as it stands. Warnke and
Proescholdt improved it by assuming the speech to be interrupted, but their
transposition of the comma to after believe is unconvincing. Bowers says 'I have no
faith in the purity of the line', but his version is at least actable as an uncompleted, if
unpredictable, sentence. Lange's theory that constant is adverbial is tenable (Abbott
§1), but does not solve the problem.

But yet, good sir, because I will not grieve you   70
With hopes to taste fruit which will never fall,
In simple truth, this is the sum of all:
My husband lives—at least, I hope he lives.
Pressed was he to these bitter wars in France.
Bitter they are to me by wanting him.   75
I have but one heart, and that heart's his due.
How can I then bestow the same on you?
Whilst he lives, his I live, be it ne'er so poor;
And rather be his wife than a king's whore.
Hammon. Chaste and dear woman, I will not abuse thee,   80
Although it cost my life if thou refuse me.
Thy husband pressed for France—what was his
name?
Jane. Ralph Damport.
Hammon.   Damport. Here's a letter sent
From France to me from a dear friend of mine,
A gentleman of place. Here he doth write   85
Their names that have been slain in every fight.
Jane. I hope death's scroll contains not my love's name.
Hammon. Cannot you read?
Jane.   I can.
Hammon.   Peruse the same.
To my remembrance such a name I read
Amongst the rest. See here.

---

71. *fruit . . . fall*] an allusion to the myth of Tantalus.

74. *Pressed*] conscripted.

75. *by wanting*] i.e., 'because I lack'.

78. *be . . . poor*] in however poor a condition.

79. *wife . . . whore*] The sentiment is not uncommon; cf. Greene's *Pandosto* (1588), 'I had rather be Meleagrus wife, and a begger, then liue in plenty, and be *Pandostos* Concubine' (sig. G1).

83. *letter*] Hammon's possession of the letter is a momentarily plausible plot device. Dekker has not worked out its full implications. He does not give us the evidence on which to judge whether Hammon is, as he claims, genuinely *misled* (xviii.46), or whether he is deliberately deluding Jane. Another matter that will not bear close examination is the length of the letter. It is said (l. 86) to include *Their names that have been slain in every fight,* yet in one battle alone *Four thousand English* were killed (viii.9). If one sought a rational explanation of the presence of Ralph's name in such a list, one might propose that he had been reported dead while actually being only badly wounded.

88. *Cannot you read?*] (not an insulting question in an age of limited literacy).

Jane.   Ay me, he's dead.   90
He's dead. If this be true, my dear heart's slain.
Hammon. Have patience, dear love.
Jane.   Hence, hence!
Hammon.   Nay, sweet Jane,
Make not poor sorrow proud with these rich tears.
I mourn thy husband's death because thou mournest.
Jane. That bill is forged. 'Tis signed by forgery.   95
Hammon. I'll bring thee letters sent besides to many
Carrying the like report. Jane, 'tis too true.
Come, weep not. Mourning, though it rise from love,
Helps not the mournèd, yet hurts them that mourn.
Jane. For God's sake, leave me.
Hammon.   Whither dost thou turn?   100
Forget the dead; love them that are alive.
His love is faded—try how mine will thrive.
Jane. 'Tis now no time for me to think on love.
Hammon. 'Tis now best time for you to think on love,
Because your love lives not.
Jane.   Though he be dead,   105
My love to him shall not be burièd.
For God's sake, leave me to myself alone.
Hammon. 'Twould kill my soul to leave thee drowned in
    moan.
Answer me to my suit, and I am gone.
Say to me yea or no.
Jane.   No.
Hammon.   Then farewell.   110
One farewell will not serve. I come again.
Come, dry these wet cheeks. Tell me, faith, sweet
    Jane,
Yea, or no, once more.

101 dead] Q2; deede Q1.
104–5 'Tis . . . love, / Because . . . not.] *Fritsche; as prose,* Q1.
105–6 Though . . . dead, / My . . . burièd.] *Fritsche; one line in* Q1.
110–14] *as verse, Fritsche; as prose,* Q1.

95. *bill*] letter, document.
108. *moan*] grief.

Jane.   Once more I say no.
Once more, be gone, I pray, else will I go.
Hammon. Nay, then, I will grow rude. By this white hand,   115
Until you change that cold no, here I'll stand
Till by your hard heart—
Jane.   Nay, for God's love, peace.
My sorrows by your presence more increase.
Not that you thus are present; but all grief   120
Desires to be alone. Therefore in brief
Thus much I say, and saying bid adieu:
If ever I wed man it shall be you.
Hammon. O blessèd voice. Dear Jane, I'll urge no more.
Thy breath hath made me rich.   125
Jane.   Death makes me poor.

                                        Exeunt.

[SCENE XIII.]
Enter HODGE *at his shop board,* RALPH, FIRK, [LACY *as*]
HANS, *and a* Boy, *at work.*

All. [*Singing*] Hey down, a-down, down-derry.
Hodge. Well said, my hearts! Ply your work today—we
loitered yesterday. To it, pell-mell, that we may live to
be Lord Mayors, or Aldermen at least.

115 rude.] Q5 (rude,); rude Q1.

---

122. *If . . . you*] Cf. Deloney, chapter II: 'if euer I loue earthly man, it shall be thee' (pp. 97–8). This also recalls *A.Y.L.I.*, V.ii.109–10: 'I will satisfy you if ever I satisfied man', which itself is based on Lodge's *Rosalynde* (1590): 'I will never marrie my selfe to woman but unto thy selfe' (*Narrative and Dramatic Sources of Shakespeare,* ed. Geoffrey Bullough, II (1958), p. 245).

0.1. *at . . . board*] See *The play on the stage,* p. 45.

1. *Hey . . . derry*] Harrison prints the second three-man's song here. These words are close to, but not exactly the same as, its refrain. Certainly the scene begins with singing, though not perhaps with a full song.

2. *Well said*] Excellent! Well done!

3. *pell-mell*] headlong, without respite.

3–4. *live to be Lord Mayors*] anticipating the news given at ll. 42–3. On the play's optimistic picture of the possibilities of social advancement, epitomised in Eyre's career, see Introduction, *passim.* The idea of apprentices achieving the highest office is used in other plays: cf., e.g., Dekker and Webster, *Northward Ho,* III.ii.131–2; Heywood, *1 Edward IV* (ed. Shepherd, I.17).

Firk. [*Singing*] Hey down a-down derry.   5

Hodge. Well said, i'faith! How sayst thou, Hans—doth not
     Firk tickle it?

Lacy [*as Hans*]. Yaw, meester.

Firk. Not so, neither. My organ-pipe squeaks this morning
     for want of liquoring. [*Sings*] Hey down a-down derry.   10

Lacy [*as Hans*]. *Forware, Firk, tow best un jolly youngster. Hort,
     ay, meester, ik bid you cut me un pair vampies for Meester
     Jeffrey's boots.*

Hodge. Thou shalt, Hans.

Firk. Master.   15

Hodge. How now, boy?

Firk. Pray, now you are in the cutting vein, cut me out a pair
     of counterfeits, or else my work will not pass current.
     [*Sings*] Hey down a-down.

---

11 *Forware*] Spencer; Forward *Q1*.

11–12 *Hort, ay, meester*] *Q1* (hort I mester); Hort 'ee, mester *Spencer*.

12 *vampies*] *(conj. George)* Bowers; vāpres *Q1*.

---

7. *tickle it*] See xi.74, n.

8. Yaw, meester] 'Yes, master.'

11–13. Forware . . . boots] 'Indeed, Firk, you are a jolly youngster. Listen, master:
I bid you cut me a pair of vamps for Master Jeffrey's boots.' The sense is clear, but
'hort I' in *Q1* is of uncertain meaning. Spencer takes it as a form of 'thee' or 'you',
but we interpret it as an intensive, perhaps related to the Dutch 'hee', meaning 'hey!'.

11. Forware] (from Dutch *voorwaar*, 'indeed').

12. vampies] The emendation was suggested by George and adopted by Bowers.
O.E.D. suggests that 'vamper' is an error for 'vampey' or 'vampy', forms of 'vamp',
which means 'the part of a boot or shoe covering the front of the foot'. Greg,
reviewing Bowers (*R.E.S.*, N.S. 5 (1954), 418), pointed out, as George had done,
that 'vampers' is recorded in 1698 in the sense of 'stockings', and that it may, like
'vamp', have referred also to shoes. This is indisputable. George's conjecture is
followed here because 'vampy' certainly had an acceptable meaning in Dekker's
time; *O.E.D.* cites Greene's *A Quip for an Upstart Courtier*: 'Beside, you will ioine a
neates leather vampey to a calues leather heele' (1592, sig. F1). But 'vampers' could
easily be right.

16. *boy*] (probably a jocular assertion of Hodge's new status rather than a just
reflection of Firk's age).

18. *counterfeits*] presumably Firk means 'copies', an identical pair of *vampies*. In
Elizabethan usage *counterfeit* did not necessarily imply an intention to deceive,
though Firk's following pun exploits this sense. Some editors have suggested,
without evidence, that *counterfeits* is an alternative technical term for 'vamps'.
Spencer, citing Kittredge, glosses 'patterns'.

pass current] (playing on the idea of *counterfeit* coins).

Hodge. Tell me, sirs, are my cousin Mistress Priscilla's shoes   20
done?

Firk. Your cousin? No, master, one of your aunts. Hang her;
let them alone.

Ralph. I am in hand with them. She gave charge that none but
I should do them for her.   25

Firk. Thou do for her? Then 'twill be a lame doing, and that
she loves not. Ralph, thou mightest have sent her to me.
In faith, I would have yerked and firked your Priscilla.
[*Sings*] Hey down a-down derry.—This gear will not
hold.   30

Hodge. How sayst thou, Firk—were we not merry at Old
Ford?

Firk. How, merry?—why, our buttocks went jiggy-joggy
like a quagmire. Well, Sir Roger Oatmeal, if I thought
all meal of that nature I would eat nothing but bag-   35
puddings.

Ralph. Of all good fortunes, my fellow Hans had the best.

Firk. 'Tis true, because Mistress Rose drank to him.

Hodge. Well, well, work apace. They say seven of the
Aldermen be dead, or very sick.   40

Firk. I care not, I'll be none.

---

22. *aunts*] (slang) whores.

24. *I . . . them*] I have them in hand, I'm getting on with them.

26. *do . . . . doing*] (bawdy, with a hit at Ralph's injury, and perhaps a further
suggestion that he is sexually impotent; see x.61.1, n.)

28. *yerked*] stitched; cf. vii.95-6, where, as here, Firk makes the word an occasion
for bawdy innuendo.

firked] See *Dram. Per.*, 19, n.

29-30. *This . . . hold*] *Gear* could have a wide range of application. Firk is
complaining that something is inadequate, or unsuccessful; but it is not clear
whether he refers to the shoe he is making, Ralph's sexual incapacities, or his own
singing. (Cf. xvi.74, 110.)

33. *jiggy-joggy*] Cf. ii.67, and n.

34. *Oatmeal*] a joking perversion of *Oatley*.

34-6. *if . . . bag-puddings*] if every meal were like that, I should be happy to eat
nothing but *meal* (punning on the *oatmeal* of which *bag-puddings* were made).
Presumably Firk is reminiscing nostalgically about the high quality of the food
(*meal*) and drink at Old Ford.

35-6. *bag-puddings*] puddings boiled in bags; a kind of haggis.

39-43. *seven . . . Mayor*] This is very convenient for the plot; its improbability
would have been less acute in times of plague (see Introduction, p. 23).

Ralph. No, nor I; but then my Master Eyre will come quickly
to be Lord Mayor.

Enter SYBIL.

Firk. Whoop, yonder comes Sybil!

Hodge. Sybil! Welcome, i'faith; and how dost thou, mad   45
wench?

Firk. Syb-whore, welcome to London.

Sybil. Godamercy, sweet Firk. Good Lord, Hodge, what a
delicious shop you have got! You tickle it, i'faith.

Ralph. Godamercy, Sybil, for our good cheer at Old Ford.   50

Sybil. That you shall have, Ralph.

Firk. Nay, by the Mass, we had tickling cheer, Sybil. And
how the plague dost thou and Mistress Rose, and my
Lord Mayor?—I put the women in first.

Sybil. Well, godamercy. But God's me, I forget myself.   55
Where's Hans the Fleming?

Firk. Hark, butter-box, now you must yelp out some
spreaken.

Lacy [as Hans]. Vat begey you, vat vod you, frister.

Sybil. Marry, you must come to my young mistress, to pull   60
on her shoes you made last.

Lacy [as Hans]. Vare ben your edle fro? Vare ben your mistress?

Sybil. Marry, here at our London house in Cornwall.

59 *you . . . you*] *Warnke and Proescholdt; gon . . . gon* Q1.
62 *edle*] *Lange;* egle Q1.
63 Cornwall] Q3 (Cornewall); Cornewaile Q1.

---

47. *Syb-whore*] (a friendly insult).
48, 50, 55. *Godamercy*] thank you.
49. *tickle it*] See xi.74, n.
51. *That . . . have*] Perhaps sarcastic; as a servant, she takes a jaundiced view of the
entertainment the household would provide; or possibly flirtatious.
55. *God's me*] a shortened form of 'God save me' (*O.E.D.* 'god', 8b).
57. *butter-box*] Cf. iv.57, n.
58. spreaken] foreign talk; cf. vii.106, where Firk uses the word as a verb.
59. *Vat . . . frister*] 'What do you want? What would you, girl?'
60–61. *pull on*] try for size.
62. Vare . . . mistress] 'Where is your noble lady? Where is your mistress?'
63. *Cornwall*] George demonstrated that the alteration to 'Cornhill' made in Q4
and by many editors is unnecessary, as the street was commonly called 'Cornewaile'
about 1600. He cites, *inter alia,* Dekker's *The Meeting of Gallants* (in *Plague Pamphlets,* p.

Firk. Will nobody serve her turn but Hans?

Sybil. No, sir. Come, Hans, I stand upon needles.   65

Hodge. Why then, Sybil, take heed of pricking.

Sybil. For that, let me alone. I have a trick in my budget.
    Come, Hans.

Lacy [as Hans]. Yaw, yaw; ik sal mit you gane.

                    Exeunt [LACY *as*] HANS *and* SYBIL.

Hodge. Go, Hans, make haste again. Come, who lacks work?   70

Firk. I, master; for I lack my breakfast. 'Tis munching time,
    and past.

Hodge. Is't so? Why then, leave work, Ralph. To breakfast.
    Boy, look to the tools. Come, Ralph. Come, Firk.   *Exeunt.*

                    [SCENE XIV.]
                Enter a Servingman.

Servingman. Let me see, now, the Sign of the Last in Tower
    Street. Mass, yonder's the house. What haw! Who's
    within?

                    Enter RALPH.

Ralph. Who calls, there? What want you, sir?

69 Exeunt] *Exit Q1.*

---

117). Bowers supported this in 'A late appearance of "Cornwall" for "Cornhill" ',
N.&Q., 194 (1950), 97–8. Nevertheless, the actress playing Sybil could properly
normalise to 'Cornhill', the form used at ii.32.

  64. *serve her turn*] do as well (the phrase often had bawdy implications; cf. *L.L.L.,*
I.i.277–9).

  65. *stand upon needles*] am impatient (proverbial: Tilley, N100; first instance,
1613).

  66. *pricking*] (with sexual innuendo).

  67. *trick*] device (sexual stratagem).

  budget] bag (bawdy; Henley and Farmer list among terms for the female organ).

  69. Yaw . . . gane] 'Yes, yes; I will go with you.'

  71. *munching time*] Cf. iv.126, n.

  1. *Sign . . . Last*] (indicating a shoemaker's shop. Shop-signs were necessarily
widely used in an age of limited literacy.)

  1–2. *Tower Street*] See Epistle, 14, n.

  2. *Mass*] by the Mass (a mild oath).

  What haw!] What ho! The spelling may indicate an affected pronunciation.

Servingman. Marry, I would have a pair of shoes made for a   5
gentlewoman against tomorrow morning. What, can
you do them?

Ralph. Yes, sir; you shall have them. But what length's her
foot?

Servingman. Why, you must make them in all parts like this   10
shoe. But at any hand, fail not to do them; for the
gentlewoman is to be married very early in the morning.

Ralph. How? By this shoe must it be made? By this? Are you
sure, sir, by this?   15

Servingman. How, 'by this' am I sure, 'by this'! Art thou in
thy wits? I tell thee, I must have a pair of shoes, dost thou
mark me? A pair of shoes, two shoes, made by this very
shoe, this same shoe, against tomorrow morning by
four o'clock. Dost understand me? Canst thou do't?   20

Ralph. Yes, sir, yes. Ay, ay, I can do't. By this shoe, you say? I
should know this shoe. Yes, sir, yes, by this shoe. I can
do't. Four o'clock. Well. Whither shall I bring them?

Servingman. To the Sign of the Golden Ball, in Watling
Street. Enquire for one Master Hammon, a gentleman,   25
my master.

Ralph. Yea, sir. By this shoe, you say?

Servingman. I say Master Hammon at the Golden Ball. He's
the bridegroom, and those shoes are for his bride.

Ralph. They shall be done, by this shoe. Well, well, Master   30
Hammon at the Golden Shoe—I would say, the Golden
Ball. Very well, very well; but, I pray you, sir, where
must Master Hammon be married?

21 Ay, ay, I] *Fritsche;* I, I, I *Q1.*

---

6. *against*] in time for.

11. *at any hand*] on any account.

14. *By this*] i.e., with this as a model.

19–20. *by four o'clock*] It seems not to have been unusual for weddings to take place
very early in the morning (cf. *R.&J.,* IV.v, and Dekker's *Satiromastix,* I.i).

23–4. *Sign . . . Street*] No inn of this name is recorded. A shop-sign may be
intended. Watling Street, running east from St Paul's, was an area of 'wealthy
drapers . . . more then in any one streete of this citie' (Stow, I.346). Perhaps Dekker
imagines Hammon as a member of this wealthy community.

Servingman. At Saint Faith's Church, under Paul's. But
    what's that to thee? Prithee, dispatch those shoes; and so,   35
    farewell.   *Exit.*
Ralph. By this shoe, said he? How am I amazed
    At this strange accident! Upon my life,
    This was the very shoe I gave my wife
    When I was pressed for France; since when, alas,   40
    I never could hear of her. It is the same,
    And Hammon's bride no other but my Jane.

Enter FIRK.

Firk. 'Snails, Ralph, thou hast lost thy part of three pots a
    countryman of mine gave me to breakfast.
Ralph. I care not. I have found a better thing.   45
Firk. A thing? Away! Is it a man's thing, or a woman's thing?
Ralph. Firk, dost thou know this shoe?
Firk. No, by my troth. Neither doth that know me. I have no
    acquaintance with it. 'Tis a mere stranger to me.
Ralph. Why, then, I do. This shoe, I durst be sworn,   50
    Once coverèd the instep of my Jane.
    This is her size, her breadth. Thus trod my love.
    These true-love knots I pricked. I hold my life,
    By this old shoe I shall find out my wife.
Firk. Ha, ha! Old shoe, that wert new—how a murrain came   55
    this ague-fit of foolishness upon thee?

---

    34. *Saint . . . Paul's*] a church in the crypt of St Paul's which, Stow (I.329) records,
'serued for the Stacioners and others dwelling in Paules Churchyard . . . and the
places neare adioyning'—including, it would seem, Watling Street.
    35. *dispatch*] hurry with.
    37. *amazed*] (stronger than in modern usage).
    40. *pressed*] conscripted.
    43. *'Snails*] God's nails! (see iv.78, n.).
    44. *countryman of mine*] person from my neighbourhood, from my part of the
world.
    to] for.
    45. *thing*] (used of both the male and female organs).
    49. *mere*] complete.
    53. *pricked*] traced with dots or holes (O.E.D. 16); cf. i.241, and n.
    I . . . life] 'as sure as I live'.
    55. *murrain*] plague.

Ralph. Thus, Firk: even now here came a servingman;
    By this shoe would he have a new pair made
    Against tomorrow morning for his mistress,
    That's to be married to a gentleman.   60
    And why may not this be my sweet Jane?
Firk. And why mayst not thou be my sweet ass? Ha, ha!
Ralph. Well, laugh and spare not. But the truth is this.
    Against tomorrow morning I'll provide
    A lusty crew of honest shoemakers   65
    To watch the going of the bride to church.
    If she prove Jane, I'll take her in despite
    From Hammon and the devil, were he by.
    If it be not my Jane, what remedy?
    Hereof am I sure, I shall live till I die,   70
    Although I never with a woman lie.   *Exit.*
Firk. Thou lie with a woman—to build nothing but Cripple-
    gates! Well, God sends fools fortune, and it may be he
    may light upon his matrimony by such a device; for
    wedding and hanging goes by destiny.   *Exit.* 75

[SCENE XV.]
Enter [LACY *dressed as*] HANS *and* ROSE, *arm in arm.*

Lacy. How happy am I by embracing thee!
    O, I did fear such cross mishaps did reign
    That I should never see my Rose again.
Rose. Sweet Lacy, since fair opportunity
    Offers herself to further our escape,   5
    Let not too over-fond esteem of me

---

61. *sweet*] (two syllables).
63. *and spare not*] as much as you please.
70. *I shall . . . die*] proverbial; Tilley, L385 (this is his first citation).
72–3. *Cripplegates*] One of the seven gateways in London Wall, so called because
cripples congregated there. Firk is making a harsh allusion to Ralph's lameness;
cf.x.61.1, and n.
73. *God . . . fortune*] proverbial; Tilley, G220.
74. *device*] means, trick.
75. *wedding and hanging goes by destiny*] proverbial; Tilley, W232.

6. *over-fond . . . me*] i.e., over-scrupulous regard for my reputation.

     Hinder that happy hour. Invent the means,
     And Rose will follow thee through all the world.
Lacy. O, how I surfeit with excess of joy,
     Made happy by thy rich perfection!   10
     But since thou payest sweet interest to my hopes,
     Redoubling love on love, let me once more,
     Like to a bold-faced debtor, crave of thee
     This night to steal abroad, and at Eyre's house,
     Who now by death of certain aldermen   15
     Is Mayor of London, and my master once,
     Meet thou thy Lacy, where, in spite of chance,
     Your father's anger, and mine uncle's hate,
     Our happy nuptials will we consummate.

                         Enter SYBIL.

Sybil. O God, what will you do, mistress? Shift for yourself.   20
     Your father is at hand. He's coming, he's coming.
     Master Lacy, hide yourself. In, my mistress! For God's
     sake, shift for yourselves.
Lacy. Your father come! Sweet Rose, what shall I do?
     Where shall I hide me? How shall I escape?   25
Rose. A man, and want wit in extremity?
     Come, come: be Hans still; play the shoemaker.
     Pull on my shoe.

          Enter [Sir ROGER OATLEY, *the former*] Lord Mayor.

17 chance] *This ed.;* change Q*1*.   19 we] Q*3*; me Q*1*.
22 yourself. In,] *Sutherland;* your selfe in Q*1*.

___

     8. *follow . . . world*] Cf. Juliet towards the end of the 'balcony' scene: 'And all my
fortunes at thy foot I'll lay, / And follow thee, my lord, throughout the world'
(*R.&J.*, II.ii.147–8).
     15–16. *Who . . . London*] Cf. xiii.39–43, and n.
     17. *chance*] Q*1*'s 'change' has not been questioned, but *chance* both makes better
sense and provides a half-rhyme with *once,* leading in to the following couplet.
     22. *yourself. In.*] The emendation is uncertain. Bowers does not adopt it, allowing
that the Q reading may 'be retained as a piece of bawdy malapropism', especially as
'Sybil elsewhere addresses Rose simply as *mistris*'. This is fair but inconclusive. The
urgency of the dramatic situation supports the emendation.

Lacy.   Mass, and that's well remembered.

Sybil. Here comes your father.

Lacy [*as Hans*]. *Forware, metress, 'tis un good skoe, it sal vel dute,*   30
     or ye sal neit betaelen.

Rose. O God, it pincheth me! What will you do?

Lacy. [*Aside*] Your father's presence pincheth, not the shoe.

Oatley. Well done. Fit my daughter well, and she shall please
     thee well.   35

Lacy [*as Hans*]. *Yaw, yaw, ik weit dat well. Forware, 'tis un good*
     skoe, 'tis gi-mait van neat's leather; se ever, mine heer.

Oatley. I do believe it.

Enter a Prentice.

What's the news with you?

Prentice. Please you, the Earl of Lincoln at the gate
     Is newly lighted, and would speak with you.   40

Oatley. The Earl of Lincoln come to speak with me?
     Well, well, I know his errand. Daughter Rose,
     Send hence your shoemaker. Dispatch, have done.
     Syb, make things handsome. Sir boy, follow me.

Exeunt [OATLEY, SYBIL, *and* Prentice].

Lacy. Mine uncle come! O, what may this portend?   45
     Sweet Rose, this of our love threatens an end.

Rose. Be not dismayed at this. Whate'er befall,
     Rose is thine own. To witness I speak truth,

---

38 *Enter a* Prentice.] *as here, Harrison; after 'heer', l. 37, Q1.*
39–40] *as verse, Fritsche; as prose, Q1.*
41 come to speak] *Fritsche;* come speake *Q1.*
44.1 *Exeunt*] *Exit. Q1.*   47 this.] *Fritsche (this;);* this *Q1.*

30–1. Forware . . . betaelen] 'Indeed, mistress, 'tis a good shoe, it will do well, or
you shall not pay for it.'

34–5. Fit . . . well] Lacy interprets this in a sexual sense.

36–7. Yaw . . . heer] 'Yes, yes, I know that well. Indeed, 'tis a good shoe, 'tis made
of neat's [cow's] leather; just look, my lord.'

38.1. *Prentice*] Presumably Dekker, in this play in which so many apprentices
figure, here uses the term loosely for a young servant. See *Dram. Per*, 21–3, n.

41. *come to speak*] 'Although such metrical tinkering is to be regarded with
suspicion, the Lord Mayor usually speaks regular verse, and the emendation is
admitted here on the odds that the Q1 compositor omitted *to* by memorial
contamination from the preceding line, *would speake with you*' (Bowers). We agree
that error is likely.

Where thou appoints the place I'll meet with thee.
I will not fix a day to follow thee,   50
But presently steal hence. Do not reply.
Love which gave strength to bear my father's hate
Shall now add wings to further our escape.   *Exeunt.*

[SCENE XVI.]
Enter [Sir ROGER OATLEY, *the former*] Lord Mayor,
and [*the* Earl of] LINCOLN.

Oatley. Believe me, on my credit I speak truth,
         Since first your nephew Lacy went to France
         I have not seen him. It seemed strange to me
         When Dodger told me that he stayed behind,
         Neglecting the high charge the King imposed.   5
Lincoln. Trust me, Sir Roger Oatley, I did think
         Your counsel had given head to this attempt,
         Drawn to it by the love he bears your child.
         Here I did hope to find him in your house;
         But now I see mine error, and confess   10
         My judgement wronged you by conceiving so.
Oatley. Lodge in my house, say you? Trust me, my lord,
         I love your nephew Lacy too too dearly
         So much to wrong his honour; and he hath done so
         That first gave him advice to stay from France.   15
         To witness I speak truth, I let you know
         How careful I have been to keep my daughter
         Free from all conference or speech of him—
         Not that I scorn your nephew, but in love
         I bear your honour, lest your noble blood   20
         Should by my mean worth be dishonourèd.

---

49. *appoints*] (a common second-person form for verbs ending in *t*; Abbott, §340).
51. *presently*] immediately.
52–3. *Love . . . wings*] a variant of the proverb 'Love will find a way' (Tilley, L531).

Sc. xvi.] The action is continuous, and some editors run this scene on with the previous one; see p. 63.
7. *head*] authority, encouragement.
18. *conference . . . of*] communication with.

Lincoln. [*Aside*] How far the churl's tongue wanders from his
    heart!
    [*To Oatley*] Well, well, Sir Roger Oatley, I believe you,
    With more than many thanks for the kind love
    So much you seem to bear me. But, my lord,   25
    Let me request your help to seek my nephew,
    Whom if I find, I'll straight embark for France.
    So shall your Rose be free, my thoughts at rest,
    And much care die which now lives in my breast.

Enter SYBIL.

Sybil. O Lord, help, for God's sake. My mistress, O, my   30
    young mistress!
Oatley. Where is thy mistress? What's become of her?
Sybil. She's gone, she's fled!
Oatley.   Gone? Whither is she fled?
Sybil. I know not, forsooth. She's fled out of doors with Hans
    the shoemaker. I saw them scud, scud, scud, apace,   35
    apace.
Oatley. Which way? What, John, where be my men? Which
    way?
Sybil. I know not, an it please your worship.
Oatley. Fled with a shoemaker? Can this be true?
Sybil. O Lord, sir, as true as God's in heaven.   40
Lincoln. [*Aside*] Her love turned shoemaker! I am glad of this.

---

28 your . . . my] *Q3;* my . . . your *Q1.*
29 lives] *Fritsche;* dies *Q1;* lies *Q2.*   33] *as verse, Wheeler; as prose, Q1.*

---

  27. *embark*] (transitive).
  28. *your . . . my*] Q3's emendation has been generally accepted, and is inescapable.
  29. *lives*] Bowers adopts Q2's unauthoritative correction 'lies', but in his 'Corrections and revisions' (IV.407) he adds a note saying that 'some critics prefer the
Warnke–Proescholdt emendation *liues* for Q1 *dies*, instead of Q2 *lies*'. He admits
that '*liues* makes a sharper contrast with *die* earlier in the line', but says that 'the sense
would appear to be insufficient evidence to decide the crux'. In fact Warnke and
Proescholdt only offer the emendation as a suggestion, but we prefer it for both sense
and sound.
  35. *scud*] rush, scurry.
  37. *John*] presumably off-stage; perhaps identified in Dekker's mind with the
Prentice of xv.38 (see n.).

Oatley. A Fleming butter-box, a shoemaker!
    Will she forget her birth, requite my care
    With such ingratitude? Scorned she young Hammon
    To love a honnikin, a needy knave?   45
    Well, let her fly. I'll not fly after her.
    Let her starve if she will. She's none of mine.
Lincoln. Be not so cruel, sir.

Enter FIRK *with shoes.*

Sybil. [*Aside*]   I am glad she's 'scaped.
Oatley. I'll not account of her as of my child.
    Was there no better object for her eyes   50
    But a foul drunken lubber, swill-belly,
    A shoemaker? That's brave!
Firk. Yea, forsooth, 'tis a very brave shoe, and as fit as a
    pudding.
Oatley. How now, what knave is this? From whence comest
    thou?   55
Firk. No knave, sir. I am Firk, the shoemaker, lusty Roger's
    chief lusty journeyman, and I come hither to take up the
    pretty leg of sweet Mistress Rose, and thus hoping your

48] *as verse, Warnke and Proescholdt; as prose Q1.*

---

42. *Fleming butter-box*] Cf. iv.57, n.
45. *honnikin*] W. W. Skeat and A. L. Mayhew (*A Glossary of Tudor and Stuart Words*, Oxford, 1914), gloss as 'a term of contempt; a despised fellow', and suggest an origin in Middle High German *hone*, a despised person. But this is their only example of the word, and another possible explanation is that it is a diminutive of 'honey', which, as an endearment, could be 'used contemptuously of a man' (*Dialect Dict.*, North Country). It might also be another contemptuous allusion to the eating habits of the Dutch (cf. 'butter-box').
51. *drunken*] the conventional accusation; cf. iv.42–7, n.
lubber] lout, layabout.
52. *brave*] (sarcastic) excellent. In the following line, Firk supposes that the word is used straightforwardly of the shoes he carries.
53–4. *as fit . . . pudding*] from the proverb 'as fit as a pudding for a friar's mouth' (Tilley, P620).
56, 57. *lusty*] (with a range of meaning including 'jolly', 'strong', and 'lustful').
57. *take up*] attend to (as a shoemaker, but with bawdy overtones).
58–62. *thus . . . Firk*] (parodying the conventional ending of a letter; cf. *Much Ado*, I.i.243–7).

worship is in as good health as I was at the making
   hereof, I bid you farewell,   60
                 Yours,
                   Firk.

Oatley. Stay, stay, sir knave.

Lincoln.   Come hither, shoemaker.

Firk. 'Tis happy the knave is put before the shoemaker, or else
   I would not have vouchsafed to come back to you. I am   65
   moved; for I stir.

Oatley. My lord, this villain calls us knaves by craft.

Firk. Then 'tis by the Gentle Craft, and to call one 'knave'
   gently is no harm. Sit your worship merry. [*Aside*] Syb,
   your young mistress—I'll so bob them, now my master,   70
   Master Eyre, is Lord Mayor of London!

Oatley. Tell me, sirrah, whose man are you?

Firk. I am glad to see your worship so merry. I have no maw
   to this gear, no stomach as yet to a red petticoat (*pointing
   to* SYBIL).

Lincoln. He means not, sir, to woo you to his maid,   75
   But only doth demand whose man you are.

63] *as verse, Wheeler; as prose, Q1.*   70 them] *Q2; then Q1.*

---

66. *moved . . . stir*] Firk puns: both words could mean 'angered', 'feel emotion', as
well as 'move from one place to another'.

67. *calls . . . craft*] *craft*, cunning. The surface meaning of Firk's statement in the
previous speech is that the second form by which he has been addressed—*shoemaker*
—is conciliatory after *knave*. It is not clear why Oatley feels that Firk's *craft* (cunning)
has turned the insult back on to his superiors. Perhaps Firk was going off at the back
of the stage, and thus, when he turns round, Oatley and Lincoln are placed *before*
him: thus *before* has a double reference to time (innocuously) and (more offensively)
to place. Sutherland suggests that Firk 'had pretended to believe that the Lord
Mayor was really addressing Lincoln when he cried "Stay, stay, Sir Knave!" '.

69. *Sit . . . merry*] Cf. 'Rest you merry'—a form of farewell.

70. *bob*] make fools of, mock.

72. *man*] servant. Firk puns by taking him to mean 'husband', as if suggesting that
Firk should marry Sybil.

73. *maw*] stomach, appetite.

74. *gear*] Cf. xiii.29–30, n. Here the relevant senses seem to be 'apparel' (and thence
a woman—cf. *red petticoat*) and 'affair', 'business'.

stomach] appetite, inclination.

red petticoat] *petticoat* was used for 'woman'. Henley and Farmer show that *a red
petticoat* was used of a rich wife; here it seems more likely to be derogatory: cf. *1H4*,
I.2.8–9.

Firk. I sing now to the tune of Rogero. Roger, my fellow, is
now my master.

Lincoln. Sirrah, knowest thou one Hans, a shoemaker?

Firk. Hans shoemaker? O yes, stay, yes, I have him. I tell you   80
what—I speak it in secret—Mistress Rose and he are by
this time—no, not so, but shortly are to come over one
another with 'Can you dance the shaking of the sheets?'
It is that Hans—[*Aside*] I'll so gull these diggers.

Oatley. Knowest thou then where he is?   85

Firk. Yes, forsooth. Yea, marry.

Lincoln. Canst thou in sadness?

Firk. No, forsooth. No, marry.

Oatley. Tell me, good, honest fellow, where he is,
And thou shalt see what I'll bestow of thee.   90

Firk. 'Honest fellow'? No, sir, not so, sir. My profession is the
Gentle Craft. I care not for seeing, I love feeling. Let me
feel it here, *aurium tenus,* ten pieces of gold, *genuum tenus,*
ten pieces of silver, and then Firk is your man in a new
pair of stretchers.   95

---

77. *Rogero*] a popular tune, to which many different ballads were sung; cf. W.
Chappell, *Popular Music of the Olden Time* (London [1855–59]; repr. New York,
1965), I.93–5.

80. *have him*] know whom you mean.

83. *the shaking . . . sheets*] the name of a dance tune, often used as the basis for a
sexual joke, as at xxi.30; Henley and Farmer define as 'the act of kind'. Cf., e.g.,
Dekker and Webster's *Westward Ho*, V.iii.28.

84. *gull*] fool.

diggers] (for information).

87. *Canst thou*] Do you know? *O.E.D.* records *can* (cf. 'ken') in this sense up to
1649.

in sadness] seriously.

90. *of*] on.

91. *'Honest fellow'? No, sir*] i.e., he is not Oatley's *fellow* (colleague, or equal).

92. *seeing . . . feeling*] i.e., it is not enough for him to *see* the money (with a bawdy
quibble).

93. *here*] i.e., on his palm.

aurium tenus . . . genuum tenus] 'up to the ears' . . . 'up to the knees'. Firk seems to
mean that for ten pieces of *gold* he will give full information, but for *silver*, only
partial. There is a pun on *tenus* and *ten*. As Sutherland points out, in William Lilly's
Short Introduction of Grammar, which Dekker probably used, '*Aurium Tenus,* Vp to
the eares', is given as an example of the genitive with *tenus* (1549, sig. C4).

95. *stretchers*] (*a*) shoe stretchers; (*b*) lies (*O.E.D.* I.2, not recorded before 1674).

Oatley. Here is an angel, part of thy reward,
    Which I will give thee, tell me where he is.
Firk. No point. Shall I betray my brother? No. Shall I prove
    Judas to Hans? No. Shall I cry treason to my corpo-
    ration? No. I shall be firked and yerked then. But give   100
    me your angel. Your angel shall tell you.
Lincoln. Do so, good fellow. 'Tis no hurt to thee.
Firk. Send simpering Syb away.
Oatley. Huswife, get you in.   *Exit* SYBIL.
Firk. Pitchers have ears, and maids have wide mouths. But   105
    for Hauns Prauns, upon my word, tomorrow morning
    he and young Mistress Rose go to this gear. They shall
    be married together, by this rush, or else turn Firk to a
    firkin of butter to tan leather withal.
Oatley. But art thou sure of this?   110
Firk. Am I sure that Paul's Steeple is a handful higher than

97 thee] Q*1*; thee; *Fritsche.*

---

96. *angel*] Cf. ix.97.
97. *tell*] (probably the subjunctive used conditionally; Abbott §364).
98. *No point*] not a bit, not at all.
99–100. *corporation*] guild.
100. *firked and yerked*] See xiii.28, n.
101. *angel . . . you*] (possibly glancing at the function of angels as message-bearers).
104. *Huswife*] hussy, wench.
105. *Pitchers . . . ears*] proverbial; 'Small pitchers have wide ears' (Tilley, P363).
maids . . . mouths] Cf. Tilley, W701, 'Women are great talkers'.
106. *Hauns Prauns*] Hauns is a common alternative spelling in Q1 for Hans. It is
preserved here because the parallel spelling 'Prauns' completes a jocular nickname
which may pun on both 'prance' (suggesting affectation) and 'prawns'.
107. *gear*] business (cf. xiii.29–30, n.).
108. *by this rush*] Steane, improbably, finds 'an allusion to rush rings, sometimes
used for weddings, often by a bridegroom who had no intention of being held by his
vows'. More likely this is a very light oath (rushes were proverbially of negligible
value), referring to rushes used to strew the floors.
109. *firkin*] a small keg.
butter . . . leather] Butter is not a tanning agent, but various fats and oils can be used
in the dressing of leather.
111. *Paul's Steeple*] The wooden spire on the top of the tower of St Paul's was
burned down in 1561, and never repaired (Stow, I.331–2). Dekker's *The Dead Term*
includes a section called 'Paul's Steeple's Complaint', couched in autobiographical
terms (1608, sigs. D2–E1; Grosart, IV.42–52). The present reference might therefore
be an attempt to place the action in Eyre's historical period. But this would be

London Stone? Or that the Pissing Conduit leaks
nothing but pure Mother Bunch? Am I sure I am lusty
Firk? God's nails, do you think I am so base to gull you?
Lincoln. Where are they married? Dost thou know the
    church?   115
Firk. I never go to church, but I know the name of it. It is a
    swearing church. Stay a while, 'tis 'Ay, by the
    Mass'—no, no, 'tis 'Ay, by my troth'—no, nor that, 'tis
    'Ay, by my faith'—that, that, 'tis 'Ay by my Faith's'
    Church under Paul's Cross. There they shall be knit like   120

---

uncharacteristic (cf. Introduction, pp. 24–6), and the term *Steeple* is probably used
here, as it frequently was, to refer to the stone tower which survived the fire: see
Sugden, who cites many instances, including several from Dekker. The tower was
285 feet high; the spire had added a further 208 feet.

112. *London Stone*] a large stone, probably of Roman origin, fixed in Candlewick
(now Cannon) Street, near St Swithin's Church, and a famous London landmark
mentioned in several plays of the period. Stow (I.224) describes it as 'pitched
vpright, a great stone . . . fixed in the ground verie deepe, fastned with bars of iron,
and otherwise so strongly set, that if Cartes do run against it through negligence, the
wheeles be broken, and the stone it selfe vnshaken . . . Some haue said this stone to be
set, as a marke in the middle of the Citie within the walles: but in truth it standeth
farre nearer vnto the river of Thames, then to the wall of the Citie.'
   Pissing Conduit] So called because of the slender stream of water it provided, the
'little Conduit, called the pissing Conduit, by the Stockes Market' (Stow, I.183) was
at the junction of Cornhill, Threadneedle Street, and Lombard Street. It was built in
1500.

113. *pure Mother Bunch*] Sutherland cites the Epistle to *Pasquils Jests and Mother
Bunches Merriments* (1604) as saying that Mother Bunch 'dwelt in Cornehill (neere
the Exchange) [and therefore near the Conduit], and sold strong Ale' (*The Shakespeare Jest Books*, ed. W. C. Hazlitt, 3 vols, London, 1864, III.9–10). Her 'slimie ale' is
mentioned in Nashe's *Pierce Pennilesse* of 1593 (McKerrow, I.173). As Sutherland
comments: 'Either Mother Bunch's strong ale was so weak as to have lent its name as
a synonym for water, or else the Conduit "leaked" very dirty brown water of the
colour of her ale.'

114. *God's nails*] See iv.78, n.

116. *I . . . church*] Legally, church-going was compulsory; but the law was often
neglected. But perhaps 'the' has been omitted before *church*. This would make a
more satisfactory antecedent for *it*.

116–17. *a swearing church*] a church whose name might be used as an oath.

117–18. *by the Mass*] Cf. xiv.2, n.

119–20. *Faith's . . . Cross*] Cf. xiv.34, n. Paul's Cross was a wooden pulpit-cross on
a stone foundation and roofed with lead, from which public sermons were delivered. It was on the north side of St Paul's near the east (St Faith's) end.

a pair of stockings in matrimony. There they'll be
incony.

Lincoln. Upon my life, my nephew Lacy walks
In the disguise of this Dutch shoemaker.

Firk. Yes, forsooth.   125

Lincoln. Doth he not, honest fellow?

Firk. No, forsooth, I think Hans is nobody but Hans, no
spirit.

Oatley. My mind misgives me now 'tis so indeed.

Lincoln. My cousin speaks the language, knows the trade.   130

Oatley. Let me request your company, my lord.
Your honourable presence may, no doubt,
Refrain their headstrong rashness, when myself,
Going alone, perchance may be o'erborne.
Shall I request this favour?

Lincoln.   This or what else.   135

Firk. Then you must rise betimes, for they mean to fall to
their 'hey-pass-and-repass, pindy-pandy, which hand
will you have?' very early.

Oatley. My care shall every way equal their haste.
This night accept your lodging in my house.   140
The earlier shall we stir, and at Saint Faith's
Prevent this giddy, hare-brained nuptial.

---

127 nobody] *Q3;* no bodie, *Q1.* Hans,] *Q3;* Hans *Q1.*

---

122. *incony*] a word of unknown origin, first found in *L.L.L.,* III.i.128; see R.
David's note in the Arden edition, where he quotes *O.E.D.*'s definition 'rare, fine,
delicate, pretty, nice' and adds: 'In Dekker's *Shoemaker's Holiday* . . . "incony" takes
on a more active sense, almost Shakespeare's "honeying".'

125. *Yes, forsooth*] Q1's designation of speaker has not been questioned by editors,
but the reply comes oddly from Firk, especially in comparison with his next remark
(ll. 127–8), and would seem to be more appropriate to Oatley. Perhaps Firk's
vacillations are part of his plan to *bob* Lincoln and Oatley (l. 70).

133. *Refrain*] restrain (a normal use).

135. *what else*] anything else.

136. *betimes*] very early; cf. xiv.12 and 19–20.

137. *hey-pass-and-repass*] a conjurer's formula, used, e.g., in making things vanish
or (more relevant here) exchange places.

pindy-pandy] like 'handy-dandy' in the game of choosing in which hand something is concealed. The allusion is to the giving of hands in marriage.

This traffic of hot love shall yield cold gains.
They ban our loves, and we'll forbid their banns.   *Exit.*
Lincoln. At Saint Faith's Church, thou sayst?   145
Firk. Yes, by their troth.
Lincoln. Be secret, on thy life.   [*Exit.*]
Firk. Yes, when I kiss your wife! Ha, ha, here's no craft in the
     Gentle Craft. I came hither of purpose with shoes to Sir
     Roger's worship, whilst Rose his daughter be coney-   150
     catched by Hans. Soft, now, these two gulls will be at
     Saint Faith's Church tomorrow morning to take Master
     Bridegroom and Mistress Bride napping, and they in
     the meantime shall chop up the matter at the Savoy. But
     the best sport is, Sir Roger Oatley will find my fellow,   155
     lame Ralph's wife, going to marry a gentleman, and
     then he'll stop her instead of his daughter. O brave,
     there will be fine tickling sport. Soft now, what have I
     to do? O, I know—now a mess of shoemakers meet at

---

144 *Exit.*] *Q3; exeunt, Q1.*   147 *Exit.*] *Q3; not in Q1.*
155–6 fellow, lame] *Fritsche;* felow lame, *Q1.*
159 know—now] (know, now) *Q1;* know now, *Bowers.*

---

143. *traffic*] business (the imagery is appropriate to the speaker).
143–4. *gains . . . banns*] (a rhyme; *banns* is spelled 'baines' in Q1, reflecting contemporary pronunciation).
146. *their*] There is something to be said for Warnke and Proescholdt's suggestion of 'my', though few subsequent editors have adopted it. Firk may, however, be joking on the lovers' *troth*.
148. *kiss your wife*] Firk's cheeky rhyme may echo a popular tag of the time.
150–51 *coney-catched*] tricked. 'Coney-catchers' were city tricksters who exploited the innocence of 'coneys' from the country inexperienced in city ways.
154. *chop up*] settle; not recorded in this sense, but related to *chop*, 'barter, give in exchange' (*O.E.D.* v², I); cf. Deloney (p. 124): 'thinking him the fittest Chapplaine to chop vp such a mariage'.
the Savoy] The Savoy Palace, on the north bank of the Thames between the Strand and the river, was destroyed in 1381, when in the possession of John of Gaunt, by Wat Tyler and his followers. At the historical time of the action of *The Shoemaker's Holiday* it was in ruins. Henry VII rebuilt it in 1505 as a hospital to house one hundred poor people. Its early-sixteenth-century chapel was much used for clandestine marriages (Sugden).
158. *tickling*] Cf. xi.74, n.
159. *mess*] group of people, especially one gathered to eat together (as, apparently, here).

    the Woolsack in Ivy Lane to cozen my gentleman of   160
lame Ralph's wife, that's true.
    Alack, alack,
    Girls, hold out tack,
    For now smocks for this jumbling
    Shall go to wrack.   *Exit.*   165

[SCENE XVII.]
Enter EYRE, [MARGERY] *his wife,* [LACY *dressed as*] HANS, *and*
ROSE.

Eyre. This is the morning, then—say, my bully, my honest
    Hans—is it not?
Lacy. This is the morning that must make us two
    Happy or miserable; therefore if you—
Eyre. Away with these ifs and ans, Hans, and these etceteras.   5
    By mine honour, Rowland Lacy, none but the King

162–5] *as verse, Fritsche; as prose, Q1.*

1 say] *Wheeler; stay Q1.*   3–4] *as verse, Spencer; as prose, Q1.*

---

160. *Woolsack . . . Lane*] a tavern in the street running north from Paternoster Row to Newgate Street.
cozen] trick.
162–5] This has only a tenuous relationship to the actual situation, and may be a snatch of a song. But such jingles at the ends of scenes are not uncommon: cf., e.g., Anthony Munday, *The Downfall of Robert Earl of Huntington*, 1601, sig. A3v–A4, etc., and *Lr.*, III.ii.81 ff.
163. *hold out tack*] hold your own, stand firm.
164. *smocks*] i.e., women, maidenheads.
for this jumbling] as a result of this disorder.
0.1. LACY dressed as HANS] i.e., wearing the clothes that he wore as Hans, but no longer disguising his identity in any other way.
1. *say*] Bowers collates the emendation and has a note justifying it: 'Although the Qq reading *stay* can be defended if we suppose that Eyre checks the eager Lacy in order to converse with him, the result may seem rather tortuous in view of the fact that the *say* phrase is common in Dekker.' Nevertheless, in all three printings his text accidentally reads 'stay', which is followed by Davies, Steane, and Palmer.
bully] comrade, friend (one of the favourite words of the Host of the Garter in *M.W.W.*). The word, implying hearty companionship, seems to have had a special vogue about 1600, and occurs also in *H5*. (See also xviii.23 and xxi.25.)
5. *ifs and ans*] (Tilley, I16).
etceteras] uncertainties (probably by parody of legal phraseology).

shall wrong thee. Come, fear nothing. Am not I Sim
Eyre? Is not Sim Eyre Lord Mayor of London? Fear
nothing, Rose. Let them all say what they can. 'Dainty,
come thou to me.' Laughest thou?   10

Margery. Good my lord, stand her friend in what thing you
may.

Eyre. Why, my sweet Lady Madgy, think you Simon Eyre
can forget his fine Dutch journeyman? No, vah! Fie, I
scorn it. It shall never be cast in my teeth that I was   15
unthankful. Lady Madgy, thou hadst never covered thy
Saracen's head with this French flap, nor loaden thy
bum with this farthingale—'tis trash, trumpery, vanity
—Simon Eyre had never walked in a red petticoat, nor
wore a chain of gold, but for my fine journeyman's   20
portagues; and shall I leave him? No. Prince am I none,
yet bear a princely mind.

Lacy. My lord, 'tis time for us to part from hence.

Eyre. Lady Madgy, Lady Madgy, take two or three of my
piecrust eaters, my buff-jerkin varlets, that do walk in   25

9–10. *Dainty . . . me.*] presumably intended to be sung, as an expression of
ebullience; there are several references to a lost tune of this name; cf., e.g., W.
Chappell, *Popular Music of the Olden Time*, 2 vols [1855–59], repr. New York, 1965,
II.517, where the ballad of Sir Richard Whittington is to be sung to this tune.

11. *stand*] act as (as usual, there are bawdy overtones to Margery's remark).

14. *vah!*] an expression of contempt.

15. *cast . . . teeth*] brought against me (as an accusation).

17. *Saracen's head*] used as a target (cf. vii.63–4, n.) and as an inn-sign; here, a
generalised insult. Dekker writes elsewhere of a rogue with 'a face staring like a
Saracen' (*Lantern and Candlelight*, Pendry, p. 219).

French flap] her French hood; cf. x.37, 150, and n.

17–18. *loaden thy bum*] Cf. x.37–8, n.

19. *red petticoat*] Cf. xi.13, and n.

21. *portagues*] Cf. vii 24, n. and 100.

21–2. *Prince . . . mind*] Cf. vii.49–50, n.

25. *piecrust eaters*] Possibly a memory of Deloney's story (pp. 160 ff.) of the affairs
of Eyre's servants, in which a venison pasty plays an important role. But since
Dekker associates shoemakers with an inn called the Woolsack (xvi.160) there may
be a connection with the famous Woolsack pies mentioned by Jonson (*The
Alchemist*, ed. F. H. Mares, Revels Plays, V.iv.41)—though Sugden makes it clear
that two different inns of the same name are involved.

buff-jerkin] an official uniform, worn by sheriffs' officers, etc. (see Linthicum, p.
240, and cf. *1H4*, I.ii.41, 45).

varlets] (his attendants).

black gowns at Simon Eyre's heels. Take them, good
Lady Madgy, trip and go, my brown Queen of Periwigs, with my delicate Rose and my jolly Rowland to
the Savoy, see them linked, countenance the marriage,
and when it is done, cling, cling together, you Ham-   30
borow turtle-doves. I'll bear you out. Come to Simon
Eyre, come dwell with me, Hans, thou shalt eat minced-
pies and marchpane. Rose, away, cricket. Trip and go,
my Lady Madgy, to the Savoy. Hans, wed and to bed;
kiss and away; go; vanish.   35

Margery. Farewell, my lord.

Rose. Make haste, sweet love.

Margery.   She'ld fain the deed were done.

Lacy. Come, my sweet Rose, faster than deer we'll run.

                                        They go out.

Eyre. Go, vanish, vanish, avaunt, I say. By the Lord of
Ludgate, it's a mad life to be a Lord Mayor. It's a stirring   40
life, a fine life, a velvet life, a careful life. Well, Simon

---

37] *as verse, Warnke and Proescholdt; as prose, Q1.*

27. *trip and go*] Cf. iv.30–1, n.
brown] presumably the colour of Margery's wig; possibly, in view of *good, delicate,*
and *jolly,* a misprint for *brave.*
27–8. *Periwigs*] Cf. x.46.
29. *Savoy*] Cf. xvi.154, n.
countenance] witness.
30. *cling*] For the sexual sense, not recorded in *O.E.D.,* see, e.g., Tourneur,
Revenger's Tragedy, I.iii.59, 'slide from the mother, and cling the daughter-in-law',
and Marston, *2 Antonio and Mellida,* I.v.8, 'clinged in sensuality'.
30–1. *Hamborow*] presumably Hamburg; but the allusion is unexplained.
31. *bear you out*] support you, stand by you.
32–3. *minced-pies*] pies containing minced meat (not sweet mince-meat).
33. *marchpane*] marzipan, or cakes made of it (a luxury).
cricket] (used as a term of endearment).
37. *deed*] (*a*) marriage; (*b*) (of love).
39. *avaunt*] begone! away!
39–40. *Lord of Ludgate*] Cf. i.173, n.
41. *velvet*] 'velvet-jacket' was a slang term for a steward or mayor (Henley and
Farmer); cf. Heywood, *1 Edward IV* (ed. Shepherd, I.17): 'spoken like a man, and
veluet-iacket' (addressed to the Lord Mayor). The phrase 'on velvet' (meaning 'in
easy circumstances') is not recorded before 1769 (*O.D.E.P.*), but *velvet* may be used
figuratively here.
careful] full of care and responsibility. 'Carefree' or 'cheerful' would be more
consonant with the rest of the sentence; but perhaps Eyre is listing the varied aspects
of his life, not simply its pleasures.

Eyre, yet set a good face on it, in the honour of Saint
Hugh. Soft, the King this day comes to dine with me, to
see my new buildings. His Majesty is welcome. He shall
have good cheer, delicate cheer, princely cheer. This   45
day my fellow prentices of London come to dine with
me too. They shall have fine cheer, gentlemanlike cheer.
I promised the mad Cappadocians, when we all served
at the conduit together, that if ever I came to be Mayor
of London, I would feast them all; and I'll do't, I'll do't,   50
by the life of Pharaoh, by this beard, Sim Eyre will be no
flincher. Besides, I have procured that upon every
Shrove Tuesday, at the sound of the pancake bell, my
fine dapper Assyrian lads shall clap up their shop win-

42–3. *Saint Hugh*] Cf. Second Song, 2, n.

44. *my new buildings*] Leadenhall. The name is conferred by the King at xxi.130–4
(see n.).

48–55. *I promised . . . away*] Dekker follows Deloney (Appendix A, p. 217) in
ascribing the institution of the Shrove Tuesday festival to Eyre. In fact, since well
before Eyre's time the Tuesday before the beginning of Lent had traditionally been
an occasion for feasting and merriment before the Lenten fast. In Dekker's time it
seems to have been particularly associated with apprentice exuberance, often leading
to riotous behaviour. Dekker himself refers to this on several occasions (e.g.,
Northward Ho, IV.iii.76–7; *Seven Deadly Sins*, 1606, sig. F2 (Grosart, II.65); *Work for
Armourers*, 1609, sig. C1v (Grosart, IV.109)).

48. *Cappadocians*] one of Eyre's frequent, grandiloquent terms for his companions.
It may be related to 'Cappadochio' (also 'caperdewsie' and 'caperdochy'), meaning
the stocks, or prison.

48–9. *served . . . conduit*] It was the custom for apprentices to forgather at the
conduits, from which they took water to their masters' houses; cf. Heywood, *The
Four Prentices of London*, and *2 If You Know Not Me* (ed. Shepherd, I.256 and II.169).

51. *by . . . Pharaoh*] Cf. i.174–5, n.

53. *pancake bell*] Dekker does not precisely ascribe the institution of the *pancake bell*
to Eyre, as Deloney does (Appendix A, p. 217). As Shrove Tuesday was a holy day
the bells rang to call the citizens to church; but they were naturally also associated
with the festivities, and the preparations for making pancakes. In 1620 John Taylor,
the Water-Poet, describes the effects of the ringing of the bell: 'Shrove Tuesday. At
whose entrance in the morning, all the whole kingdome is in quiet, but by that time
the clocke strikes eleuen, which (by the helpe of a knauish Sexton) is commonly
before nine, then there is a Bell rung, call'd *The Pancake Bell*, the sound whereof
makes thousands of people distracted, and forgetfull eyther of manners or humani-
tie' (*Jack à Lent*, 1620, sig. B2).

54. *Assyrian lads*] 'jolly good fellows' (Sugden).

clap up] shut (appropriate to the wooden window-flaps which formed the
shop-counters).

dows and away. This is the day, and this day they shall   55
do't, they shall do't.
    Boys, that day are you free. Let masters care,
And prentices shall pray for Simon Eyre.   *Exit.*

[SCENE XVIII.]
Enter HODGE, FIRK, RALPH, *and five or six* Shoemakers,
all with cudgels, or such weapons.

Hodge. Come, Ralph. Stand to it, Firk. My masters, as we are
the brave bloods of the shoemakers, heirs apparent to
Saint Hugh, and perpetual benefactors to all good fellows, thou shalt have no wrong. Were Hammon a king
of spades, he should not delve in thy close without thy   5
sufferance. But tell me, Ralph, art thou sure 'tis thy
wife?

Ralph. Am I sure this is Firk? This morning, when I stroked
on her shoes, I looked upon her, and she upon me, and
sighed, asked me if ever I knew one Ralph. 'Yes', said I.   10
'For his sake', said she, tears standing in her eyes, 'and for
thou art somewhat like him, spend this piece of gold.' I
took it. My lame leg and my travel beyond sea made me
unknown. All is one for that. I know she's mine.

Firk. Did she give thee this gold? O glorious, glittering gold.   15
She's thine own. 'Tis thy wife, and she loves thee; for,
I'll stand to't, there's no woman will give gold to any

57–8] *as verse, Fritsche; as prose, Q1.*

---

57. *Let masters care*] i.e., the masters will have to put up with it, to take responsibility themselves.

2. *bloods*] kin; valiant comrades.

4–5. *king of spades*] an allusion to the playing-card, introduced for the sake of
word-play with *delve. Spade* could also mean 'eunuch'; perhaps Hodge means 'if he
were very powerful *(king)* though entirely harmless (a eunuch) . . .'.

5. *delve . . . close*] (bawdy).

6. *sufferance*] consent.

8. *stroked*] eased.

17–19. *there's . . . silver to*] a kind of mock-proverb, stating the obvious in jocularly
formulaic fashion.

man but she thinks better of him than she thinks of them
she gives silver to. And for Hammon, neither Hammon
nor hangman shall wrong thee in London. Is not our old   20
master, Eyre, Lord Mayor? Speak, my hearts.

All. Yes, and Hammon shall know it to his cost.

Enter HAMMON, [a Servant] *his man,* JANE, *and others.*

Hodge. Peace, my bullies. Yonder they come.

Ralph. Stand to't, my hearts. Firk, let me speak first.

Hodge. No, Ralph, let me. Hammon, whither away so early?   25

Hammon. Unmannerly rude slave, what's that to thee?

Firk. To him, sir? Yes, sir, and to me, and others. Good
    morrow, Jane, how dost thou? Good Lord, how the
    world is changed with you, God be thanked.

Hammon. Villains, hands off! How dare you touch my
    love?   30

All [the Shoemakers]. Villains? Down with them. Cry 'Clubs
    for prentices!'

Hodge. Hold, my hearts. Touch her, Hammon? Yea, and
    more than that, we'll carry her away with us. My
    masters and gentlemen, never draw your bird-spits.   35
    Shoemakers are steel to the back, men every inch of
    them, all spirit.

All of Hammon's side. Well, and what of all this?

Hodge. I'll show you. Jane, dost thou know this man? 'Tis
    Ralph, I can tell thee. Nay, 'tis he, in faith. Though he be   40

19–20. *Hammon nor hangman*] 'A double pun: (1) the similar sound; (2) the
Hammon in the play and the Haman in the Book of Esther, who having prepared a
gallows fifty cubits high for his enemy was strung up on it himself' (Steane).

22.1. *others*] i.e., servants 'of Hammon's side' (l. 38).

23. *bullies*] Cf. xvii.1, n.

26. *rude*] rough (stronger than the modern sense).

31. *Cry*] It is just possible that this is a direction to the actors which has been
accidentally printed as part of the spoken text.

31–2. *Clubs for prentices!*] a rallying-cry; the apprentices enjoyed a fray. Cf. *H8*,
V.iv.51–4: 'that woman, who cried out "Clubs!" when I might see from far some
forty truncheoners draw to her succour'.

35. *bird-spits*] (figurative) rapiers. (Cf. *fiddlestick*, *R.&J.*, III.i.51; *toasting-iron*, *King
John*, IV.iii.99; also *R.&J.*, IV.iii.56: 'spit his body / Upon a rapier's point'.)

lamed by the wars, yet look not strange, but run to him;
　　fold him about the neck, and kiss him.
Jane. Lives then my husband? O God, let me go,
　　Let me embrace my Ralph!
Hammon.　　　　　　　　　What means my Jane?
Jane. Nay, what meant you to tell me he was slain?　　　　45
Hammon. Pardon me, dear love, for being misled.
　　[*To Ralph*] 'Twas rumoured here in London thou
　　wert dead.
Firk. Thou seest he lives. Lass, go, pack home with him.
　　Now, Master Hammon, where's your mistress your
　　wife?　　　　　　　　　　　　　　　　　　　　50
Servant. 'Swounds, master, fight for her. Will you thus lose
　　her?
All [*the Shoemakers*]. Down with that creature! Clubs! Down
　　with him!
Hodge. Hold, hold!　　　　　　　　　　　　　　　55
Hammon. Hold, fool! Sirs, he shall do no wrong.
　　Will my Jane leave me thus, and break her faith?
Firk. Yea, sir, she must, sir, she shall, sir. What then? Mend it.
Hodge. Hark, fellow Ralph. Follow my counsel. Set the
　　wench in the midst, and let her choose her man, and let　　60
　　her be his woman.
Jane. Whom should I choose? Whom should my thoughts
　　affect
　　But him whom heaven hath made to be my love?
　　[*To Ralph*] Thou art my husband, and these humble
　　weeds
　　Makes thee more beautiful than all his wealth.　　　　65
　　Therefore I will but put off his attire

---

41. *look . . . strange*] do not look at him as if you did not know him (O.E.D. 'strange', 11e).
46. *misled*] See xii.83, n.
48. *pack*] be off.
51. *'Swounds*] By God's wounds.
53. *creature*] (a stronger insult than now) 'toady'.
62. *affect*] love.
64. *weeds*] (his shoemaker's clothes, contrasted with Hammon's wedding finery).
66. *his attire*] i.e., the wedding clothes that Hammon has evidently paid for.

Returning it into the owner's hand,
And after ever be thy constant wife.

Hodge. Not a rag, Jane. The law's on our side. He that sows in
    another man's ground forfeits his harvest. Get thee   70
    home, Ralph. Follow him, Jane. He shall not have so
    much as a busk point from thee.

Firk. Stand to that, Ralph. The appurtenances are thine own.
    Hammon, look not at her.

Servant. O 'swounds, no.   75

Firk. Bluecoat, be quiet. We'll give you a new livery else.
    We'll make Shrove Tuesday Saint George's Day for
    you. Look not, Hammon. Leer not. I'll firk you. For thy
    head now—one glance, one sheep's eye, anything at
    her. Touch not a rag, lest I and my brethren beat you to   80
    clouts.

Servant. Come, Master Hammon, there's no striving here.

Hammon. Good fellows, hear me speak. And, honest
    Ralph,
    Whom I have injured most by loving Jane,
    Mark what I offer thee. Here in fair gold   85
    Is twenty pound. I'll give it for thy Jane.

69–70. *He that . . . harvest*] not recorded as a proverb; but cf. Tilley, G470: 'Who builds upon another's ground loses both mortar and stones.'

72. *busk point*] lace for tying down a bodice, 'often used as a type of something of small value' (*O.E.D.*). They were also used as lovers' favours (Linthicum, p. 178), and at weddings (see Deloney, *Jack of Newbury*: 'shee was led to Church betweene two sweet boyes, with Bride laces and Rosemary tied about their silken sleeues' (Lawlis, p. 29)).

73. *appurtenances*] (a legal term) belongings, appendages.

76. *Bluecoat*] the servant's traditional blue livery.

77–8. *We'll . . . for you*] The threat to give a new livery may be simply a threat of dismissal. *Shrove Tuesday* will thus become *Saint George's Day* because on that day domestic servants traditionally looked for new employment. There may also be a more physical threat: the blue coat will be stained with blood, red being the colour of St George's cross.

78. *firk*] See *Dram. Per.*, 19, n.

For] for the sake of, at peril of.

79. *one*] i.e., not one.

sheep's eye] amorous look (Tilley, S323).

81. *clouts*] rags.

82. *no striving*] i.e., no point in resisting.

85–6. *Here . . . pound*] It is clear from ll. 97 and 105–6 that Hammon produces the gold and lays it down.

If this content thee not, thou shalt have more.
Hodge. Sell not thy wife, Ralph. Make her not a whore.
Hammon. Say, wilt thou freely cease thy claim in her,
 And let her be my wife?   90
All [the Shoemakers]. No, do not, Ralph!
Ralph. Sirrah Hammon, Hammon, dost thou think a shoe-
 maker is so base to be a bawd to his own wife for
 commodity? Take thy gold, choke with it! Were I not
 lame, I would make thee eat thy words.   95
Firk. A shoemaker sell his flesh and blood—O indignity!
Hodge. Sirrah, take up your pelf, and be packing.
Hammon. I will not touch one penny. But in lieu
 Of that great wrong I offerèd thy Jane,
 To Jane and thee I give that twenty pound.   100
 Since I have failed of her, during my life
 I vow no woman else shall be my wife.
 Farewell, good fellows of the Gentle Trade.
 Your morning's mirth my mourning day hath made.
       Exeunt [HAMMON *and* Servants].
Firk. [*To Servant going out*] Touch the gold, creature, if you   105
 dare. You're best be trudging. Here, Jane, take thou it.
 Now let's home, my hearts.
Hodge. Stay, who comes here? Jane, on again with thy mask.

  Enter [the Earl of] LINCOLN, [Sir ROGER OATLEY, *the*
   former] Lord Mayor, *and* Servants.

Lincoln. Yonder's the lying varlet mocked us so.
Oatley. Come hither, sirrah.   110
Firk. Ay sir, I am sirrah. You mean me, do you not?

---

 92. *Sirrah*] (contemptuous).
 94. *commodity*] profit.
 97. *pelf*] money (contemptuous).
 102. *I vow . . . wife*] See Introduction, p. 36.
 104.1 *Servants*] i.e., the one who has spoken, and the *others* (l. 22.1) 'of Hammon's side' (l. 38).
 105. *creature*] Cf. l. 53, n.
 108. *mask*] Elizabethan ladies frequently wore masks as a protection against the sun, and on certain social occasions. Jane's mask, however, is primarily a dramatic device which makes it possible for Oatley to mistake her for Rose.

Lincoln. Where is my nephew married?

Firk. Is he married? God give him joy, I am glad of it. They
have a fair day, and the sign is in a good planet, Mars in
Venus.   115

Oatley. Villain, thou told'st me that my daughter Rose
This morning should be married at Saint Faith's.
We have watched there these three hours at the least,
Yet see we no such thing.

Firk. Truly, I am sorry for't. A bride's a pretty thing.   120

Hodge. Come to the purpose. Yonder's the bride and bridegroom you look for, I hope. Though you be lords, you
are not to bar by your authority men from women, are
you?

Oatley. See, see, my daughter's masked.

Lincoln.   True, and my nephew,   125
To hide his guilt, counterfeits him lame.

Firk. Yea, truly, God help the poor couple; they are lame and
blind.

Oatley. I'll ease her blindness.

Lincoln.   I'll his lameness cure.

Firk. [*Aside, to the Shoemakers*] Lie down, sirs, and laugh! My   130
fellow, Ralph, is taken for Rowland Lacy, and Jane for
Mistress Damask Rose—this is all my knavery!

Oatley. [*to Jane*] What, have I found you, minion!

Lincoln. [*to Ralph*]   O base wretch!
Nay, hide thy face; the horror of thy guilt
Can hardly be washed off. Where are thy powers?   135
What battles have you made? O yes, I see

114–15. *sign . . . Venus*] astrologically faulty. 'The planet is found in the sign, not
the sign in the planet, nor is Mars a sign. Planets of good luck in opposition were
generally held to produce an evil influence; but Firk apparently means to say that
Mars and Venus were in conjunction, and therefore all was well' (Sutherland).

117. *Saint Faith's*] Cf. xiv. 34, n.

120. *A bride's . . . thing*] Firk cheekily pretends to believe that Oatley simply
wanted to watch a wedding.

127–8. *lame and blind*] perhaps an echo of Luke xiv.21: 'bring in hither the poore,
and the maymed, and the halt, and the blind'.

132. *Damask Rose*] a variety of rose, punning on Rose's name.

133. *minion*] See ix. 62, n.

135. *powers*] troops, soldiers.

Thou fought'st with shame, and shame hath conquered
  thee.
This lameness will not serve.

Oatley.   Unmask yourself.

Lincoln. [*to Oatley*] Lead home your daughter.

Oatley. [*to Lincoln*]   Take your nephew hence.

Ralph. Hence? 'Swounds, what mean you? Are you mad? I   140
  hope you cannot enforce my wife from me. Where's
  Hammon?

Oatley. Your wife?

Lincoln. What Hammon?

Ralph. Yea, my wife; and therefore the proudest of you that   145
  lays hands on her first, I'll lay my crutch cross his pate.

Firk. To him, lame Ralph!—Here's brave sport!

Ralph. Rose, call you her? Why, her name is Jane. Look here
  else. [*He unmasks her.*] Do you know her now?

Lincoln. Is this your daughter?

Oatley.   No, nor this your nephew.   150
  My Lord of Lincoln, we are both abused
  By this base crafty varlet.

Firk. Yea, forsooth, no 'varlet', forsooth, no 'base', forsooth I
  am but mean. No 'crafty' neither, but of the Gentle
  Craft.   155

Oatley. Where is my daughter Rose? Where is my child?

Lincoln. Where is my nephew Lacy married?

Firk. Why, here is good laced mutton, as I promised you.

Lincoln. Villain, I'll have thee punished for this wrong.

Firk. Punish the journeyman villain, but not the journeyman   160
  shoemaker.

Enter DODGER.

153–4. '*base*' . . . *mean*] punning on 'bass' and on *mean* as the middle part in a piece
of musical harmony.

158. *laced mutton*] a prostitute (Tilley, M1338, 'He loves laced mutton'). The term
seems to be suggested to Firk by the name *Lacy,* and to be no more than his ribald
way of referring to Jane in order to annoy Lincoln.

160. *journeyman villain*] obscure, but possibly alluding to the Poor Law legislation
of 1597. Firk's *journeyman villain* may pun on 'journey-man villein', meaning a
wandering labourer, liable to punishment under the new law, in contrast to the
journeyman (qualified) craftsman.

Dodger. My lord, I come to bring unwelcome news.
>   Your nephew Lacy and [*to Oatley*] your daughter
>   Rose
>   Early this morning wedded at the Savoy,
>   None being present but the Lady Mayoress.   165
>   Besides, I learnt among the officers
>   The Lord Mayor vows to stand in their defence
>   'Gainst any that shall seek to cross the match.
Lincoln. Dares Eyre the shoemaker uphold the deed?
Firk. Yes, sir, shoemakers dare stand in a woman's quarrel, I   170
>   warrant you, as deep as another, and deeper, too.
Dodger. Besides, his Grace today dines with the Mayor,
>   Who on his knees humbly intends to fall
>   And beg a pardon for your nephew's fault.
Lincoln. But I'll prevent him. Come, Sir Roger Oatley,   175
>   The King will do us justice in this cause.
>   Howe'er their hands have made them man and wife,
>   I will disjoin the match, or lose my life.

>   *Exeunt* [*the* Earl of LINCOLN, OATLEY, *and* DODGER].

Firk. Adieu, Monsieur Dodger! Farewell, fools! Ha, ha! O, if
>   they had stayed, I would have so lammed them with   180
>   flouts! O heart, my codpiece point is ready to fly in
>   pieces every time I think upon Mistress Rose—but let
>   that pass, as my Lady Mayoress says.
Hodge. This matter is answered. Come, Ralph, home with
>   thy wife; come, my fine shoemakers, let's to our mas-   185

---

166. *officers*] (of the City); liverymen.

170–1. *shoemakers . . . deeper, too*] (bawdy).

170. *quarrel*] It may be relevant that Henley and Farmer list 'quarry' among slang terms for the female organ.

172. *his Grace*] i.e., the King.

179. *Monsieur*] (presumably a sneer at Dodger's affectation).

180. *lammed*] beaten, thrashed.

181. *flouts*] insults, mockery.

codpiece point] lace holding together the front of the breeches.

182–3. *let . . . says*] By drawing attention to his own device of the catch-phrase, Dekker momentarily turns the comedy upon himself.

184. *answered*] settled.

ter's the new Lord Mayor, and there swagger this
Shrove Tuesday. I'll promise you wine enough, for
Madge keeps the cellar.

All. O rare! Madge is a good wench.

Firk. And I'll promise you meat enough, for simpering Susan   190
keeps the larder. I'll lead you to victuals, my brave
soldiers. Follow your captain. O brave! Hark hark!

        Bell rings.

All. The pancake bell rings, the pancake bell. Tri-lill, my
hearts!

Firk. O brave! O sweet bell! O delicate pancakes! Open the   195
doors, my hearts, and shut up the windows. Keep in the
house, let out the pancakes. O rare, my hearts! Let's
march together for the honour of Saint Hugh to the
great new hall in Gracious Street corner, which our
master the new Lord Mayor hath built.   200

Ralph. O, the crew of good fellows that will dine at my Lord
Mayor's cost today!

Hodge. By the Lord, my Lord Mayor is a most brave man.
How shall prentices be bound to pray for him and the
honour of the Gentlemen Shoemakers! Let's feed and be   205
fat with my lord's bounty.

Firk. O musical bell still! O Hodge, O my brethren! There's
cheer for the heavens—venison pasties walk up and

---

208 pasties] *Q2*; pastimes *Q1*.

186. *swagger*] show ourselves off, flaunt ourselves (in the manner that Mistress
Quickly could not abide (*2H4*, II.iv)).

188. *Madge*] (obviously not Margery Eyre).

190. *meat*] food.

193. *pancake bell*] Cf. xvii.53, n.

Tri-lill] partly an imitation of the sound of the bell; also a drinking call: 'The
tinker . . . poured it down his throat merrily and crying "Trillil!" ' (*The Wonderful
Year*, Pendry, p. 62).

196. *shut . . . windows*] Cf. xvii. 54, n.

196–7. *Keep . . . house*] Precise meaning is overwhelmed by Firk's verbal exuberance. There seems to be no implication of remaining indoors; rather the house is to
be locked up (as in the previous sentence) while its occupants come outside (with the
pancakes) for the communal festival.

198–9. *the great . . . corner*] Leadenhall (cf. xvii.44). The building remains anonymous until the King confers a name on it at xxi.130–4 (see n.).

208. *pasties*] If Q2's emendation needed support it could be found in Deloney (p.
158): 'bring me forth the Pastie of Venison'.

down piping hot like sergeants; beef and brewis comes
marching in dry fats; fritters and pancakes comes troll-   210
ing in in wheelbarrows, hens and oranges hopping in
porters' baskets, collops and eggs in scuttles, and tarts
and custards comes quavering in in malt shovels.

Enter more Prentices.

All. Whoop, look here, look here!
Hodge. How now, mad lads, whither away so fast?   215
First Prentice. Whither?—why, to the great new hall! Know
you not why? The Lord Mayor hath bidden all the
prentices in London to breakfast this morning.
All. O brave shoemaker! O brave lord of incomprehensible
good fellowship! Hoo, hark you, the pancake bell rings!   220
Cast up caps.
Firk. Nay, more, my hearts, every Shrove Tuesday is our
year of jubilee; and when the pancake bell rings, we are

---

209. *piping hot like sergeants*] i.e., puffing in energetic pursuit of duty.
brewis] Cf. iv.2, n.
210. *dry fats*] vats used to hold dry things as opposed to liquids.
trolling] trundling.
211. *hens*] All the other foods—*beef and brewis, fritters and pancakes, collops and eggs,
tarts and custards*—are natural pairs. Though *hens and oranges* is not an impossible
combination, Q1's 'hennes' may be a misreading of 'lemons'.
212. *collops and eggs*] eggs fried on bacon. The day before Shrove Tuesday was
called Collop Monday.
scuttles] dishes, platters.
213. *malt shovels*] capacious shovels used in the preparation of malt.
219. *incomprehensible*] boundless.
220. *Hoo*] O.E.D. first records the exclamation in *A.&C.* (1606), II.vii.141.
220.1. *Cast up caps*] a normal expression of communal excitement. In Deloney,
after the feast is over, the apprentices '(in token of thankfulnesse) flung vp their Caps,
giuing a great showt' (Appendix A, p. 218). Caps were particularly associated with
apprentices: cf. Heywood, *The Four Prentices of London* and *1 Edward IV* (ed.
Shepherd, II.174, I.17), and Jonson, Chapman, Marston, *Eastward Ho* (New Mermaid edition, II.ii.30).
221–7. *every Shrove Tuesday . . . Saint Hugh's Holiday . . . for ever*] On Dekker's
suggestion to his audience that Eyre had instituted their Shrove Tuesday holiday, see
Introduction, pp. 41–3 and Appendix B. Dekker himself invents the phrase *Saint
Hugh's Holiday* to increase the association with shoemaking by a reference to its
patron saint.
222. *year of*] annual. (This use is not recorded in *O.E.D.*)

as free as my Lord Mayor. We may shut up our shops
and make holiday. I'll have it called 'Saint Hugh's
Holiday'.   225
All. Agreed, agreed—'Saint Hugh's Holiday'!
Hodge. And this shall continue for ever.
All. O brave! Come, come, my hearts; away, away.
Firk. O eternal credit to us of the Gentle Craft! March fair,
my hearts. O rare!   *Exeunt.*   230

[SCENE XIX.]
Enter KING *and his train over the stage.*

King. Is our Lord Mayor of London such a gallant?
Nobleman. One of the merriest madcaps in your land.
Your Grace will think, when you behold the man,
He's rather a wild ruffian than a Mayor.
Yet thus much I'll ensure your Majesty: 5
In all his actions that concern his state
He is as serious, provident, and wise,
As full of gravity amongst the grave,
As any Mayor hath been these many years.
King. I am with child till I behold this huffcap.   10
But all my doubt is, when we come in presence,
His madness will be dashed clean out of countenance.
Nobleman. It may be so, my liege.
King.   Which to prevent,
Let someone give him notice 'tis our pleasure
That he put on his wonted merriment.   15
Set forward.
All. On afore!   *Exeunt.*

---

230. Exeunt] A march-out is obviously called for.

0.1. over the stage] Cf. i.246.2, n. This seems to have been a regular way of staging
this kind of royal entry; cf. *2H4*, V.v.5: 'Trumpets sound, and the King, and his
traine passe ouer the stage . . .' (Q, 1600).
5. *ensure*] assure.
6. *state*] official position.
10. *with child*] (Tilley, C317) in suspense.
huffcap] swashbuckler, swaggering fellow.
11. *doubt*] fear, anxiety.

[SCENE XX.]
Enter EYRE, HODGE, FIRK, RALPH, *and other*
Shoemakers, *all with napkins on their shoulders.*

Eyre. Come, my fine Hodge, my jolly Gentlemen Shoemakers—soft, where be these cannibals, these varlets
my officers? Let them all walk and wait upon my
brethren; for my meaning is that none but shoemakers,
none but the livery of my company shall in their satin   5
hoods wait upon the trencher of my sovereign.

Firk. O, my lord, it will be rare.

Eyre. No more, Firk. Come, lively. Let your fellow prentices
want no cheer. Let wine be plentiful as beer, and beer as
water. Hang these penny-pinching fathers, that cram   10
wealth in innocent lamb-skins. Rip, knaves! Avaunt!
Look to my guests.

Hodge. My lord, we are at our wits' end for room. Those
hundred tables will not feast the fourth part of them.

Eyre. Then cover me those hundred tables again, and again,   15

---

2. *cannibals*] presumably no more than another of Eyre's bombastic epithets,
though perhaps, in relation to 'piecrust eaters' (xvii.25), carrying a complaint about
his *varlets'* greed.

3. *officers*] Cf. xviii. 166, n.

4. *brethren*] i.e., his fellow shoemakers; cf. l. 40, etc.

5–6. *livery . . . sovereign*] There may be a memory here of Holinshed's report of the
return home of Henry V after Agincourt: 'The mayor of London, and the aldermen,
apparelled in orient-grained scarlet, and four hundred commoners clad in beautiful
murrey (well mounted and trimly horsed, with rich collars and great chains) met the
King' (*Shakespeare's Holinshed*, ed. Richard Hosley, New York, 1968, p. 135).

5. *livery*] livery men, retainers.

satin hoods] Vividly coloured hoods were worn by members of the livery
companies on formal occasions; see W. Herbert, *The History of the Twelve Great
Livery Companies of London*, 2 vols (London, 1836–7), I. 65–6.

8. *fellow prentices*] Dekker seems to forget the earlier introduction of Firk as a
journeyman (i. 133).

10. *penny-pinching fathers*] skinflints.

11. *innocent lamb-skins*] Harrison says 'parchment deeds', interpreting 'invest
money in property instead of spending it on good cheer'. Sutherland seems more
likely to be right when he glosses 'purses', citing Dekker's *Old Fortunatus*, where
Fortunatus addresses his purse as a 'leather mint admirable: an Indian mine in a
Lambs skinne' (I.i.334).

Rip] Look sharp! (cf. vii. 68).

13–14. *My . . . them*] suggested by Deloney; see Appendix A, p. 217.

till all my jolly prentices be feasted. Avoid, Hodge; run,
Ralph; frisk about, my nimble Firk; carouse me fathom
healths to the honour of the shoemakers. Do they drink
lively, Hodge? Do they tickle it, Firk?

Firk. Tickle it? Some of them have taken their liquor stand-   20
ing so long that they can stand no longer. But for meat,
they would eat it an they had it.

Eyre. Want they meat? Where's this swag-belly, this greasy
kitchen-stuff cook? Call the varlet to me. Want meat!
Firk, Hodge, lame Ralph, run, my tall men, beleaguer   25
the shambles, beggar all Eastcheap, serve me whole
oxen in chargers, and let sheep whine upon the tables
like pigs for want of good fellows to eat them. Want
meat! Vanish, Firk! Avaunt, Hodge!

Hodge. Your lordship mistakes my man Firk. He means their   30
bellies want meat, not the boards; for they have drunk
so much they can eat nothing.

Enter [LACY *dressed as*] HANS, ROSE, *and* [MARGERY,
EYRE'S] *wife.*

Margery. Where is my lord?
Eyre. How now, Lady Madgy?
Margery. The King's most excellent Majesty is new come; he   35
sends me for thy honour. One of his most worshipful
peers bade me tell thou must be merry, and so forth—
but let that pass.

---

16. *Avoid*] get moving!
17–18. *carouse . . . healths*] drink deep.
19. *tickle it*] See xi. 74, n.
21. *meat*] food.
23. *swag-belly*] Cf. iv.6, n.
24. *kitchen-stuff*] Cf. vii.51, n.
25. *tall*] brave, fine; cf. i.174.
beleaguer] besiege.
26. *shambles*] meat-stalls.
Eastcheap] the principal London meat-market; cf. vii.70.
27. *chargers*] large plates.
32.] Rhys, followed by many editors, inserts the second three-man's song here.
35. *new*] just.

Eyre. Is my sovereign come? Vanish, my tall shoemakers, my
   nimble brethren. Look to my guests, the prentices. Yet   40
   stay a little. How now, Hans—how looks my little
   Rose?

Lacy. Let me request you to remember me.
   I know your honour easily may obtain
   Free pardon of the King for me and Rose,   45
   And reconcile me to my uncle's grace.

Eyre. Have done, my good Hans, my honest journeyman.
   Look cheerly. I'll fall upon both my knees till they be as
   hard as horn but I'll get thy pardon.

Margery. Good my lord, have a care what you speak to his   50
   Grace.

Eyre. Away, you Islington whitepot. Hence, you hopperarse,
   you barley pudding full of maggots, you broiled carbonado. Avaunt, avaunt, avoid, Mephistophilus! Shall
   Sim Eyre learn to speak of you, Lady Madgy? Vanish,   55
   Mother Miniver-Cap, vanish! Go, trip and go, meddle
   with your partlets and your pishery-pashery, your flews

55 learn] *Q3;* leaue *Q1.*

---

47. *Have done*] say no more.

52. *Islington whitepot*] *Whitepot* was a dish made of milk or cream boiled with eggs, flour, spices, etc. Islington, still at this time a rural village, and a favourite place for Londoners' outings, had many dairies, and its cakes and creams are alluded to by several writers of the period (Sugden).

hopperarse] large-buttocks (*O.E.D.*, 'hopper-arsed', citing *c.* 1700; also *Dialect Dict.*); alluding to the pyramidal shape of a mill hopper.

53. *barley pudding*] a kind of savoury sausage.

53–4. *broiled carbonado*] piece of fish, flesh, or fowl scored across and grilled.

54. *Avaunt . . . Mephistophilus*] Pistol has an apostrophe to Mephistophilus (*M.W.W.*, I.i.117), and Juniper, in Jonson's *The Case is Altered*, says 'avoid, Mephistophilus' (II.iv). Such uses of the name in the mouths of huffing characters are no doubt influenced by the popularity of Marlowe's *Dr Faustus*.

56. *Mother Miniver-Cap*] presumably her cap is trimmed with miniver (ermine) for this great occasion. In Dekker's *Satiromastix* the character called Mistress Miniver is scornfully referred to as 'Widow *Miniuer*-caps' (IV.ii.123).

trip and go] Cf. iv. 30–1, n.

57. *partlets*] collars, ruffs.

pishery-pashery] Cf. i.125, and n.; here seems to be used contemptuously of fine clothing.

flews] properly, the large chaps of a deep-mouthed hound; here used for the flaps of a hood or skirt.

and your whirligigs! Go, rub, out of mine alley! Sim
Eyre knows how to speak to a pope, to Sultan Soliman,
to Tamburlaine an he were here. And shall I melt, shall I   60
droop before my sovereign? No! Come, my Lady
Madgy; follow me, Hans; about your business, my
frolic freebooters. Firk, frisk about, and about, and
about, for the honour of mad Simon Eyre, Lord Mayor
of London.   65
Firk. Hey for the honour of the shoemakers!   *Exeunt.*

[SCENE XXI.]
A long flourish or two. Enter KING, Nobles, EYRE,
[MARGERY] *his wife,* LACY [*dressed as himself*],
ROSE. LACY *and* ROSE *kneel.*

King. Well, Lacy, though the fact was very foul
Of your revolting from our kingly love
And your own duty, yet we pardon you.
Rise, both; and, Mistress Lacy, thank my Lord Mayor
For your young bridegroom here.   5
Eyre. So, my dear liege, Sim Eyre and my brethren the
Gentlemen Shoemakers shall set your sweet Majesty's
image cheek by jowl by Saint Hugh for this honour you
have done poor Simon Eyre. I beseech your Grace

---

58. *whirligigs*] whirling or spinning toys, etc.; used in *Nashes Lenten Stuffe* to mean
a fantastic idea (McKerrow, III.178); here, perhaps, frills or furbelows.

rub . . . alley] in the game of bowls, a *rub* is an obstacle in the bowling-alley.
Presumably Eyre addresses his wife as such an obstacle, though *rub* could also mean
'be off!'.

59–60. *Sultan . . . Tamburlaine*] Eastern tyrants dramatised in Kyd's *Soliman and
Perseda* (1589–92) and Marlowe's *Tamburlaine* (1587).

63. *frolic*] jolly.

freebooters] plunderers, pirates (another instance of Eyre's bombast, perhaps punning on -*booters* and 'shoemakers'.

Sc. xxi.] At xviii.197–200, 216 the impression has been given that the feast is to
take place at the Leadenhall, but l. 125 below suggests that it is imagined in Eyre's
house, as in Deloney (Appendix A, p. 217).

1. *fact . . . foul*] The normal punishment for the soldier deserting his duty in
wartime would be execution (cf. viii.43, and n.). The pardon Lacy receives (followed at l. 115 by his knighthood) is an appropriate prelude to the 'holiday' mood of
the final scene.

    pardon my rude behaviour. I am a handicraftsman, yet   10
    my heart is without craft. I would be sorry at my soul
    that my boldness should offend my King.
King. Nay, I pray thee, good Lord Mayor, be even as
    merry
    As if thou wert among thy shoemakers.
    It does me good to see thee in this humour.   15
Eyre. Sayst thou me so, my sweet Diocletian? Then, hump!
    Prince am I none, yet am I princely born! By the Lord of
    Ludgate, my liege, I'll be as merry as a pie.
King. Tell me, in faith, mad Eyre, how old thou art.
Eyre. My liege, a very boy, a stripling, a younker. You see not   20
    a white hair on my head, not a grey in this beard. Every
    hair, I assure thy Majesty, that sticks in this beard Sim
    Eyre values at the King of Babylon's ransom. Tamar
    Cham's beard was a rubbing-brush to't. Yet I'll shave it
    off and stuff tennis balls with it to please my bully King.   25

14 As] *Fritsche; as* Q1.

---

    11. *craft*] guile.
    16. *Diocletian*] The Roman emperor figures, unsympathetically, in Deloney, Part One, chapter iii. Eyre chooses the name for sound rather than sense.
    hump] an interjection of indeterminate meaning, but here (as in ll. 28 and 35) obviously a cry of exultation and probably, like 'hem!', a drinking cry or 'a call to swallow a draught' (A. R. Humphreys, note to new Arden edition of *2H4*, II.iv.30). Dramatists of the period represent such cries in various spellings; the actor has the responsibility of conveying the general mood rather than representing Dekker's particular form of the word.
    17. *Prince . . . born*] See vii.49–50, n. Eyre's use of his catch-phrase before the King draws attention to the presence of two 'monarchs' in this scene (see Introduction, p. 43).
    18. *merry . . . pie*] Tilley, P281 (*pie*, magpie).
    20. *younker*] young man, especially a fashionable one. Eyre's humorous pretence that he is young recalls Falstaff (*1H4*, II.ii.82).
    21–3. *Every . . . ransom*] repeated from vii.40–1.
    23. *King of Babylon*] used here as the type of a very rich man.
    23–4. *Tamar Cham's beard*] *Tamar Cham* is Timur, or Jenghis, Khan, the ruler of Tartary, or China, and a legendary hero. A play, now lost, called *1 Tamar Cam*, is recorded by Henslowe as having been acted on 6 May 1596 and on ten later occasions that year. Perhaps something special was made of the hero's beard; in *Ado* Benedick offers to fetch 'a hair off the great Cham's beard' (II.i.237–8).
    24. *rubbing-brush*] scrubbing-brush (with short hairs).
    25. *stuff . . . it*] In Elizabethan tennis (different from lawn tennis) the ball was made of leather stuffed normally with dog's hair. Cf. *Ado*: 'the old ornament of his cheek

King. But all this while I do not know your age.

Eyre. My liege, I am six-and-fifty year old; yet I can cry 'hump' with a sound heart for the honour of Saint Hugh. Mark this old wench, my King. I danced the shaking of the sheets with her six-and-thirty years ago,   30
and yet I hope to get two or three young Lord Mayors ere I die. I am lusty still, Sim Eyre still. Care and cold lodging brings white hairs. My sweet Majesty, let care vanish. Cast it upon thy nobles. It will make thee look always young, like Apollo, and cry 'Hump!'—Prince   35
am I none, yet am I princely born.

King. Ha, ha! Say, Cornwall, didst thou ever see his like?

Nobleman. Not I, my Lord.

        Enter [*the* Earl of] LINCOLN *and* [Sir ROGER OATLEY,
                the former] Lord Mayor.

King.   Lincoln, what news with you?

Lincoln. My gracious Lord, have care unto yourself,
    For there are traitors here.

All.   Traitors? Where? Who?   40

Eyre. Traitors in my house? God forbid! Where be my officers? I'll spend my soul ere my King feel harm.

37 Ha, ha!] *as a line on its own, Fritsche.*

---

hath already stuffed tennis-balls' (III.ii.40–2). This mention of tennis-balls before the King might be an allusion to the Dauphin's notorious gift to Henry V, shown in the second scene of Shakespeare's play.

bully] See xvii.1, n. and xviii.23; cf. Pistol in H5, IV.i.48, also using the word of a king. In both plays the word epitomises the comradeship of king and subject.

29–30. *danced . . . sheets*] Cf. xvi.83, n.

30. *six-and-thirty . . . ago*] Cf. Deloney: 'what a chance haue wee had within these thirty yeares' (Appendix A, p. 217).

31. *get*] beget.

32–3. *Care . . . hairs*] Cf. Tilley, C82: 'Care brings grey hair'; cf. also Epistle, 19–20, n.

35. *Apollo*] (as the symbol of youthful male beauty).

39–40. *My gracious lord . . . traitors here*] In both situation and words the moment of Lincoln's hurried arrival before the King to declare his nephew (and heir) a traitor recalls R2, V.iii.39–40 in which York also arrives hurriedly before the King to declare his son (and heir) a traitor: 'My liege, beware; look to thyself; / Thou hast a traitor in thy presence here.'

42. *spend*] give up, sacrifice.

King. Where is the traitor, Lincoln?

Lincoln [*indicating Lacy*].   Here he stands.

King. Cornwall, lay hold on Lacy. Lincoln, speak.
    What canst thou lay unto thy nephew's charge?   45

Lincoln. This, my dear liege. Your Grace to do me honour
    Heaped on the head of this degenerous boy
    Desertless favours. You made choice of him
    To be commander over powers in France;
    But he—

King.   Good Lincoln, prithee, pause a while.   50
    Even in thine eyes I read what thou wouldst speak.
    I know how Lacy did neglect our love,
    Ran himself deeply, in the highest degree,
    Into vile treason.

Lincoln.   Is he not a traitor?

King. Lincoln, he was. Now have we pardoned him.   55
    'Twas not a base want of true valour's fire
    That held him out of France, but love's desire.

Lincoln. I will not bear his shame upon my back.

King. Nor shalt thou, Lincoln. I forgive you both.

Lincoln. Then, good my liege, forbid the boy to wed   60
    One whose mean birth will much disgrace his bed.

King. Are they not married?

Lincoln.   No, my liege.

Both.   We are.

King. Shall I divorce them, then? O, be it far
    That any hand on earth should dare untie
    The sacred knot knit by God's majesty.   65
    I would not for my crown disjoin their hands
    That are conjoined in holy nuptial bands.
    How sayst thou, Lacy? Wouldst thou lose thy Rose?

Lacy. Not for all India's wealth, my sovereign.

King. But Rose, I am sure, her Lacy would forgo.   70

43 traitor, Lincoln?] *Q3* (Traitor Lincolne?); traytor? Lincolne. *Q1*.
69 India's] *Rhys;* Indians *Q1*.

---

    47. *degenerous*] degenerate.
    65. *sacred knot*] The metaphor is common, e.g. 'this godly knot', 'An Homily of
the State of Matrimony', *Certain Sermons or Homilies* (London, 1851), p. 535.

Rose. If Rose were asked that question, she'ld say no.

King. You hear them, Lincoln?

Lincoln.   Yea, my liege, I do.

King. Yet canst thou find i'the heart to part these two?

      Who seeks, besides you, to divorce these lovers?

Oatley. I do, my gracious Lord. I am her father.   75

King. Sir Roger Oatley, our last Mayor, I think?

Nobleman. The same, my liege.

King.   Would you offend love's laws?

      Well, you shall have your wills. You sue to me

      To prohibit the match. Soft, let me see,

      You both are married, Lacy, art thou not?   80

Lacy. I am, dread sovereign.

King.   Then, upon thy life,

      I charge thee not to call this woman wife.

Oatley. I thank your Grace.

Rose.   O my most gracious Lord!   *Kneel.*

King. Nay, Rose, never woo me. I tell you true,

      Although as yet I am a bachelor,   85

      Yet I believe I shall not marry you.

Rose. Can you divide the body from the soul,

      Yet make the body live?

King.   Yea, so profound?

      I cannot, Rose, but you I must divide.

      Fair maid, this bridegroom cannot be your bride.   90

---

76. *our last Mayor*] On the compression of the time-scheme see Introduction, p. 23.

77. *offend*] offend against.

85. *as yet . . . bachelor*] Though it has been used in arguments over the identity of the King, the line's dramatic purpose overrides any possible historical significance. Henry V was married in 1420, five years after his return to London from the Agincourt victory (cf. xx.5–6, n.); Henry VI was married in 1444, the year before the historical Simon Eyre became Lord Mayor. See also Introduction, p. 24.

87–8. *Can . . . live?*] The relationship between body and soul was a common topic of philosophical, theological, and medical debate; cf., e.g., K. S. Datta, 'New Light on Marvell's "A Dialogue between the Soul and Body"', *Ren.Q.*, 32 (1969), 246 n.

90. *Fair . . . bride*] Fritsche and many later editors alter to 'This fair maid, bridegroom, cannot be your bride'. As early as 1928, Sutherland had pointed out that 'bride was used in the sixteenth century of both sexes'. Bowers says the same, yet both Davies and Steane, while preserving the original reading, attempt to explain it away as facetiousness; cf. *O.E.D.*, 'bride', 2: 'by 15th and 16th c. denoting also a bridegroom; =spouse'.

Are you pleased, Lincoln? Oatley, are you pleased?
Both. Yes, my Lord.
King.   Then must my heart be eased;
          For, credit me, my conscience lives in pain
          Till these whom I divorced be joined again.
          Lacy, give me thy hand. Rose, lend me thine.   95
          Be what you would be. Kiss now. So, that's fine.
          At night, lovers, to bed. Now, let me see,
          Which of you all mislikes this harmony?
Oatley. Will you then take from me my child perforce?
King. Why, tell me, Oatley, shines not Lacy's name   100
          As bright in the world's eye as the gay beams
          Of any citizen?
Lincoln.   Yea, but, my gracious Lord,
          I do mislike the match far more than he.
          Her blood is too too base.
King.   Lincoln, no more.
          Dost thou not know that love respects no blood,   105
          Cares not for difference of birth or state?
          The maid is young, well born, fair, virtuous,
          A worthy bride for any gentleman.
          Besides, your nephew for her sake did stoop
          To bare necessity and, as I hear,   110
          Forgetting honours and all courtly pleasures,
          To gain her love became a shoemaker.
          As for the honour which he lost in France,
          Thus I redeem it: Lacy, kneel thee down.
          Arise Sir Rowland Lacy. Tell me now,   115
          Tell me in earnest, Oatley, canst thou chide,
          Seeing thy Rose a lady and a bride?

---

97. *lovers, to bed*] Cf. *M.N.D.*, V.i.353.

104–20.] This episode resembles the one in *All'sW.* (II.iii) in which Bertram refuses Helena on the grounds of her low birth, and the King argues against him. But the date of *All'sW.* is in dispute, and the resemblances are not so close as to prove indebtedness either way.

105. *love . . . blood*] Cf. Tilley, L505, 'Love has no respect of persons'.

107–8. *The maid . . . gentleman*] Cf. *All'sW.*, II.iii.119–20 ('If she be / All that is virtuous') and 129–31 ('She is young, wise, fair; / In these to nature she's immediate heir; / And these breed honour').

Oatley. I am content with what your Grace hath done.
Lincoln. And I, my liege, since there's no remedy.
King. Come on, then, all shake hands. I'll have you friends.   120
　　Where there is much love, all discord ends.
　　What says my mad Lord Mayor to all this love?
Eyre. O, my liege, this honour you have done to my fine
　　journeyman here, Rowland Lacy, and all these favours
　　which you have shown to me this day in my poor house,   125
　　will make Simon Eyre live longer by one dozen of
　　warm summers more than he should.
King. Nay, my mad Lord Mayor—that shall be thy name—
　　If any grace of mine can length thy life,
　　One honour more I'll do thee. That new building   130
　　Which at thy cost in Cornhill is erected
　　Shall take a name from us. We'll have it called
　　The Leaden Hall, because in digging it
　　You found the lead that covereth the same.
Eyre. I thank your Majesty.
Margery.　　　　　　　God bless your Grace.   135
King. Lincoln, a word with you.

　　Enter HODGE, FIRK, RALPH, *and more* Shoemakers.

---

121. *Where . . . ends*] Cf. Tilley, L521: 'Love makes all hard hearts gentle.' Fritsche emended the short line to read 'so much love' but Warnke and Proescholdt rejected the emendation, saying: '*Where* may be pronounced as a disyllable.' This is supported by Abbott, §480.

130–4. *That . . . same*] The building referred to at xvii.44 and xviii.198–9 is now named; on the significance of the ceremony, see Introduction, pp. 42–3. Leadenhall, at the south-east corner of the intersection of Gracechurch Street and Cornhill, was remembered as Eyre's principal benefaction to the City. Stow (II.174) interrupts his list of Lord Mayors to add a note on it against Eyre's name. Eyre was the rebuilder rather than the founder: the name is recorded as early as 1296 (Stow, II.295—editor's note), and the hall was given to the City by Sir Richard Whittington in 1411 (Stow, I.153). Stow (I.154) records Eyre's rebuilding in 1419, twenty-five years before he became Lord Mayor. Eyre's hall, however, was the one familiar to Elizabethan Londoners: Stow notes that he 'builded it of squared stone, in forme as now it sheweth', and translates the Latin memorial inscription in the 'fayre and large chappell' to 'The honourable and famous Marchant, *Simon Eyre,* founder of this worke, once Maior of this Citie' (I.154). Deloney also records Eyre's building of the Leadenhall (see ll. 158–9, n.). The King's explanation of the origin of the name appears to be only legendary.

Eyre. How now, my mad knaves! Peace, speak softly.
    Yonder is the King.
King. With the old troop which there we keep in pay
    We will incorporate a new supply.   140
    Before one summer more pass o'er my head,
    France shall repent England was injurèd.
    What are all those?
Lacy.   All shoemakers, my liege,
    Sometimes my fellows. In their companies
    I lived as merry as an emperor.   145
King. My mad Lord Mayor, are all these shoemakers?
Eyre. All shoemakers, my liege; all gentlemen of the Gentle
    Craft, true Trojans, courageous cordwainers. They all
    kneel to the shrine of holy Saint Hugh.
All [the Shoemakers]. God save your Majesty!   150
King. Mad Simon, would they anything with us?
Eyre. [*To the Shoemakers*] Mum, mad knaves, not a word. I'll
    do't, I warrant you. [*To the King*] They are all beggars,
    my liege, all for themselves; and I for them all on both
    my knees do entreat that for the honour of poor Simon   155
    Eyre and the good of his brethren, these mad knaves,
    your Grace would vouchsafe some privilege to my new
    Leaden Hall, that it may be lawful for us to buy and sell
    leather there two days a week.
King. Mad Sim, I grant your suit. You shall have patent   160
    To hold two market days in Leaden Hall.

---

150 *All [the Shoemakers].* God save your Majesty!] Q3 (*All.* God saue your Maiesty.);
All God saue your maiesty all shoomaker. Q1.

139–42. *With . . . injurèd*] The lines are spoken to Lincoln and mark the intrusion
of external reality into Eyre's 'holiday' (cf. Introduction, p. 43).
    141–2. *Before . . . repent*] Cf. *2H4*, V.v.106–8: 'I will lay odds that, ere this year
expire, / We bear our civil swords and native fire / As far as France.'
    144. *Sometimes*] once, formerly.
    145. *as merry . . . emperor*] Tilley, K54: 'as merry as a King'.
    148. *Trojans*] Cf. iv.121–2, n.
    150.] Bowers follows Warnke and Proescholdt in believing Q1's 'all shoomaker'
to be a stage direction incorporated in the text. Davies says: 'Perhaps it is best
regarded as an emphatic reply to the King's question, ". . . are all these shoemakers?".' This also is possible.
    158–62. *lawful . . . Fridays*] On the significance of this explanation of the origin of
the Leadenhall market, see Introduction, pp. 42–3. Deloney records that

Mondays and Fridays, those shall be the times.
Will this content you?
All [the Shoemakers]. Jesus bless your Grace!
Eyre. In the name of these my poor brethren shoemakers, I   165
    most humbly thank your Grace. But before I rise, seeing
    you are in the giving vein, and we in the begging, grant
    Sim Eyre one boon more.
King. What is it, my Lord Mayor?
Eyre. Vouchsafe to taste of a poor banquet that stands sweetly   170
    waiting for your sweet presence.
King. I shall undo thee, Eyre, only with feasts.
    Already have I been too troublesome;
    Say, have I not?
Eyre. O my dear King, Sim Eyre was taken unawares upon a   175
    day of shroving which I promised long ago to the
    prentices of London.
    For, an't please your Highness, in time past
    I bare the water-tankard, and my coat
    Sits not a whit the worse upon my back.   180

---

178 *For . . . past] Warnke and Proescholdt; as prose with previous line, Q1.*

'Sir *Simon Eyer* built *Leaden-Hall,* appointing that in the middest thereof, there should be a Market kept euery Monday for Leather, where the Shoomakers of *London,* for their more ease, might buy of the Tanners' (Appendix A, p. 218). According to Stow, Eyre had built Leadenhall 'for a common Garner of corne to the vse of this Citie' (I.110); he records its diverse uses as a storehouse and increasingly as a market (I.153–60). By the 1590s it was one of the principal London markets where various commodities, especially wool, were sold. That leather was among them is clear from Greene's *Quip for an Upstart Courtier* (1592, E4*v*), though Dekker exaggerates its importance. (Stow does not mention leather among the goods sold at Leadenhall, and places the principal London leather-market in Southwark (II.59).) Dekker's addition of Friday to the Monday market day mentioned by Deloney is fictitious (Lange, p. 99).

167. *the giving vein]* Cf. *R3,* IV.ii.120, where this phrase is strikingly used; *vein,* mood.

170. *banquet]* (often used of dessert at the end of a feast, which seems the appropriate sense here: cf. *sweetly).*

172. *undo . . . feasts]* make you poor in no other way than with the cost of feasts.

175–8] This speech's fluctuations between prose and verse are probably, as Bowers says, 'the result of incomplete working over in Dekker's foul papers'.

176. *shroving]* merrymaking (as at Shrovetide, as here).

176–85. *I promised . . . prentices]* Cf. xvii.48–55, n.

179–85. *I bare . . . prentices]* Cf. xvii. 48–9, n.

179. *tankard]* here, a vessel for carrying water, with a bung or *stopple* (l. 183).

And then upon a morning some mad boys—
It was Shrove Tuesday even as 'tis now—
gave me my breakfast, and I swore then by the stopple
of my tankard if ever I came to be Lord Mayor of
London, I would feast all the prentices. This day, my   185
liege, I did it, and the slaves had an hundred tables five
times covered. They are gone home and vanished.
Yet add more honour to the Gentle Trade:
Taste of Eyre's banquet, Simon's happy made.

King. Eyre, I will taste of thy banquet, and will say   190
I have not met more pleasure on a day.
Friends of the Gentle Craft, thanks to you all.
Thanks, my kind Lady Mayoress, for our cheer.
Come, lords, a while let's revel it at home.
When all our sports and banquetings are done,   195
Wars must right wrongs which Frenchmen have
begun.

Exeunt.

FINIS.

188–9 *Yet add . . . happy made*] *Q3; as prose, Q1.*

---

196. *Wars . . . begun*] Cf. Introduction, pp. 43–4.

Dekker's Use of *The Gentle Craft*

Dekker's use of Thomas Deloney's *The Gentle Craft* in shaping the plot of *The Shoemaker's Holiday* is discussed in section 3 of the Introduction to this edition. *The Gentle Craft* is a collection of prose tales published in two parts and containing, so the title-page of the first surviving edition of Part I informs us, 'many matters of delight, very pleasant to be read: shewing what famous men haue beene Shoomakers in time past in this Land, with their worthy deeds and great Hospitality. Declaring the cause why it is called the *Gentle Craft:* and also how the Prouerbe first grew; *A Shoomakers sonne is a Prince borne.*' Uncertainty remains with regard to the date of publication of Deloney's work. The earliest surviving edition of Part I is dated 1627; only one copy survives, in the University of Sheffield library. The earliest complete text of Part II, of which two copies survive, one in the British Library and one in the Bodleian, was printed in 1639; a few fragments of an earlier edition are in the Folger Library in Washington. On 19 October 1597, however, 'a booke called the gentle craft intreating of Shoomakers' was entered in the Stationers' Register. Some time before 14 August 1600 the second part must have appeared, or there would have been no point in referring to the 'fyrste part' in a Stationers' Register entry of that date. After a consideration of all the evidence, Merritt E. Lawlis (in the edition cited on p. xii), upon whose work this account is based, suggests that the publication of Part I came late in 1597 and of Part II in 1598. All copies of these first editions, and, we may safely surmise, of other editions before those of 1627 and 1639, have disappeared, read out of existence by the popular audience to which they were directed.

Apart from the casual echoes noted in the commentary and the general similarities of mood described in the Introduction (pp. 17–18), Dekker's main debt was to the second and third stories of Part I of *The Gentle Craft,* the story of Crispine and Crispianus and the story of Simon Eyre. The first of these occupies chapters five to nine of Deloney's work. It is set in Kent in what seems to be the period of the Roman occupation (though a Christian friar appears in a later episode), and recounts the adventures of two Kentish princes, Crispianus and Crispine, who, fleeing from the tyranny of the Emperor Maximinus, take refuge with a shoemaker of Faversham and are bound apprentice to him. Five years pass, the boys prove adept at the trade, and their master prospers, becoming shoemaker to the Emperor and his family. After a number of visits to the imperial palace (which is apparently situated in Kent), Crispine falls in love with the Emperor's daughter Ursula and is secretly married to her, after he has confessed to her the secret of his royal birth. When it becomes clear that she is expecting his child, Crispine reveals the truth of his parentage to his master and mistress and they arrange for his wife to be conveyed secretly to their house, where the child is born. In the meantime, the elder brother Crispianus has been conscripted for the wars in Gaul, where he shows remarkable valour against the Persian invaders and returns home with honour and fame. He is welcomed by the Emperor, who, on learning the truth of his parentage, renounces his former enmity to the princes' family. The intercession of Crispianus ensures the forgiveness of Crispine and Ursula, whose son is saluted, more than once, with the motto that 'a shoemaker's son is a prince born', and harmony is restored with a final song in which we learn that 'Shoomakers made Holiday' at the happy outcome of these events.

The story of Simon Eyre occupies Deloney's chapters ten to fifteen, though it is twice interrupted (in chapters twelve and fourteen) by an account of the affairs of Eyre's household servants. Deloney constructs Eyre's career in four stages: his purchase of the ship's cargo, which begins his rise to wealth; the feast to which he is invited by the Lord Mayor, following his financial success; his elevation to the rank of sheriff; and his becoming Lord Mayor and feasting the apprentices of London. Between stages two and three and three and four Deloney diverts us with the lively story of the attempts of John the Frenchman, Haunce the Dutchman, and Nicholas the Englishman, three of Eyre's journeymen, to wed

Mistress Eyre's maid Florence, 'a jolly, lusty wench'. This story builds up to an amusing climax when John and Nicholas get Haunce drunk on the night he is to be married to Florence; Nicholas is about to take his place when John has him arrested on a trumped-up charge, but is then deprived of the chance of taking the bridegroom's role himself by the sudden, and wholly unexpected, appearance of his long-lost wife from France.

Deloney's four chapters concerned directly with Eyre are Dekker's closest source for *The Shoemaker's Holiday* and are here reprinted, by permission of Indiana University Press and Oxford University Press, from the edition of Merritt E. Lawlis.

CHAPTER X. How Sir *Simon Eyre* being at first a Shoomaker, became in the end Mayor of *London*, through the counsell of his wife: and how he broke his fast euery day on a Table that he said he would not sell for a thousand pounds: and how he builded *Leaden Hall*.

Our English Chronicles doe make mention, that somtime there was in the honourable Citie of *London* a worthy Maior known by the name of Sir *Simon Eyre*, whose fame liueth in the mouthes of many men to this day, who albeit he descended of meane parentage; yet by Gods blessing in the end hee came to be a most worthy man in the Common-wealth.

This man being brought yong out of the North Countrey, was bound prentice to a shoomaker bearing then the name of the *Gentle-Craft* (as still it doth.) His Master beeing a man of reasonable wealth, set many Iourny-men and Prentices to work, who followed their busines with great delight, which quite excludeth all wearines, for when seruants doe sit at their work like dromedaries, then their minds are neuer lightly vpon their busines: for it is an old prouerb;

> They proue seruants kind and good,
> That sing at their busines like birds in the wood.

Such fellowes had this yong Lad, who was not behind with many northerne Iigs, to answer their sothern Songs. This youth being the yongest prentice in the house, as occasion serued, was often sent to the Conduit for water, where in short time he fell acquainted with many other prentices comming thither for the same intent.

Now their custome was so, that euery Sunday morning diuers of these prentices did vse to go to a place neer the conduit, to break their fast with pudding Pies, and often they would take *Simon* along with them: but vpon a time it so fell out, that when he should draw mony to pay the shot with the rest, that he had none: whereupon hee merrily said vnto them: My faithfull friends, and Conduit companions, treasurers of the Water-tan-kerd, and maine pillars of the pudding-house; I may now compare my purse to a barren Doe, that yeelds the Keeper no more good then her empty carcasse: or to a bad nut, which being opened hath neuer a kernell: therefore, if it wil please you to pardon me at this time, and excuse me for my part of the shot, I do here vow vnto you, that if euer I come to be Lord Maior of this City, I will giue a breakfast vnto all the Prentices in London.

We will take your word (quoth they) and so they departed.

It came to passe, that Simon hauing at length worn out his yeers of Apprentiship, that he fell in loue with a Maiden that was a neere neighbor vnto him, vnto whom at length he was maried, and got him a shop, and laboured hard daily, and his yong wife was neuer idle, but straight when she had nothing to doe, she sate in the shop and spun: and hauing liued thus alone a yeere or thereabout, and hauing gathered somthing together, at length he got him some prentices, and a Iourni-man or two, and he could not make his ware so fast as he could haue sold it, so that he stood in great need of a Iourny-man or two more.

At the last, one of his seruants spying one go along the street with a fardell at his back, called to his Master, saying, Sir, yonder goes S. Hughes bones, twenty pounds to a peny.

Run presently (quoth he) and bring him hither.

The boy running forth called to the man, saying; Good fellow, come hither, here is one would speake with you.

The fellow being a Frenchman, that had not long bin in England, turning about, said: Hea, what you sea? Will you speake wed me, Hea? what you haue? tell a me, what you haue, hea?

And with that comming to the stall, the good man askt him if hee lackt work.

We par ma foy, quoth the Frenchman.

Hereupon Simon tooke him in, and to worke he went merrily, where he behaued himselfe so well, that his Master made good account of him, thinking he had beene a Batcheller; but in the end it was found otherwise.

This man was the first that wrought vpon the low cut shoo with the square toe, and the latchet ouerthwart th'instep, before which time in England they did weare a hie shoo that reached aboue the ankles, right after the manner of our husbandmens shooes at this day, saue onely that it was made very sharpe at the toe turning vp like the taile of an Island dog: or as you see a cock cary his hinder feathers.

Now it is to bee remembred, that while Iohn Deneuale dwelt with Simon Eyre, it chanced that a Ship of the Ile of Candy was driuen vpon our Coast, laden with all kind of Lawnes and Cambrickes, and other linnen cloth: which commodities at that time were in London very scant, and exceeding deare: and by reason of a great leake the ship had got at Sea, being vnable to saile any further, he would make what profit he could of his goods here.

And being come to London, it was Iohn Deneuales chance to meet him in the streetes, to whom the Merchant (in the Greeke tongue) demanded where he might haue lodging, for hee was one that had neuer bin in *England* before; and being vnacquainted, wist not whither to goe: but while he spake Greeke, *Iohn Deneuale* answered him still in French, which tongue the Merchant vnderstood well: and therfore being glad that he had met with one that could talke to him, he declared vnto him what tempests hee had indured at Sea, and also how his ship lay vpon the Coast with such commodities as he would sell.

Truly sir, quoth *Iohn,* I am my selfe but a stranger in this Country, and vtterly vnacquainted with Merchants, but I dwell with one in the City that is a very honest man, and it may be that hee can helpe you to some that will deale with you for it, and if you thinke it good, I will moue him in it, and in the meane space, Ile bring you where you may haue very good lodging, and tomorrow morning I will come to you againe.

Sir, said the Merchant, if you please to do me that fauour, ile not only be thankfull vnto you for the same, but also in most honest sort will content you for your paines: and with that they departed.

Now so soone as *Iohn* the Frenchman came home, he moued this matter vnto his Master, desiring him that hee would doe what he could for the Merchant. When his Master had heard each circumstance, noting therwith the want of such commodities in the Land, cast in his mind as he stood cutting vp his worke, what were best to be done in this case, saying to his man *Iohn,* I will thinke vpon it betwixt this and the morning, and then I will tell thee my minde: and therewithall casting downe his cutting Knife, hee went out of his shop into his chamber, and therein walking vp and downe alone very sadly ruminating hereon: he was so farre in his muse, that his wife sending for him to supper two or three times, he nothing regarded the maides call, hammering still this matter in his head.

At last his wife came to him saying: Husband, what meane you that you doe not come in to supper? why speak you not man? Hear you good husband, come away, your meat will be cold: but for all her words, hee staid walking vp and downe still like a man that had sent his wits a wool-gathering: which his wife seeing, pulled him by the sleeue, saying: Why husband in the name of God, why come you not? will you not come to supper to night? I called you a good while agoe.

Body of me, wife (said he) I promise thee I did not heare thee.

No, faith, it seemeth so (quoth she) I maruell whereupon your mind runneth.

Beleeue me wife, quoth he, I was studying how to make my selfe Lord Maior, and thee a Lady.

Now God helpe you (quoth she) I pray God make vs able to pay euery man his owne, that we liue out of debt and danger, and driue the woolfe from the doore, and I desire no more.

But wife, said he, I pray thee now tell me, Doest thou not thinke that thou couldst make shift to beare the name of a Lady, if it shold be put vpon thee?

In truth husband (quoth she) ile not dissemble with you, if your wealth were able to beare it, my mind would beare it well enough.

Well wife (replied he) I tell thee now in sadnesse, that if I had money, there is a commodity now to be bought, the gaines whereof would be able to make me a gentleman for euer.

Alas husband, that dignity your trade allowes you already, being a squire of the *Gentle-Craft,* then, how can you be lesse than a gentleman, seeing your son is a Prince borne?

Tush wife (quoth he) those titles do only rest in name, but not in nature: but of that sort had I rather be, whose lands are answerable to their vertues, and whose rents can maintaine the greatnes of their minds.

Then sweet husband, tell me, said his wife, tell me, what commodity is that which you might get so much by? I am sure your selfe hath some mony, and it shal go very hard but ile procure friends to borrow one forty shillings, and beside that, rather then you shall lose so good a bargain, I haue a couple of crowns that saw no sun since we were first maried, and them also shall you haue.

Alas wife (said *Simon*) all this comes not neare that matter: I confess it would do some good in buying a few backs of leather, but in this thing it is nothing: for this is Merchandise that is precious at this time and rare to be had, and I heare whosoeuer that will haue it, must lay downe 3000. pounds ready mony. Yea wife, and yet thereby he might get three and three thousand pounds profit.

His wife hearing him say so, was inflamed with desire therof, as women are (for the most part) very couetous: that matter running still in her mind, she could scant find in her heart to spare him time to goe to supper, for very eagernesse to animate him on to take that bargaine vpon him. Wherefore, so soone as they had supt, and giuen God thanks, she called her husband, saying: I pray you come hither I would speake a word with you: That man is not alwaies to bee blamed that sometimes takes counsell of his wife: though womens wits are not able to comprehend the greatest things, yet in doubtfull matters they often helpe on a sudden.

Well wife, what meane you by this (said her husband?)

In truth quoth she, I would haue you plucke vp a mans heart, and speedily chop vp a bargaine for these goods you speake of.

Who I? quoth he, which way should I doe it, that am not able for three thousand pounds, to lay downe three thousand pence?

Tush man, quoth shee, what of that? euery man that beholds a man in the face, knows not what he hath in his purse; and whatsoeuer he be that owes the goods, he will, no doubt, be content to stay a month for his mony, or three weekes at the least: and I promise you, to pay a thousand pounds a week, is a pretty round payment, and I may say to you, not much to be misliked of.

Now husband, I would haue you in the morning goe with *Iohn* the Frenchman to the Grecian Merchant, and with good discretion driue a sound bargaine with him, for the whole fraught of the ship, and thereupon giue him halfe a dozen Angells in earnest, and eight and twenty dayes after the deliuery of the goods, condition to deliuer him the rest of his money.

But woman (quoth hee) doest thou imagine that he would take my word for so weighty a masse of money, and to deliuer his goods vpon no better security?

Good Lord, quoth she, haue you no wit in such a case to make shift? Ile tell you what you shall doe: Be not knowne that you bargaine for your owne selfe, but tell him that you doe it in the behalfe of one of the chiefe Aldermen in the City; but beware in any case, that you leaue with him your owne name in writing, hee being a Grecian cannot read English: and you haue no need at all to shew *Iohn* the Frenchman, or if thou shouldst, it were no great matter, for you can tell well enough that he can neither write nor read.

I perceiue Wife (quoth he) thou wouldst faine be a Lady, and worthy thou art to be one, that dost thus imploy thy wits to bring thy husbands profit: but tell me, if he should be desirous to see the Alderman to confer with him, how shall we do then?

Iesus haue mercy vpon us (quoth she) you say women are fooles, but me seemeth men haue need to be taught sometimes. Before you come away in the morning, let *Iohn* the Frenchman tell him, that the Alderman himselfe shall come to his lodging in the afternoon; and receiuing a note of all the goods that be in the ship, he shall deliuer vnto him a Bil of his hand for the payment of his money, according to that time. Now sweetheart (quoth she) this Alderman shall be thine owne selfe, and ile goe borrow for thee all things that are necessary against that time.

Tush (quoth her husband) canst thou imagine, that he seeing me in the morning, will not know me againe in the afternoon?

O husband, quoth she, he will not know thee, I warrant thee: for in the morning thou shalt goe to him in thy doublet of sheepe-skins, with a smutched face, and thy apron before thee, thy thumb-leather and hand-leather, buckled close to thy wrist, with a foule band about thy necke, and a greasie cap on thy head.

Why woman (quoth he) to goe in this sort will be a discredit to me, and make the Merchant doubtfull of my dealing: for men of simple attire are (God wot) slenderly esteemed.

Hold your peace good husband (quoth she) it shall not be so with you, for *Iohn* the Frenchman shall giue such good report to the Merchant for your honest dealing (as I praise God hee can doe no lesse) that the Grecian will rather conceiue the better of you, then otherwise: iudging you a prudent discreet man, that will not make a shew of that you are not, but go in your attire agreeable to your trade. And because none of our folkes shall be priuy to our intent, to morrow weele dine at my coosin *Iohn Barbers*, in S. *Clements* Lane, which is not far from the *George* in *Lumbard* street, where the Merchants strangers lie. Now Ile be sure that all things shall be ready at my coosin *Iohns*, that you shall put on in the afternoone. And there he shall first of all with his sizzers, snap off all the superfluous haires, and fashion thy bushie beard after the Aldermans graue cut: then shall he wash thee with a sweet Camphire Ball, and besprinkle thine head and face with the purest Rosewater; then shalt thou scoure thy pitchy fingers in a bason of hot water, with an ordinary washing ball: and all this being done, strip thee from these common weeds, and Ile put thee on a very faire doublet of tawny sattin, ouer which thou shalt haue a Cassock of branched damask, furred round about the skirts with the finest foynes, thy breeches of blacke Veluet, and shooes and stockings fit for such array: a band about thy neck, as white as the driuen snow, and for thy wrists a pretty paire of cuffes, and on thy head a cap of the finest blacke: then shalt thou put on a faire gown, welted round with veluet, and ouerthwart the backe thwart it shal be with rich foine, with a paire of sweet gloues on thy hands, and on thy fore-finger a great seale ring of gold.

Thou being thus attired Ile intreat my coosin *Iohn Barber*, because he is a very hansome yong man, neat and fine in his apparell (as indeed all Barbers are) that he would take the paines to waite vpon you vnto the merchants, as if he were your man, which he wil do at the first word. And when you come there, tis not for you to vse many words, because one of you cannot vnderstand the other, so that it will be sufficient with outward curtesie, one to greet another; and he to deliuer vnto you his notes, and you to giue to him your bill, and so come home.

It doth my heart good, to see how trimly this apparell doth become you, in good faith husband, me seemes in my mind, I see you in it already, and how like an Alderman you will looke, when you are in this costly array. At your returne from the Merchant, you shal put off all these clothes at my coosins againe, and come home as you did goe forth. Then tell *Iohn* the Frenchman, that the Alderman was with the Merchant this afternoon; you may send him to him in the morning, and bid him to command that his ship may bee brought downe the Riuer: while she is comming about, you may giue notice to the linnen Drapers, of the Commodities you haue comming.

Enough Wife (quoth he) thou hast said enough, and by the grace of God Ile follow thy counsell, and I doubt not but to haue good fortune.

CHAPTER XI. How *Simon Eyre* was sent for to my Lord Mayors to supper, and shewing the great entertainment that he and his wife had there.

Anon after, supper time drew neare, she making her selfe ready in the best manner she could deuise, passed along with her husband vnto my Lord Maiors house: and being entred into the great Hall, one of the Officers there certified to my Lord Maior, that the great rich Shoomaker and his wife were already come. Whereupon the Lord Maior in courteous manner came into the Hall to *Simon*, saying: You are most heartily welcome good Master *Eyre*, and so is your gentle bedfellow.

Then came forth my Lady Maioresse and saluted them both in like manner, saying: Welcome good Master *Eyer* and Mistresse *Eyer* both, and taking her by the hand, set her downe among the Gentlewomen there present.

Sir (quoth the Lord Maior) I vnderstand you are a Shoomaker, and that it is you that hath bought vp all the goods of the great Argozy.

I am indeed my Lord of the *Gentle-craft*, quoth hee, and I praise God, all the goods of that great Argozy are my owne, when my debts are paid.

God giue you much ioy of them, said the Lord Maior, and I trust you and I shall deale for some part thereof. So the meat being then ready to be brought in, the guests were placed each one according to his calling. My Lord Maior holding *Simon* by the hand, and the Ladie Maioresse holding his wife, they would needs haue them sit neare to themselues, which they then with blushing cheekes refusing, my Lord said thus vnto them, holding his cap in his hand:

Master *Eyer* and Mistresse *Eyer*, let me intreat you not to be troublesome, for I tell you it shall be thus: and as for these Gentlemen here present, they are all of mine old acquaintance, and many times wee haue bin together, therefore I dare be the bolder with them: and albeit you are our neighbour also, yet I promise you, you are strangers to my Table, and to strangers common courtesie doth teach vs to shew the greatest fauour, and therefore let mee rule you in mine house, and you shall rule me in yours.

When *Simon* found there was no remedy, they sate them downe, but the poore woman was so abashed, that shee did eate but little meat at the Table, bearing herselfe at the table with a comely and modest countenance: but what she wanted in outward feeding, her heart yeelded to with inward delight and content.

Now so it was, many men that knew not *Simon*, and seeing him in so simple attire sit next my Lord, whisperingly asked one another what he was. And it was enough for *Simons* wife with her eyes and eares, to see and hearken after euery thing that was said or done.

A graue wealthy Citizen sitting at the table, spake to *Simon* and said; Sir in good will I drink to your good health, but I beseech you pardon mee, for I know not how to call your name.

With that my Lord Maior answered him, saying: his name is Master *Eyer*, and this is the Gentleman that bought all the goods that came in the blacke Swan of Candy, and before God, though he sit heere in simple sort, for his wealth, I doe verily beleeue he is more sufficient to bear this place then my selfe. This was a man that was neuer thought vpon, liuing obscure amongst vs, of none account in the eies of the world, carying the countenance but of a Shoomaker, and none of the best sort neither, and is able to deale for a bargaine of fiue thousand pounds at a clap.

We do want many such Shoomakers (said the Citizen), and so with other discourse droue out supper.

At what time rising from the Table, *Simon* and his wife receiuing sundry salutations of my lord Maior and his Lady, and of all the rest of the worshipfull guests, departed home to their owne house: at what time his wife made such a recitall of the matters; how brauely they were entertained, what great cheare was there, also what a great company of Gentlemen and Gentlewomen were there, and how often they dranke to her husband and to her, with diuers other circumstances, that I beleeue, if the night had beene six months long, as it is vnder the North Pole, shee would haue found talke enough till morning.

Of a truth (quoth she) although I sate close by my Ladies side, I could eat nothing for very ioy, to heare and see that we were so much made of. And neuer giue me credit husband, if I did not heare the Officers whisper as they stood behind me, and all demanded one of another, what you were, and what I was: O quoth one, doe you see this man? marke him well, and marke his wife well, that simple woman that sits next my Lady: What are they? What are they quoth another? Marrie this is the rich Shoomaker that bought all the goods in the great Argozie: I tell you there was neuer such a Shoomaker seene in *London* since the City was builded. Now by my faith (quoth the third) I haue heard much of him today among the Merchants in the street, going betweene the two Chaines: Credit me husband, of mine honesty this was their communication. Nay, and doe you not remember when the rich citizen dranke to you (which craued pardon, because hee knew not your name) what my Lord Maior said? Sir (quoth he) his name is Master *Eyer*, did you marke that? and presently thereupon he added these words: This is the Gentleman that bought, and so forth. The Gentleman vnderstood you, did you heare him speake that word?

In troth wife (quoth he) my Lord vttered many good words of me, I thanke his honor, but I heard not that.

No (quoth she) I heard it wel enough: for by and by he proceeded further, saying: I suppose, though he sit here in simple sort, hee is more sufficient to beare this charge then my selfe. Yea thought I, he may thanke his wife for that, if it come so to passe.

Nay, said *Simon*, I thanke God for it.

Yea, and next him, you may thanke me (quoth she.) And it did her so much good to talke of it, that I suppose, if she had liued to this day, she should yet be prating thereof, and if sleepe did not driue her from it.

And now seeing that *Simon* the Shoomaker is become a Merchant, we will temper our tongues to giue him that title, which his customers were wont to doe, and from henceforth call him Master *Eyer*, who, while he had his affaires in hand, committed the gouernment of his shop to *Iohn* the Frenchman, leauing him to be a guide to his other seruants, by meanes of which fauour, *Iohn* thought himselfe at that time to be a man of no small reputation.

CHAPTER XIII. How Master *Eyer* was called vpon to be Sheriffe of *London*, and how he held his place with worship.

In this space Master *Eyer* following his businesse, had sould so much of his merchandize as paid the Grecian his whole mony: and yet had rested to himselfe three times as much as hee had sold, whereof hee trusted some to one Alderman, and some to another, and a great deale amongst substantiall Marchants; and for some had much readie mony, which he imployed in diuers merchandizes, and became Aduenturer at Sea, hauing (by Gods blessing) many a prosperous voyage, whereby his riches daily increased.

It chanced vpon a time, that being in a studie, casting vp his accounts, he found himselfe to bee clearly worth 12. or 13. thousand pounds, which he finding to be so, he called his wife to him, and said: The last day I did cast vp my accounts, and I finde that Almighty God of his goodnesse hath lent me thirteen thousand pounds to maintaine vs in our old age; for which his gracious goodnesse towards vs, let vs with our whole hearts giue his glorious Maiestie eternall praise; and therewithall pray vnto him, that we may so dispose thereof, as may be to his honour, and the comfort of his poore members on earth, and aboue our neighbours may not bee puffed vp in pride, that while wee thinke on our wealth, we forget not God that sent it vs, for it hath bin an old saying of a wise man, That abundance groweth from riches, and disdaine out of abundance: of which God giue vs grace to take heed, and grant vs a contented mind.

So soone as he had spoken this, they heard one knocking hastily at doore: whereupon hee sent *Florence* to see who it was, the Maiden comming againe, told her Master it was one of my Lord Maiors Officers that would speake with him. The Officer being permitted to come in, after due reuerence, he said: Sir, it hath pleased my Lord Maior, with the worshipfull Aldermen his brethren, with the counsell of the whole Communaltie of the honourable Citie, to chuse your worship Sheriffe of *London* this day, and haue sent me to desire you to come and certifie your mind therin, whether you be contented to hold the place or no.

Master *Eyer* hearing this, answered he would come to his Honor and to their Worships incontinent, and resolue them what hee was minded to doe; and so the Officer departed.

His wife, which all this while listened vnto their talke, hearing how the case stood, with a ioyfull countenance meeting her husband, taking him about the necke with a louing kisse, said, Master Sheriffe, God giue thee ioy of thy name and place.

O wife (quoth he) my person is farre vnworthy of that place, and the name farre exceedes my degree.

What, content your selfe good husband (quoth shee) and disable not your selfe in such sort, but bee thankfull vnto God for that you haue, and doe not spurn at such promotion as God sendeth vnto you; the Lord bee praysed for it, you haue enough to discharge the place whereto you are

called with credit: and wherefore sendeth God goods but therewithall to
doe him and your country seruice?

Woman (quoth he) it is an old Prouerb, Soft fire makes sweet mault: for
such as take things in hand rashly, repent as suddenlie: to bee Sheriffe of
London it is no little cost. Consider first (said he) what house I ought to
haue, and what costly ornaments belong thereto, as hanging of Tapistrie,
cloth of Arras, and other such like, what store of Plate and Goblets of Gold,
what costlie attire, and what a chargeable traine, and that which is most of
all, how greatlie I shall stand charge beside to our Soueraigne Lord the
King, for the answering of such prisoners as shall be committed to my
custody, with an hundred matters of such importance, which are to such an
Office belonging.

Good Lord Husband (quoth she) what neede all these repetitions? you
neede not tell me it is a matter of great charge: notwithstanding I verily
thinke many heretofore haue with great credit discharged the place, whose
wealth hath not in any sort been answerable to your riches, and whose wits
haue bin as mean as your owne: Truly sir, shall I be plaine? I know not any
thing that is to be spoken of, that you want to performe it, but only your
good will: and to lacke good will to doe your King and Countrie good
were a signe of an vnworthy subiect, which I hope you will neuer be.

Well wife (said her husband) thou dost hold mee here with prittle
prattle, while the time passeth on, tis high time I were gone to Guildhall, I
doubt I shal appear too vnmannerly, in causing my Lord Maior and the rest
to stay my leisure.

And hee hauing made himselfe ready, meet to goe before such an
Assembly as he went vnto, he went out of doore, at what time his wife
called after him, saying: and holding vp her finger.

Husband, remember, you know what I haue said: take heed you
dissemble not with God and the world, looke to it husband.

Goe to, goe to, get you in quoth he, about your businesse, and so away
he went.

So soone as he was gone out of sight, his wife sent one of her men after
him to Guild hall to hearken and hear, whether her husband held his place
or no; and if he do, bring me word with all possible speed.

I will Mistris, quoth her man.

Now when Master *Eyer* came to Guild-hall, the Lord Maior and his
brethren bade him heartily welcome, saying: Sir, the communaltie of the
Citie hauing a good opinion of you, haue chosen you for one of our
sheriffes for this yeare, not doubting but to find you a fit man for the place.

My good Lord, quoth he, I humbly thanke the City for their courtesie
and kindnesse, and I would to God my wealth were answerable to my
good will, and my ability were able to beare it. But I finde my selfe
insufficient; I most humbly desire a yeere respite more, and pardon for this
present.

At these words, a graue Commoner of the City standing vp, with due reuerence spake thus vnto the Maior: My good Lord, this is but a slender excuse for Master *Eyre* to make: for I haue often heard him say, and so haue diuers others also, that he hath a Table in his house, whereon he breakes his fast euery day, that he will not giue for a thousand pounds: wherefore (vnder your Lordships correction) in my simple iudgement, I thinke he that is able to spare a thousand pounds in such a dead commoditie, is very sufficient to be Sheriffe of *London*.

See you now, quoth my Lord, I muse Master *Eyer*, that you will haue so lame an excuse before vs as to take exceptions at your owne wealth, which is apparently proued sufficient; you must know Master *Eyer*, that the Commons of *London* haue searching eies, and seldome are they deceiued in their owne opinion, and therefore looke what is done, you must stand to.

I beseech you my Lord, quoth Master *Eyer,* giue mee leaue to speake one word. Let it be granted, that I will not giue my Table whereon I breake my fast for a thousand pounds, that is no consequence to proue it is worth so much; my fancy to the thing is all: for doubtlesse no man here would giue me a thousand shillings for it when they see it.

All is one for that, quoth my Lord Maior, yet dare I giue you as much wine as you will spend this yeare in your Shriualtie to let mee haue it.

My good Lord quoth he, on that cóndition I will hold my place, and rest no longer troublesome to this company.

You must hold, said my Lord, without any condition or exceptions at all in this matter: and so they ended.

The Assembly being then broken vp, the voice went, Master *Eyer* is Sheriffe, Master *Eyer* is Sheriffe. Whereupon the fellow that Mistris *Eyer* sent to obserue how things framed, ranne home in all hast, and with leaping and reioycing said: Mistris, God giue you ioy, for you are now a Gentlewoman.

What, quoth she, tell me sir sawce, is thy Master Sheriffe, or no? and doth hee hold his place?

Yes Mistris, hee holds it now as fast as the stirrop doth the shooe while we sow it.

Why then (quoth she) I haue my hearts desire, and that I so long looked for, and so away she went.

Within a while after came her husband, and with him one of the Aldermen, and a couple of wealthy Commoners, one of them was he that gaue such great commendations of his Table, and comming to his dore, he said, You are welcome home good Master Sheriffe.

Nay, I pray you come in and drinke with me before you goe.

Then said he, Wife, bring me forth the Pastie of Venison, and set me heere my little Table, that these Gentlemen may eate a bit with me before they goe.

His wife which had beene oft vsed to this terme, excused the matter, saying; The little Table! good Lord husband, I doe wonder what you will doe with the little Table now, knowing that it is vsed already? I pray you good husband, content your selfe, and sit at this great Table this once. Then she whispered him in the eare, saying; What man, shall we shame our selues?

What shame (quoth he?) tell not me of shame, but do thou as thou art bidden, for we are but three or foure of vs, then what should wee doe troubling the great Table?

Truly (answered shee) the little Table is not readie: now good husband let vs alone.

Trust me, we are troublesome guests (said the Alderman) but yet we would faine see your little Table, because it is said to bee of such price.

Yea, and it is my mind you shall, quoth Master *Eyer*: therefore he called his wife againe, saying: Good wife, dispatch and prepare the little Table: for these Gentlemen would faine haue a view of it.

Whereupon his wife seeing him so earnest, according to her wonted manner, came in; and setting herselfe downe on a lowe stoole, laid a faire Napkin ouer her knees, and set the Platter with the pastie of Venison therupon, and presently a chaire was brought for Master Alderman, and a couple of stooles for the two Commoners: which they beholding, with a sudden and hearty laughter, said; Why Master Sherife, is this the table you held so deare?

Yes truly, quoth hee.

Now verily, quoth they, you herein haue vtterly deceiued our expectation.

Euen so did you mine, quoth hee, in making me Sheriffe: but you are all right heartily welcome, and I will tell you true, had I not thought wondrous well of you, you had not seene my Table now. And I thinke, did my Lord Maior see it as you doe, he would repent his bargaine so hastily made. Notwithstanding I account of my Table neuer the worse.

Nor haue you any cause (quoth they) and so after much pleasant talke, they departed, spreading the fame of Master Sheriffes little table ouer the whole Citie.

But you must now imagine, that a thousand cares combred the Sheriffe, in prouiding all things necessarie for his Office: at what time he put off his Shoomakers shop to one of his men, and set vp at the same time the signe of the Blacke Swan swimming vpon the Sea, in remembrance of that Ship, that first did bring him his wealth: and before that time the signe of the Blacke Swanne was neuer seene nor knowne in any place in or about the Citie of *London*.

CHAPTER XV. How Master Alderman *Eyer* was chosen Lord Maior of
London, and how he feasted all the Prentices on Shroue-tuesday.

Within a few yeeres after, Alderman *Eyer*, being chosen Lord Maior of *London*, changing his copie, hee became one of the Worshipfull Company of Drapers, and for this yeare hee kept a most bountifull house. At this time it came into his minde what a promise once hee made to the Prentices, being at breakfast with them at their going to the Conduit, speaking to his Lady in this wise: Good Lord (quoth he) what a chance haue wee had within these thirty yeares? and how greatly hath the Lord blessed vs since that? blessed be his Name for it.

I doe remember, when I was a yong prentice, what a match I made vpon a Shroue-tuesday morning, being at the Conduit, among other of my Companions; trust me wife (quoth he) tis worth the hearing. And Ile tell thee how it fell out.

After we had filled our Tankards with water, there was some would needs haue me set downe my Tankard, and goe with them to breakfast (as many times before I had done) to which I consented: and it was a breakefast of Pudding-pies. I shall neuer forget it: But to make short, when the shot came to be paid, each one drew out his money, but I had not one penny in my purse, and credit I had none in the place; which when I beheld, being abashed, I said; Well my Masters, doe you giue me my breakfast this time; and in requitall thereof, if euer I be Maior of *London,* Ile bestow a breakfast on all the Prentices of the Citie: these were the words, little thinking (God wot) that euer it would come to passe: but such was the great goodnesse of our God, who setteth vp the humble, and pulleth downe the proud, to bring whom he pleaseth to the seat of honor. For as the scripture witnesseth, *Promotion commeth neither from the East, nor from the West, but from him that is the giuer of all good things, the mighty Lord of heauen and earth:* Wherefore wife seeing God hath bestowed that vpon me that I neuer looked for; it is reason that I should performe my promise: and being able now, Ile pay that which then I was not able to do: for I would not haue men say that I am like the Ebon tree, that neither beares leaues nor fruit. Wherefore wife, seeing that Shroue-tuesday is so neere at hand, I will vpon that day performe my promise; which vpon that day I made.

Truly, my Lord (quoth she) I shall bee right willing therunto.

Then answered my Lord, As thou dost loue me let them lacke neither Pudding-Pies nor Pancakes, and looke what other good cheare is to be had, Ile referre all to your discretion.

Hereupon great prouision was made for the prentices breakfast: and Shrouetuesday being come, the Lord Maior sent word to the Aldermen, that in their seuerall Wards they should signifie his minde to the Citizens, to craue their fauours, that their Prentices might come to his house to breakfast; and that for his sake they might play all the day after.

Whereupon it was ordered, that at the ringing of a Bell in euery Parish, the Prentices should leaue worke, and shut in their shops for that day, which being euer since yearly obserued, it is called the Pancake bell. The prentices being all assembled my Lord Maiors house was not able to hold them, they were such a multitude; so that besides the great Hall, all the Garden was beset with Tables, and in the backeside Tables were set, and euery other spare place was also furnished: so that at length, the Prentices were all placed; and while meate was bringing in, to delight their eares, as well as to feede their bodies, and to drowne the noise of their pratlings, Drums and Trumpets were pleasantly sounded: that being ended, the Waits of the City, with diuers other sorts of Musicke played also to beguile the time, and to put off all discontent.

After the first seruice, were all the Tables plentifully furnished with Pudding-pies and Pancakes, in very plentifull manner, and the rest that remained was giuen to the poore. Wine and Ale in very great measure they had giuen; insomuch, that they had no lacke, nor excesse to cause them to be disordered. And in the middest of this their merriment, my Lord Maior in his skarlet gowne, and his Lady in like manner went in amongst them, bidding them all most heartily welcome, saying vnto them, that his promise so long agoe made, he hath at length performed. At what time they (in token of thankfulnesse) flung vp their Caps, giuing a great showt, and incontinently they all quietly departed.

Then after this, Sir *Simon Eyer* builded *Leaden-Hall,* appointing that in the the middest thereof, there should be a Market-kept euery Monday for Leather, where the Shoomakers of *London,* for their more ease, might buy of the Tanners, without seeking any further. And in the end, this worthy man ended his life in *London* with great Honour.

The Play's Title

The form of the play's main title on the title-page of the first quarto of 1600—'The Shomakers Holiday'—provides the modern editor with an interesting problem. The absence of the apostrophe, permitted by Elizabethan orthography, conceals three possible meanings, and the provision of modern spelling and punctuation necessarily entails a choice among them. Is this 'the shoemakers' holiday', a holiday for the shoemakers; or is it (in the same form but with a rather wider significance) 'the shoemakers' holiday', the holiday inaugurated by the shoemakers but open to everyone; or is it 'the Shoemaker's holiday', Eyre's holiday, the festival established by the play's main character? It is clearly not the first. In his story of Crispine and Crispianus Deloney describes the foundation of a feast confined to men of the Gentle Craft as the shoemakers celebrate the marriage of Crispine and the Princess Ursula: 'at which time the Shoomakers in the same towne made holiday. . . . And euer afterward, vpon that day at night the Shoomakers make great cheare and feasting, in remembrance of these two Princely brethren: and because it might not be forgotten, they caused their names to be placed in the Kalender for a yeerly remembrance, which you shall find in the moneth of October, about three daies before the Feast of *Simon* and *Iude*' (ed. Lawlis, p. 137). This is indeed a holiday of limited scope, the feast of the patron saints of the exclusive company of shoemakers. The marriage that ends Dekker's play, on the other hand, is celebrated on Shrove Tuesday, and exclusiveness becomes inclusiveness as the final scenes partake of the general revelry of that great apprentice holiday of Elizabethan London (see commentary to xvii.48–55). The feast that ends the play is open to everyone: '*all* the prentices in London' (xviii.217) have been invited; there is no suggestion that the feast, and the holiday, are for Eyre's trade alone.

Of the two other possible meanings for Dekker's title, both are clearly possible. As he and his companions prepare for the final feast, Hodge predicts that when future apprentices remember the origins of their Shrove Tuesday holiday they will 'be bound to pray for him [Eyre] and the honour of the Gentlemen Shoemakers' (xviii.204). Both Eyre and his Company are inextricably linked in this tribute, both take the credit for the establishment of a holiday that is both 'the Shoemaker's' and 'the shoemakers' '; to choose between its two possible forms is to restrict the title's meaning. But the modern editor can hardly offer both forms on his title-page, and a choice has to be made. In favour of ascribing the foundation of the holiday to all the shoemakers in general is Firk: it will bring 'eternal credit to us of the Gentle Craft' and he even wants it renamed 'Saint Hugh's holiday' (xviii.229, 224). Firk, however, is anxious, as always, to assert the glory of his calling, particularly so here as he revels before a crowd of apprentices who are not all privileged to belong to his trade. In fact the invitation to the feast that they are all celebrating has come from Eyre himself, with Firk only basking in the reflected glory of his former master. Nor would his sentiments find any very immediate echo in the play's first audiences, for the Shrove Tuesday festivities were not known to Firk's Elizabethan successors by the name he suggests.

One arrives, then, at the third possibility, and it seems appropriate that the play's title should endorse the fact that the great feast with which it ends is the gift of the one man who has controlled its mood throughout. The 'crew of good fellows' converging on Eyre's Leadenhall for the final scene 'will dine at my Lord Mayor's cost', and it is of the 'brave lord of incomprehensible good fellowship' that they shout as they go to enjoy Eyre's hospitality (xviii.201, 219). The dominance of Eyre's world that has become gradually more apparent throughout the play, the establishment of his mood of 'good fellowship', altogether takes over in these final scenes. With Eyre as its founder, host, and presiding genius, Dekker projects the mood of the play's last feast into the everyday world of his audience, linking it with their great annual holiday: 'every Shrove Tuesday is our year of jubilee; and when the pancake bell rings, we are as free as my Lord Mayor. . . . And this shall continue

for ever' (xviii.221). The mood is finally confirmed by the arrival
of the King himself, first talking of Eyre as he approaches his feast
(sc. xix), then endorsing all Eyre's actions and granting all his
requests, and finally agreeing to 'taste of Eyre's banquet' at which
'Simon's happy made' (xxi.189). The presiding dominance of Eyre
is indisputable as the play here ends in holiday revelry. It is a holiday
that his energy, success, and optimism have established, and it is
proper that this should be reflected in the form of the play's title.
The cheerful support of his fellow craftsmen has been indispensable
throughout, of course, but fundamentally this has been Eyre's play,
The Shoemaker's Holiday.

Index to the Commentary

The following list is necessarily selective. Words and phrases are referred to their first annotated occurrence in the play. An asterisk indicates that the note provides information beyond that given in *O.E.D.* or other standard reference works.